Hiv&
Human
Rights

HIV & Human Rights

Legal and Policy Perspectives on HIV and Human Rights in the Caribbean

Edited by

George Alleyne

and

Rose-Marie Belle Antoine

UNIVERSITY OF THE WEST INDIES PRESS
Jamaica • Barbados • Trinidad and Tobago

University of the West Indies Press
7A Gibraltar Hall Road, Mona
Kingston 7, Jamaica
www.uwipress.com

A catalogue record of this book is available
from the National Library of Jamaica.

ISBN 978-976-640-314-0

Printed in the United States of America.

Cover design by Robert Harris based on a concept by Ajibola Oyeleye.

Contents

Foreword

HIV and Human Rights

The struggle to ensure the human rights of Caribbean people has been a consistent theme in the history of this region. Over the last two decades, Caribbean people have sought to overcome stigma and discrimination based on race, ethnicity, class and gender. The advent of HIV in the mid-1980s introduced a new form of prejudice that built up the previous discriminations and led to human rights abuses based on sexuality, sexual orientation and HIV status. The violations and exclusions experienced by many Caribbean citizens affected by HIV have had adverse social and economic impacts. More important, stigma and discrimination have negatively affected the health of persons living with HIV.

The Symposium on HIV and Human Rights brought together a unique mix of political, legal, social and health leaders. The chapters presented in this book (all drawn from the symposium) attest to the determination in the region to change the social norms that sanction homophobia, violence against women and prejudice against persons living with HIV. The goal is to remove the legal frameworks that allow arbitrary discrimination-based sexual behaviour and sexual orientation.

The Caribbean could be one of the first regions to end its AIDS epidemic, as it did with polio in the 1990s. To do so, it must address the human rights challenges – stigma, discrimination and punitive laws – that prevent Caribbean people from being able to access health care, seek an education, continue in employment and enjoy their sexuality without fear of penal sanctions. HIV requires Caribbean societies to look closely at issues they have preferred not to discuss – matters considered too socially and politically sensitive – if they are to achieve not only their HIV targets but also the principle of equality, which was core to the independence movement in all Caribbean countries.

The symposium marked a welcome and brave step towards ensuring that all Caribbean citizens are seen as equal and allowed to contribute to and benefit from the development of their region.

Ernest Massiah
Director, Caribbean Regional
Support Team, UNAIDS

A Word from UNAIDS

Dear Colleagues and Friends,

It is wonderful that the hard work and exciting reflections that went into the Symposium on HIV and Human Rights (held 13–14 September 2010 at the University of West Indies in Barbados) is being captured in this publication. From what I have heard about the symposium, it was not a general discussion about HIV and human rights. Rather, those present went straight to some of the hardest challenges faced by the epidemic in the Caribbean – high levels of HIV-related stigma, violence against women and gender inequality, pervasive homophobia, and difficult economic and migration conditions. Participants at the symposium knew that all these issues must be dealt with if we are to achieve the vision of the UNAIDS strategy "Getting to Zero" (2011–15), promulgated for the global response to HIV. That vision involves "zero new infections, zero AIDS-related deaths and zero discrimination".

Over the years, it has become increasingly clear that we will not succeed against HIV or achieve universal access to HIV prevention, treatment, care and support where there are high levels of stigma and discrimination or punitive legal environments. For these reasons, the UNAIDS strategy calls on all to *advance human rights and gender equality* as one of three strategic directions for the AIDS response – the others being to *catalyse the new phase of treatment, care and support* and to *revolutionize prevention*. Under these strategic directions, UNAIDS is supporting governments and civil society in taking on the HIV-related human rights and gender equality issues that hold us back in our efforts to reach all those in need of HIV prevention and treatment.

This symposium was one of the first ever region-wide meetings in the Caribbean that specifically focused on these issues. The meeting provided a great opportunity for dialogue and strategizing among leaders in government, parliament, civil society, international organizations and academia to find better ways to reduce HIV-related stigma, protect against discrimination, and build legal and social capacity to protect the human rights of people living with HIV and those vulnerable to HIV infection. It highlighted certain concrete actions built on current initiatives, such as the Law, Ethics and Human Rights project by the Pan Caribbean Partnership against HIV and AIDS (PANCAP) and Canadian International Development Agency (CIDA) and the initiative by the Caribbean Community (CARICOM) on regional legislation and policy, as well as the work of academic institutions and civil society organizations on HIV and human rights.

I see the efforts of the first Symposium on HIV and Human Rights in the Caribbean region as a powerful illustration of the human rights leadership so urgently needed in the response to HIV. This need was clearly reaffirmed at the High Level Meeting on HIV and AIDS in June 2011, at which member states of the UN General Assembly, including those from the Caribbean, reaffirmed in the "2011 UN Political Declaration on HIV/AIDS" the centrality of human rights in the AIDS response.

I assure you of my personal commitment and that of UNAIDS to continue supporting the realization of health, dignity and rights for all in the response to HIV in the Caribbean and around the world and wish you all success in your important work against HIV.

Michel Sidibe
Executive Director, UNAIDS

Acknowledgements

The editors would like to thank the following persons who made indispensable contributions to the production of this book and without whom the work could not have borne fruit: our two student research assistants, D'Andra Lewars and Danielle Turnquest, who painstakingly added background material and corrected citations for the several chapters; our experienced in-house proofreader Professor Gilbert Kodilinye, who cast a piercing and expert eye over our offerings; Jennifer Hinkson, who was instrumental in providing administrative support for the conference that produced the various texts; graphic artist Ajibola Oyeleye, who provided the cover concept; and the highly valued assistant to Sir George Alleyne, Silvia Sanchez, who had the unenviable task of doing everything else that needed to be done and was not.

The original symposium was supported and the production of this book was financed through generous grants from UNAIDS. We also thank the University of the West Indies Press and its editorial team for their work and their support of our cause toward human rights in relation to HIV.

Introduction

George Alleyne

Chancellor and Professor Emeritus, University of the West Indies

Origins of the Human Rights Symposium

This symposium had its genesis in a discussion on HIV and the law hosted by Dr Karen Sealey in the UNAIDS Caribbean Secretariat in July 2008. The idea was to examine those aspects of the law and legal practice that negatively impact the lives of people living with HIV or AIDS (PLWHA) and also impede the efforts to prevent and control the HIV epidemic. The late Robert Carr was a strong proponent for a seminar to be held under the aegis of the University of the West Indies. He argued, as he had done on several previous occasions, that much of the discrimination being experienced by persons with HIV should be cast in a historical context, given that this was the year of the bicentennial of the abolition of the slave trade. He posited that it was an extreme incongruity that a people who would be remembering the abolition of the worst possible example of human degradation, stigmatization and discrimination should be embracing any form of discrimination. Even worse was having such discrimination enshrined in laws, even though in many cases such laws ran counter to the constitutions to which countries pointed proudly as evidence of their independence and embrace of human rights. One participant in the discussion argued strongly that the redress would not come through the political route but essentially through the courts.

It was finally agreed that one way to discuss the problem and make an impact on decision-makers would be to convene a seminar/symposium under the aegis of the region's premier academic institution – the University of the West Indies – bringing together a range of stakeholders, academics, practising politicians, PLWHA, the business sector, national HIV and AIDS coordinators, organized labour, and international organizations.

The symposium was developed in conjunction with the Faculty of Law of the University of the West Indies and several other stakeholders. It is fair to admit that there was a measure of scepticism about the symposium, in that it was accepted that there was already a rich and diverse literature on HIV and human rights and many of the persons affected had said often and loudly that their human rights were being abused with little or no substantive response. The governments of the world had made several commitments on human rights and HIV. The most recent at that time was the "Political Declaration on HIV/AIDS" in 2006, which stated, "The full realization of all human rights and fundamental freedoms for all is an essential element in the global response to the HIV and AIDS pandemics, including in the areas of prevention, treatment, care and support, and recognize that addressing stigma and discrimination is also a critical element in combating the global HIV/AIDS pandemic." The governments committed themselves "to intensifying efforts to enact, strengthen or enforce, as appropriate, legislation, regulations and other measures to eliminate all forms of discrimination against and to ensure the full enjoyment of all human rights and fundamental freedoms by people living with HIV and members of vulnerable groups, in particular to ensure their access to, inter alia, education, inheritance, employment, health care, social and health services, prevention, support and treatment, information and legal protection, while respecting their privacy and confidentiality; and developing strategies to combat stigma and social exclusion connected with the epidemic".

This powerful language has not been translated into actions that have resulted in the diminution of the problem in the Caribbean. Indeed, the recent publication of UNAIDS's "Keeping Score 3" indicates there is "a lot of talk around human rights but very little change on the ground. All countries have integrated some elements of human rights in their national response to HIV; however, in many instances, new policies were not approved or implemented."[1]

A snapshot of the HIV-related legal environment in the Caribbean in 2010 reveals the following:

- 56 per cent of countries report no legal protection against HIV-related discrimination.
- 75 per cent of countries report laws and regulations that present obstacles to HIV services for vulnerable population groups.
- 69 per cent of countries criminalize same-sex activities among consenting adults. These include Antigua and Barbuda, Barbados, Belize, Dominica, Grenada, Guyana, Jamaica, St Kitts and Nevis, St Lucia, St Vincent and the Grenadines, and Trinidad and Tobago.
- 81 per cent of countries criminalize some aspects of sex work.

- 19 per cent of countries have HIV-related travel restrictions.
- 19 per cent of countries have HIV-specific laws that criminalize HIV transmission.

The clear and evident concern for human rights in the Caribbean had led to many initiatives, some of which are detailed in the presentations made at the symposium and included in the chapters that follow. There was concern that the debate in the Caribbean had tended to conflate the human rights of those PLWHA with the human rights of groups vulnerable to infection with HIV, especially men who have sex with men (MSM). It should be pointed out that the discourse in the Caribbean has generally been full of statements of discrimination without there being any good data on the extent of such discrimination and whether or not it interferes with the efforts to control the epidemic (although the latter opinion has become standard dogma almost universally).

Organization and Goals

The symposium was organized under the sponsorship of the University of the West Indies, the Pan Caribbean Partnership against HIV and AIDS (PANCAP) and UNAIDS. The participants were drawn from almost every possible stakeholder group. They included PLWHA; PANCAP staff; university academics, principally from the Faculty of Law; representatives from the ministries of health, including ministers of health; senior politicians, including the acting prime minister of Barbados; nongovernmental organizations (NGOs), which focused on HIV and human rights; directors of national AIDS programmes; international organizations such as United Nations Development Programme (UNDP), International Labour Organization (ILO), United Nations Programme on HIV/AIDS (UNAIDS), Pan American Health Organization (PAHO) and Organization of American States (OAS); the media; the business community; and organized labour.

The stated goal was to influence policymakers and the judiciary through symposium materials that spoke to the issues of HIV and human rights and encouraged steps that might be taken to ameliorate the situation. The expected results included the following:

- Sensitization of the judiciary and senior policymakers to the issue of HIV and human rights in the context of the Caribbean experience
- Advocacy for including HIV issues within the current established human rights and social services programmes of governments

- Reduction of stigma and discrimination against PLWHA
- Recommendation of strategies for governments to move the human rights agenda forward in relation to PLWHA

The Political Dimension

The critical importance of the political approach to the issue was underscored by the presence of the acting prime minister of Barbados, who gave the keynote address and spoke to some of the legal implications of HIV and human rights. He traced the history of the epidemic, noting the initial moral strictures against those whose lifestyles were thought to be conducive to not only contracting but also spreading the disease. He proceeded to expand on the notion of rights and posited, "The sense which I think most appropriate to present purposes is that in which the use of the word 'right' connotes the existence of a duty in someone else to make claims to that right effective."

He then went on to outline the fundamental rights that are enshrined in the Constitution of Barbados, which include protection against discrimination. He also indicated that since Barbados is a signatory to many relevant international conventions, they should encourage the prohibition of discrimination, including in situations where such discrimination arises as a result of serious illness. He made the point that the nondisclosure of a person's status makes the task of protecting against discrimination more difficult.

Two ministers of health adopted different approaches to the issue of HIV and human rights. There was acceptance of the fact that discrimination and human rights abuses do occur. They emphasized the phenomenon of the discrimination which was shown to exist in the health services. However, it was also posited that politicians are themselves products of the society and often simply reflect the prejudices of that society. A strong call was made for the studied engagement and education of parliamentarians, since some are willing, if properly supported, to lead on contentious issues such as human rights. The point was made that parliamentarians have to see rights as indivisible and not advocate for the rights of one or another segment of society. Politicians are often divided over the issue of promoting certain individuals' rights while alienating the general public. The symposium was reminded that a parliamentarian who loses his or her seat for whatever reason is ineffective as a political force. Special attention has to be paid to the use of public health measures, which can be justified even when applied to stigmatized groups. One minister's call for attention to women's rights and especially their sexual and reproductive rights was an echo of the concern addressed by one of the PLWHA presenters.

Undoubtedly, political sensitivity surrounds the issue of HIV and rights. While it is acknowledged that rights are enshrined in the constitution, there is also recognition that these constitutional provisions are not enough to protect PLWHA. Parliaments and parliamentarians represent a source of change, but we must encourage the willing few to adopt the leadership necessary to enact other laws that will give full protection to PLWHA.

Reflections of PLWHA

The contribution of PLWHA was varied, but it was salutary that there was an attempt to describe what, on the basis of varied experiences, could be done to address the issues of rights and discrimination. One view was that there should and could be no separation of the rights of PLWHA from the rights of other persons. The international declarations made for the indivisibility of rights and the natural query was why, after universal agreement on these rights, they were still being abused. The widespread problems in the Caribbean were highlighted. For example, it was noted that if the rights of PLWHA are abused, the region would never fully address the kinds of rights that are intrinsic to the Treaty of Chaguaramas, the basic document of the Caribbean community that underpins the Caribbean integration movement. How would it be possible to accept the rights of Caribbean people to move freely in the region when other, perhaps conflicting rights were not being observed? The answer seemed to lie in the fact that the necessary political actions were stymied by a lack of support at the popular level as a result of social norms, values and attitudes.

This political paralysis accounted for the fact that there was a poor Caribbean track record of sanctions against human rights violations. By calling for special attention to the human rights abuses endured by PLWHA, we could examine if they were being targeted and therefore further marginalized and discriminated against. Naturally, some were impatient with the disjuncture between political rhetoric and actual practice.

The issues of discrimination, human rights abuse and access to treatment were explored as a personal narrative. While it was accepted that discrimination was present and harmful before treatment was available, its existence represented a real barrier to access to treatment when such treatment did become available. As one speaker noted, "Arguably people with AIDS died more from shame, isolation and loneliness in those days than the disease itself. Fear and ignorance fanned the flames of discrimination, the mortality rate soared and the future looked uncertain." Vigorous and sustained advocacy and the presence of a strong Caribbean Regional Network of People Living with HIV/AIDS (CRN+) were presented as one approach to enhancing access to treatment. It was proposed that this twin approach might also engage people at all levels – from the political directorate, to the private sector, to the positive community itself – and help to reduce the stigma, discrimination and abuse of human rights.

An interesting contribution from a Greater Involvement of People Living with HIV/AIDS (GIPA) coordinator focused on the need to train PLWHA to understand their rights with the thesis that "absence of this self-determination may lead to social exclusion and the violation of fundamental rights", and "the rights-based approach to HIV and AIDS can be enhanced when [PLWHA] are sensitized and trained to understand and recognize their role as part of the wider citizenry". The training programme described starts from the position that it is the PLWHA who must be most engaged and aggressive in participating in the decision-making that affects them directly, and it is they who have a particular stake in achieving goal 6 of the Millennium Development Goals, which speaks to halting and reversing the spread of HIV by 2015. It is not enough to depend on the goodwill of the concerned and sympathetic citizenry. Thus there is the need for training of PLWHA to provide them with tools for this role.

The programme of capacity building is led by an HIV-positive coordinator, thus giving tangible expression to the thesis that it is the infected and directly affected who must have a stronger voice in all aspects of the HIV programmes. The proposal is for the training of successive groups of HIV-positive recruits who, through adequate selection and appropriate training, will achieve the comfort level to allow them to be community facilitators and activists and eventually participate in the national HIV-Related Discrimination Reporting and Redress System, which was established to collect cases of stigmatization and discrimination and provide redress. The results of this innovative approach were not available but clearly could be of tremendous significance and, if successful nationally, could perhaps be replicated regionally. One of the critical elements for success will be the continued psychosocial support needed by the cadre recruited to perform this role. The approach would serve to strengthen the network of PLWHA and supplement their collective work.

Several different concerns of PLWHA were manifest in a small research study that investigated the sexual and reproductive rights of HIV-positive women. It is sometimes forgotten that this is an area in which abuse often goes undetected. Sexual and reproductive rights extend to all women and men, irrespective of HIV status, but the problem is made complex in the presence of HIV infection. Health services are sometimes the worse perpetrators of abuse in this area. The young HIV-positive mother faces the problem of disclosure and a lifetime of balancing the needs related to her sex and sexuality with the public perceptions of her HIV status.

Although the sample was small and clearly not representative of the general population, it revealed data that are in keeping with those gathered elsewhere. The health services were only moderately responsive to the needs of these HIV-positive young women with respect to contraceptive choices, infant feeding and postpartum family referrals. The high level of physical violence against them was striking, and it was remarkable that there was little or no counselling in this area. It is perhaps a manifestation of their level of agency that only one-third of the women had disclosed their HIV status to their partners.

The discussion of the experiences of PLWHA centred for the most part on how the Commonwealth Caribbean institutions were responding tardily to the HIV epidemic or, in some cases, responding in a manner that was frankly inimical to prevention and control. One view was that the institutions, such as the health care system, that were built under colonialism were inherently prejudicial to the rights of the poor and the marginalized, such as PLWHA. It was not uncommon, for example, to hear that HIV-positive women had abrogated their right to have children. They represented another face of the inequality of power relations in our societies. An opposite view was that our "sins" are not a result of our colonial heritage but are of our own creation. The problem is the basic fear of openly addressing HIV, which obviously touches on sensitive moral issues.

HIV, Human Rights and the Law

The legal aspects of HIV and human rights were addressed by academic lawyers, and the opening sentence of the discourse on human rights in the Caribbean constitutions gives some insight into the nature of the argument:

> The Member states of the Caribbean Community, including the British Overseas Territories, stand in the tradition of written, democratic constitutionalism: the idea of a democratic polity is constituted and regulated by a written fundamental law, founded on the principle of the separation of powers, and containing a set of basic human rights which constrain the exercise of legitimate governmental powers by the agencies of the State and are legally enforceable in favour of the citizen through the practice of judicial review by an independent judiciary. It is for this reason that the typical Caribbean constitution may be dubbed a constitution of rights and the community that that constitution constitutes, a community of rights.

There is a well-reasoned argument that human rights norms derive from an appreciation of the intrinsic dignity of the person, and the constitution sets out certain provisions that form essential human rights and represent the moral legitimacy of the state. To the extent that all persons are equal and possessors of the same dignity, human rights are universal. The essential human rights that are enshrined in all democratic constitutions are life, autonomy and liberty. The right to life is obvious. Autonomy relates to the power to make one's own critical decisions.

Liberty entails the ability to make one's own life choices, provided there is no interference with the liberty of another. Health is one of the requirements for life, and the state has the responsibility to provide the wherewithal to ensure that the individual has the option to pursue a healthy existence. As stated in article 11 of the American Declaration on the Rights and Duties of Man – the world's first *international human rights instrument* of a general nature – "Every person has the right to the preservation of his health through sanitary and social measures relating to food, clothing, housing and medical care, to the extent permitted by public and community resource."[2]

The West Indian constitutions guarantee basic human rights to all citizens, and it is posited that the state cannot justifiably favour the rights of one part of the citizenry over another. The rights of the minority, in the exercise of their personhood, have to be protected as well. As an eminent Indian jurist put it, "The law is, theoretically at least, a product of majoritarian moral beliefs – a statute enacted by a representative legislature elected through majority vote. It makes little sense for a court to use that same conventional morality to review an expression of it by the legislature. Constitutional guarantees would lose their significance if these are given conventional – that is – majoritarian interpretation. A right against the majority only when the majority agrees with it is not much of a right."[3]

There was discussion of the infamous "savings law clauses", which bar pre-existing laws from being declared inconsistent with the rights enshrined in the constitution. The unconstitutionality of one example of such a law, which criminalizes same-sex relations, has been argued successfully in India.

Many now accept that existing laws that criminalize same-sex relations run counter to basic but theoretical precepts of human rights. There appear to be two possible resolutions to the problem of making such rights a reality. The parliaments could declare such laws unconstitutional and abolish them. This is unlikely, given that parliaments tend to be guardians of and a reflection of public majoritarian morality rather than constitutional morality. The other more likely option is for the courts to rule that such laws are subject to judicial review.

Pragmatic approaches to HIV and human rights were presented with special emphasis on employment. It was argued that human rights is conceived as a "legalistic, juristic concept, confined strictly to the constitutional mores of a particular jurisdiction", but note must also be taken of the popular concept of human rights embraced as an entitlement. The important point was made that the Caribbean constitutions are no more and no less than reflections of our societies and are silent on the rights of particular groups or individuals, although they claim to represent the rights of all citizens. It is thus unrealistic to rely solely on constitutional provisions to address discrimination or injury perceived or suffered by certain groups. The concern of vulnerable groups, which may indeed be victims of discrimination, cannot be addressed adequately through a "human rights approach" based on constitutional provisions. As was argued, "While rights conjure up the idea of constitutional protection, it may well be that some of the so-called rights about which we speak are located outside of the boundaries of the constitution. Therefore, there needs to be a proactive legislative agenda separate from the constitution that will be in accord with the most fundamental human rights." This is a pragmatic approach to addressing any denial of human rights and one that is likely to be more effective than attempting the Herculean task of constitutional reform, desirable though that may be.

The rights of migrant persons were discussed, stressing that international human rights law speaks clearly to the rights of noncitizens. HIV persons should not be deemed "undesirable" in the context of immigration nor in any context. Because constitutional considerations are not applicable in the private law context, which embraces employment issues, the approach has to be the development and practice of ordinary legislation related to HIV in the context of fairness and justice.

While the importance of national laws is accepted, attention has to be drawn to the several bodies of regional and international human rights law for protecting the human rights and fundamental freedoms of all persons and certainly for addressing the problems of discrimination against PLWHA. The case of Jamaica was highlighted, since it is one of the parties involved in the American Convention on Human Rights. This convention outlines the rights to equal protection of the law, personal liberty and security of person, life and personal integrity, freedom of movement and residency, security of person, and freedom of thought and expression. The question may be posed as to the value and pertinence of these conventions when states quite openly deny their citizens these rights.

In direct relevance to this, it was pointed out that the Inter-American Commission on Human Rights and the Inter-American Court of Human Rights

represent two bodies within the Organization of American States (OAS) created to promote the observance and defence of human rights in the Americas.
Currently, six Caribbean states have ratified the American Convention on
Human Rights. The recommendations of the commission and the decisions
of the court have been instrumental in assisting member states to re-examine
their legislation and policies. It was pointed out that human rights activists in
the Caribbean make little use of these instruments, and indeed the court has
yet to adjudicate on a petition involving the denial of the human rights of a
Caribbean person with HIV.

Caribbean Programmes to Address Stigma and Discrimination

It is not that there has not been concern about the legal aspects of stigma and
discrimination in the Caribbean. The priority area 1 of the Caribbean Regional
Strategic Framework is "advocacy, policy development and legislation".[4] To
fulfil that mandate, PANCAP developed, with the aid of Canadian International
Development Agency (CIDA), the "HIV/AIDS Law Ethics and Human Rights"
project. The major components of the project included country assessments, law
and policy reform and the enhancement of legal aid services. Regional model
codes of practice were developed, as was a code of practice for psychosocial
practitioners. A number of Caribbean policies and declarations were developed.
Several regional consultations were held, and as a result of this, the PANCAP
Regional Stigma and Discrimination Unit was established to attempt to collect
data on the extent and nature of the problem. One interesting development
was the support of two subregional groups of legal practitioners, supporting
PLWHA in seeking redress for abuses of their human rights.

Another outcome of the project was the documentation of widespread
stigmatizing and discriminatory legal and policy measures by a number of
governments, as has been mentioned previously. These included compulsory
screening of several groups of persons, pre-employment screening and mandatory testing of persons seeking work permits. There was a detailed country-by-
country analysis of antidiscrimination legislation, constitutional protections,
public health law, confidentiality, criminal law, immigration, education and
human rights of prisoners.

Human rights desks were established in six countries in 2005. However,
after five years, a review showed that only three of the five were functioning. All are seriously constrained financially, and the inadequacy of training
and physical location made them less than effective. The need for a reporting
mechanism to address stigma and discrimination is clear, as documenting violations is an essential step in encouraging policy change and the monitoring of

the relevant laws and policies. However, it is doubtful that this approach made any significant difference in the countries in which it was tried. One interesting and progressive development was the formation of a Caribbean Human Rights Defenders Network, and the idea was put forward that existing activist groups such as Jamaicans for Justice could lend technical cooperation to the newly formed network.

Private Sector Concerns

The role of the private sector was the subject of active discussion. A point was forcibly made that it is not the responsibility of the business enterprise to determine or act on human rights issues. Rather, it is the role of governments to establish the rights of individuals through constitutional means, and business should follow such prescriptions. However, it is possible to avoid violations of the human rights of PLWHA in business, especially in the workplace, as it is in the interest of all parties that there should be no discrimination there. The International Labour Organization (ILO) Code of Conduct represented an ideal template for developing appropriate roles for businesses and employees with respect to HIV and the rights of PLWHA. The Barbados AIDS Foundation presented a charter as a guide to the best practices in regard to HIV and the workplace. The point was made very strongly that it was not enough to depend on the volition of the employers. There was need for the nongovernment actors, or civil society and organized labour, to be much more aggressive in holding governments accountable for the gaps between the constitutional provisions in regard to human rights and the practice of discrimination. Indeed, it was argued that governments were not entirely guilt free with respect to the latter.

Another nongovernment actor is the media, and it was pointed out that the Caribbean Broadcast Media partnership on HIV had as one of its key sustainability objectives the building of partnerships at regional and country levels to sustain action to reduce stigma and discrimination. It had established a formal partnership with the regional stigma and discrimination unit and would be developing human rights PSAs to be used by more than one hundred broadcasters in twenty-four countries.

The case of the insurance industry was posed as a special problem. PLWHA complained of discrimination with regard to life and other forms of insurance. The industry complained that it could not obtain the actuarial data necessary to offer its products. Part of the onus lies with the medical profession and its diffidence with regard to the accuracy of death certification. It was agreed that a conference between the parties should be held to establish the data needs and the method of obtaining them.

Final Reflections: Reducing the Gap between "Promise and Reality"

The timing of the workshop was felt to be significant, as it coincided with the decision in the Caribbean to strive for universal access to prevention, care and treatment. The realization of that decision was impeded by the gap between the promise and the reality of the human rights agenda that would make universal access possible. The workshop gave some leads as to how to close that gap. One idea posed that there should not be reliance on the constitutional affirmation of human rights but rather on the pragmatic approach of developing legislation needed to make them real. There needed to be some institutional focal points to enhance the effort to improve the human rights situation of PLWHA. In addition, a coordinating agency, such as PANCAP, should be important in facilitating the concerted action of the many groups which had HIV as their raison d'être. Caribbean strategic planning for HIV should embrace the protection of human rights. Governments are obviously of critical importance, but in the end, it will take the concerted effort of all those present and many other like-minded individuals and groups to effectively advance the human rights agenda in the Caribbean both in general and with specific reference to HIV.

Notes

1. UNAIDS, "Keeping Score 3: The Voice of the Caribbean People", 2011.
2. Basic Documents Pertaining to Human Rights in the InterAmerican System OEA/Ser.L.V/II.82 doc6.Rev1at 17 (1992).
3. Justice Ajit Prakash Shah, "De-Criminalization of Anti-Sodomy Law in India: Tackling the Issues of Constitutional Morality, Public Health and Individual Rights" (presented at the first Commonwealth HIV Human Rights lecture, London, 30 November 2010, for World AIDS Day), http://www.aidsalliance.org/includes/document/WAD_Justice_Shah.pdf.
4. Pan-Caribbean Partnership on HIV and AIDS, *The Caribbean Regional Strategic Framework for HIV/AIDS 2002–2006*, http://www.caricom.org/jsp/projects/hiv-aidsstrategicframework.pdf.

Part 1

A Social Engineering Approach to HIV

Conceptual and Policy Issues

Chapter 1

HIV, AIDS and Human Rights

A Barbados Governmental Perspective

Freundel J. Stuart

Prime Minister of Barbados

HIV and AIDS have become a haunting presence in our societies. In 1981, acquired immune deficiency syndrome (AIDS) was first recognized among homosexual men in the United States. In 1983, the etiological agent, the human immunodeficiency virus (HIV), was identified.[1] HIV becomes AIDS when the immune system is seriously damaged.[2] In 1984, the first case in Barbados was identified.[3] A most relevant and timely issue is that of HIV and its intersection with human rights. We do ourselves no good if we pretend that this is a challenge that we can afford to ignore. It is therefore appropriate to confront its implications, legal and otherwise, for the way that we live in Barbados and the wider Caribbean.

Since the very future of our societies seemed threatened by the disease, the government was forced to get involved and at least try to slow its spread. Since 2003, the government of Barbados has been making antiretroviral (ARV) drugs available to persons living with the disease, free of cost.[4] Fortunately this has resulted in a 50 per cent reduction of the death rate and a similar reduction of the sick rate.[5]

It has to be emphasized, however, that even though people are living longer with the virus, one must be careful not to equate that fact with the finding of a cure. People continue to be infected, which results in an even larger demand for the resources available for the treatment of the disease. The fact that infected persons not only are living longer but also seem to be leading normal lives raises necessarily and understandably the issue of the rights to which these persons are entitled – hence the link between HIV and human rights and the need to discuss this issue.

HIV, AIDS and the Gay Stereotype

At the time of its earliest manifestations, the general population tended to associate the contraction of HIV with the homosexual lifestyle. Since this lifestyle did not coincide with the general society's brand of righteousness, it was easy for some members of the society to relegate persons living with HIV to the lonely status of social pariahs journeying, ineluctably, to deserved perdition.[6]

Since, according to those who arrogated to themselves the right to occupy the judgement seat, the gay lifestyle was both sinful and wrong, there could be no compromise on this issue. To do otherwise would be to court, senselessly, the fate that befell Sodom and Gomorrah. For this school, the issue was an ethical one, and since these ethics derived their energy and legitimacy from the Bible, these spokespersons thought they were just discharging their responsibilities as faithful ambassadors of the Almighty.

No attempt was made then, and I daresay that very little attempt is made now, to consider that it might just be that practitioners of this lifestyle were responding to the irresistible promptings of nature, with the result that imputing fault to them satisfied no known definition of fairness.[7] Further, even if these practitioners were pursuing this lifestyle as a result of nurture, in which case they may have been exercising some measure of choice, the right to choose in these circumstances should be protected as long as its exercise did not interfere with the rights of others.[8] These purists ignored the important fact that difference does not necessarily imply a relationship of superiority and inferiority, or good and bad, or blamelessness and blameworthiness.

Once it was discovered that the disease did not seek out by preference only those who practised the gay lifestyle, there was a realization that we were all potentially at risk, and attitudes towards the disease softened. In fact, we now know that HIV may be contracted by any individual engaged in any form of unprotected sexual intercourse with an individual who is HIV positive, from blood transfusions with HIV infected blood or from intravenous drug use with needles used by an infected individual; it can also be transferred from an infected pregnant mother to her unborn baby or to a baby through the mother's breast milk. These circumstances appear to have led to some softening of attitudes.

HIV, AIDS and Human Rights

The word *right*, as lawyers generally use the term, connotes the existence of a duty of someone else if the exercise of that right is to have real meaning. Put differently, there is a correlative relationship between the word *right* and the word *duty*. Of course, the word is used in other senses as well. There are times when it means no more than *liberty*, such as if I say, "I have a right to wear my hair long or short." This statement means that I am at liberty to decide that issue and nothing more. At other times, the word means nothing more than *power*, such as if I say, "The government has the right to raise or lower taxes." That statement means that the government is vested with power to both raise and lower taxes. At still other times the word means nothing more than *immunity*, such as if I say, "Ambassador John Smith has a right not to be subjected to legal process." That right of immunity would derive, of course, from his status as a diplomat. The sense which I think most appropriate for our present purposes is that in which the use of the word *right* connotes the existence of a duty of someone else to make claims to that right effective.

The fundamental rights to which all Barbadians are entitled are enshrined in chapter 3 of the Constitution of Barbados and are as follows: the right to life, liberty and security; the right to protection of the privacy of his or her home and other property and protection from deprivation of property without compensation; the right to the protection of the law; and the right to freedom of conscience, expression, and assembly and association. These rights apply without regard to race, place of origin, political opinions, colour, creed or sex but are subject to respect for the rights of others and for the public interest.[9]

In 1967, Barbados became a member of the Organization of American States, and subscription to the charter included an obligation to respect the fundamental rights of the individual as elaborated in the 1948 American Declaration of the Rights and Duties of Man. In 1973, Barbados acceded to the International Convention on Civil and Political Rights and in 1982 ratified the American Convention on Human Rights, which had come into force in 1978. None of these instruments, either in letter or in spirit, permits Barbados or any other subscribing state expressly or by implication to discriminate against persons, whether citizens or not.[10] Indeed, the preamble to the Constitution of Barbados and other Caribbean states affirms belief in the dignity and worth of the human person and an unshakeable faith in fundamental rights and freedoms.[11]

The fact is HIV and AIDS are illnesses. Though it is simple to understand, it requires constant repetition. No person should be discriminated against be-cause of illness. In determining rights in relation to HIV, we should be very mindful of this fact and the responsibilities of the state in this regard.

The principal arena in which human rights issues are played out is in the relationship between the state and the citizen.[12] Since that relationship is nec-essarily an unequal one – the state controlling an apparatus of coercion to which the citizen must invariably submit – governments tend to be held to the highest possible standards when the citizen or subject has reason to complain that his or her rights are being breached or undermined. Human rights issues are essentially public law issues. In that regard, they are to be distinguished from private law issues which define the relationship between individuals and groups in their day-to-day interactions with one another. The issues that press serious claims for the attention of the state are those of prevention, treatment, care and support. No credible attempts can be made in the area of prevention in the absence of a clear identification of the groups that are most vulnerable to infection and the spreading of the disease. The state can best approach the discharge of this remit by, as a matter of policy, effectively regulating places frequented, occupied or used by these groups (e.g., places like brothels where sex workers ply their trade).[13] In this way, the health of those who provide sexual services and those who purchase those services will be properly and professionally addressed.

An important target group is also the youth of the region, who are becoming sexually active at ever younger ages. They must be encouraged to pay greater attention to health care, especially since thoughtless experimentation is more likely among members of this group.[14] There is also the question of our correctional facilities and penal institutions, where HIV transmission requires urgent and carefully planned intervention and management. I believe Professor E.R. Walrond in his respected report[15] canvassed, ably, some of these issues and has placed Barbados firmly in his debt. As earlier indicated, steps taken in the area of treatment have been bearing fruit and the government is committed to the continued pursuit of this path. In the area of care and support, every opportunity to build upon the progress being made will be fully explored.

HIV, AIDS, Discrimination and State Response

Because of the unfortunate early association of HIV and AIDS with sexual behaviour thought to be outside the mainstream, it has not attracted the sympathy and understanding which illness ordinarily does. Securely planted in the minds of those living with the disease, therefore, is the belief that they will not be treated favourably in society if their status becomes known. They believe, and not without justification, that they will be discriminated against.

Discrimination is ultimately a question of evidence, and in the case of a person living with HIV, if he or she alleges discrimination, the burden of proof will rest on him or her to produce evidence of the legally required standard to support the allegation made.[16] The decisions of the courts of law are, invariably, based on the strength of the evidence adduced at trial.

Another obstacle for persons living with HIV is the inescapable peril of living in societies that are as small and highly personalized as the societies in the Caribbean. This often means that information travels very quickly and not always very accurately. The result usually is that privacy is, more often than not, a luxury. Further, once a stigma of whatever kind is attached to a person, there is little scope available for him or her to leave one area and migrate to another to, as it were, make a fresh start. Living in small, highly personalized societies, therefore, makes the situation faced by persons living with HIV even more unbearable.[17]

Unlike in the case of the social category we identify sometimes as "the disabled", at other times as "the differently abled" and at still others as "persons with disabilities", where the status is always known because, in most cases, the disability can be easily seen, HIV may often not manifest itself outwardly in a physical sense. Further, there exists no legal duty on the part of persons living with HIV to make their status known to those with whom they interact. It is not, therefore, beyond the realm of probability that what a person living with HIV privately interprets as discrimination is nothing more than an innocent, nonbiased encounter.

How then do we tread our way through this labyrinth? It seems to me that if, as American courts have held, the word *discriminate* means no more than "to treat unfavourably because of", persons living with HIV can only legitimately allege discrimination if they can prove that, in their particular case, their status was contemplated, either directly or indirectly, and therefore fuelled an unjust or unfavourable decision or situation. If the rights of the person living with HIV or AIDS are to awaken a correlative duty in others, that duty can be discharged more effectively if those called to it are not only aware of the duty but also aware of what its effective discharge will entail.[18]

In all this, leadership is the responsibility of the state through its various organs and agencies. The constitution outlaws discrimination based on certain characteristics, and the many international treaties to which we have subscribed reinforce that position.[19] However, HIV or AIDS is not a specifically protected ground. The passage of antidiscrimination legislation on this issue, while potentially very useful, will be cheated of effective results so long as the duty of disclosure remains an undecided issue.[20]

The protection of the human rights of persons living with HIV will require legislative support. Policymakers must be as passionate about what persons living with HIV should have a right to achieve as they are about what persons living with HIV have a right to be protected from. Where legislation that enables these persons to more fully actualize their God-given potential is thought desirable or necessary, its drafting and passage must be accorded the appropriate sense of urgency.[21]

The arbiters in all this will be the courts of law to which we all submit when we think our rights have been infringed. While it is true that our judiciary system is expected to be strong, enlightened and independent, it is never expected to do more than dispense justice according to law, as distinct from justice according to whim, caprice or sentiment. Justice according to law requires that people be held culpable only when in breach of mandated duties of which they should be aware.

Conclusion

We live in a region in which a person will now routinely and unabashedly disclose that he or she is diabetic or hypertensive. These diseases attract neither stigma nor reproach. We have not yet reached the stage where a person will routinely and unabashedly disclose that he or she is HIV positive. Diabetes and hypertension are described as chronic, noncommunicable diseases. HIV is a communicable virus with a pronounced social stigma attached to it. This distinction heightens our responsibility as governments and caregivers to those who are its hapless victims.

A better understanding of HIV and AIDS that leads to a more sympathetic treatment of those suffering with these illnesses and continuing public education at all levels that focuses on how we should treat our fellow man, HIV sufferer or not, are the ultimate and best guarantees of the observance and preservation of fundamental human rights for all. We should aim to achieve this. I hope that the rights and freedoms of a fragile humanity can benefit from much-needed enlargement as a result of the much-needed deliberations on these issues.

Notes

1. UNAIDS, "A History of the HIV/AIDS Epidemic with Emphasis on Africa" (prepared for Workshop on HIV/AIDS and Adult Mortality in Developing Countries, UNAIDS, Population Division, Department of Economic and Social Affairs, United Nations Secretariat, New York, 8–13 September 2003), 6–7, http://www.un.org/esa/population/publications/.../UNAIDS _WHOPaper2.pdf.

2. If you have fewer than two hundred CD4 cells or if your CD4 percentage is less than 14 per cent, you have AIDS. If you get an *opportunistic infection*, you

have AIDS. See "What Is AIDS?", http://www.aids.org/topics/aids-factsheets/aids-background-information/what-is-aids.

3. E. Massiah, T.C. Roach, C. Jacobs, A.M. St. John, V. Inniss, J. Walcott and C. Blackwood, "Stigma, Discrimination, and HIV/AIDS Knowledge among Physicians in Barbados", *Rev Panam Salud Publica/Pan Am J Public Health* 16, no. 6 (2004): 397, http://journal.paho.org/index.php?a_ID=296.

4. National HIV/AIDS Commission, "UNGASS Country Progress Report 2010: Barbados" (reporting period January 2008 to December 2009, March 2010), 36.

5. Allison Ramsay, "Stigma and Discrimination Hinder HIV/AIDS Fight", *Barbados Advocate*, 27 June 2010, http://www.barbadosadvocate.com/newsitem.asp?more=local&NewsID=11049.

6. Peter Richards, "Still Fighting HIV Stigma after 30 Years", *Inter-Press Service*, 16 September 2010, http://ipsnews.net/news.asp?idnews=52860. See also Richard Parker and Peter Aggleton, "HIV/AIDS-Related Stigma and Discrimination: A Conceptual Framework and an Agenda for Action", study prepared for the Horizons Program, Population Council, 2002, http://www.popcouncil.org/pdfs/horizons/sdcncptlfrmwrk.pdf.

7. The nature versus nurture debate concerns whether sexual orientation is a result of genetics (nature) or personal experiences (nurture).

8. The right to choose in pursuing one's sexual orientation is not specifically protected under our constitutions. However, in some jurisdictions, it has been possible to extend the protection regarding sex to include sexual orientation. This approach has not yet been tested in Barbados.

9. Additionally, they echo the familiar provisions of the Universal Declaration of Human Rights adopted by the UN General Assembly in 1948, and their content was influenced by the provisions of the European Convention on Human Rights of 1950. The European Convention on Human Rights had in fact applied to Barbados and other Caribbean countries since in 1953 the United Kingdom had made a declaration pursuant to that convention extending its application to its colonies, which, of course, included Barbados.

10. The international treaties that address human rights, such as the Universal Declaration of Human Rights, do not expressly mention HIV and AIDS. However, specific human rights that are protected in these documents are relevant to HIV and AIDS and therefore are means by which the human rights of people living with HIV or AIDS are protected. These include, inter alia, the right to nondiscrimination, the right to health and the right to work. See also Program on International Health and Human Rights, François-Xavier Bagnoud Center for Health and Human Rights, Harvard School of Public Health and the International Council of AIDS Service Organizations (ICASO), "HIV/AIDS and Human Rights in a Nutshell: A Quick and Useful Guide for

Action, as Well as a Framework to Carry HIV/AIDS and Human Rights Actions Forward" (2004), 4–5.

11. Even though discrimination on certain grounds is protected in the Constitution of Barbados, discrimination towards people living with HIV or AIDS is not a protected ground of discrimination.

12. The Bill of Rights in the Commonwealth Caribbean constitutions acts under the state action doctrine, which means that it governs only violations between the state and the citizens rather than between private individuals.

13. In Barbados, the Ministry of Labour launched a policy and code of practice on HIV, AIDS and other life-threatening illnesses in the public sector on 28 October 2009.

14. National HIV/AIDS Commission, "UNGASS Country Progress Report 2010", 14.

15. E.R. Walrond, "Report on the Legal, Ethical and Socio-Economic Impact of HIV/AIDS in Barbados" (June 2004).

16. Barbados does not have specific HIV and AIDS legislations but its Industrial Relations Code of Practice, which is a nonbinding but persuasive document, prohibits discrimination on the ground of HIV or AIDS.

17. Richards, "Still Fighting HIV Stigma".

18. The discrimination policy for individuals with HIV must take into consideration the notion of privacy and disclosure on the part of people living with HIV or AIDS.

19. The constitution outlaws discrimination only on certain grounds. There is no general principle of equality or nondiscrimination.

20. The question should be considered as to whether confidentiality as a legal principle is necessarily a good objective because a culture of silence can be dangerous and lead to further prejudice. Rose-Marie Belle Antoine, "Charting a Legal Response to HIV/AIDS and Work from the Perspective of Vulnerability", in *Sexuality, Social Exclusion and Human Rights*, ed. C. Barrow, M. de Bruin and R. Carr (Kingston: Ian Randle, 2009), 47. In some Commonwealth Caribbean territories such as the Bahamas and Jamaica, HIV and AIDS cases require notification, which call for the compulsory reporting of the full name, age, sex address, occupation and place of employment of the infected person. Under the Barbados model, more anonymity and confidentiality is secured as cases are reported to only one individual – a senior officer at the Ministry of Health.

21. The failure of governments to protect the rights of people living with HIV or AIDS through legislation or to enforce existing protective legislation may be considered discrimination by nonaction.

Chapter 2

Reflections on Reducing the Gap between "Promise and Reality"

Edward Greene

Special UN Envoy on HIV

The Symposium on HIV and Human Rights was significant in many ways. It was organized at a time when policymakers and practitioners in the Caribbean region were beginning to strive for universal access to prevention, care and treatment for people living with HIV or AIDS (PLWHA). Among the perquisites for achieving this objective are reducing stigma and removing outdated and punitive legislative environments. The symposium highlighted the need for bold leadership in advocating a human rights agenda, responsive governments and a vigilant civil society. It focused on strategies for closing the gap between the promise and the reality of human rights with special reference to HIV. This chapter alone is by no means a comprehensive summary of the symposium. It was initially presented at the end of the engaging and dynamic sessions and was originally intended to provide some reflections on the way forward in closing this gap.

As a first principle, the symposium agreed that the essence of human rights is rooted in the Universal Declaration of Human Rights (simply the Universal Declaration)[1] enunciated by the United Nations in 1948. That instrument provides a blueprint for other conventions, declarations and outcome documents from UN high-level meetings. Hence the rights of PLWHA, workers, women, children and vulnerable groups all fall under the umbrella of the Universal Declaration. Recommendation no. 200 of the ILO on HIV and the workplace[2] fully illustrates the comprehensive elements of human rights.

The principle of the indivisibility of human rights that was stressed in the presentation by Professor Simeon McIntosh on the West Indies constitution (chapter 6) reinforces the message conveyed in the keynote address by Prime

Minister Freundel Stuart (chapter 1). It provides a point of reference for understanding the paradox of the gap between promise and reality.

Many of the symposium presenters explored how and why this gap is
sustained. Human rights are prescribed in the constitutional instruments
and are supposed to be upheld by the legal system. In practice, however,
breaches prevail in the application of human rights shaped by national conventions and cultural mores and dignity and respect can be lost. Distortions
of the human rights principles were illustrated in the symposium presentations on discrimination and access. These distortions lead to countervail-
ing actions with contradictory results. The reason for this dilemma is that
the instruments for guaranteeing and safeguarding the rights of PLWHA,
embedded in the universal declaration, are also elements enshrined in the
West Indies constitution, but the applications within the latter have "seeds
for failure" because of the emphasis that is placed on diversity rather than
indivisibility.

Reducing and even eliminating the gap between promise and reality requires some specific and targeted steps. One option is to apply the principle
of human rights to public health. The Directing Council of the Pan American
Health Organization (PAHO), for example, has enunciated the goal of equity
in health. This translated into specific applications that would create the basis
for solidarity among health practitioners within health systems and could
make a difference in the patterns of treatment, care and support for PLWHA.
This is enunciated in the WHO Global Response to HIV/AIDS (1996) and the
more recent championing of universal access to prevention, care treatment
and support for PLWHA by the UNAIDS Global Task Team (2007).

There is a need to promote some institutional focal points and programmatic best practices that would consolidate the public health approach to
human rights. The recent attempts to establish a Caribbean Public Health
Agency – an attempt to merge five regional health institutions into one
agency – has the potential to influence the human rights agenda. Its objectives
include the following: (1) provide strategic direction in analysing, defining and
responding to public health issues in order to prevent diseases; (2) respond
to health emergencies; and (3) support solidarity in health.

Responding to the challenge thrown out by Brendan Bain, we must identify "who is responsible" for advancing the mission to reduce the gap between
promise and reality. Focusing specifically on HIV and human rights in the
Caribbean, that responsibility inevitably falls to the Pan Caribbean Partnership
against HIV and AIDS (PANCAP), the acknowledged authority for coordinating the regional HIV response. But PANCAP could not function effectively
without the support of UNAIDS, PAHO, the other UN systems and other

developing partners who are part of the driving force in the application of the "Caribbean Regional Strategic Framework", accepted as the guiding principles for the region's accelerated approach to HIV.

While the identification of a coordinating agency in PANCAP is vital to a collective and sustainable response, there is need for supporting agencies, to which we have already referred, and facilitating agencies to ensure the connectivity between regional and national programmes. The national AIDS programmes; the national and regional business coalitions for HIV; and groups like the Caribbean Regional Network of People with HIV/AIDS (CRN+), the Caribbean Council on Vulnerable Communities, and the Caribbean Broadcast Media Partnership for HIV/AIDS are vital. These organizations, together with faith-based institutions, youth groups and cultural icons, connect up with stakeholders at the national level.

Working with and through its supporters and facilitators and networking at the international and the national levels, PANCAP is in the best position to advocate for the implementation of the indivisibility principle. This is especially the case when it could base its advocacy on empirical information that would demonstrate the extent to which stigma and discrimination fuels the spread of the disease and how a more appropriate human rights agenda could contribute to increasing the value of human capital to the region's economic development. The University of the West Indies HIV/AIDS Response Program (UWIHARP) and other research and training institutions play critical roles in reducing the gaps.

The PANCAP approach helps to advance the cause of human rights for PLWHA and has the best chance for success, as it provides supportive leaders at the national level with a legitimate point of reference.

If the proposed trajectory for closing the gap between promise and reality is acceptable, then it is necessary to re-examine the "Caribbean Regional Strategic Framework" with the goal of incorporating a human rights element. This would provide the missing link in the Caribbean regional strategic framework and enhance the ethics and human rights component. An opportunity needs to be created to move this initiative forward perhaps at an anniversary celebration of PANCAP. It is consistent with the recommendations put forward by Susan Timberlake (chapter 3), with a model championed by UNAIDS.

I think if we are intent on making HIV and human rights more meaningful, it may be useful to establish a human rights committee which will bring together representatives of the PANCAP coordinating unit, PLWHA, the legal community, the universities (coordinated by the University of the West Indies), the stigma and discrimination unit and the Inter-American Commission on Human Rights. These would compose a specialized engine of PANCAP to move the human rights programmes forward in keeping with the recommendations from this symposium.

It is essential to identify a special role for our governments. They are critical to the political will required for consolidating and accelerating approaches to human rights. They need to see their roles in three ways: First, they need to respect human rights generally – specifically, the rights of PLWHA and those affected by HIV or AIDS. Second, they should protect those rights by providing redress against discrimination. Third, governments should play a critical role in establishing the appropriate legislative, administrative, budgetary and judicial measures to create effective changes in human rights approaches – specifically with respect to HIV.

In the introduction, Sir George Alleyne says that we all must play a part in responding to and fostering changes in human rights policies and practices. I fully endorse these sentiments and have put forward the case for PANCAP to play the lead role in marshalling the regional resources to achieve the goals of this symposium.

I join the other delegates for commending Sir George for his creative leadership and for marshalling this distinguished group of researchers and practitioners to grapple with the sensitive issues related to HIV and human rights. Hopefully the recommendations will be speedily converted into actions.

Notes

1. UN General Assembly, *Universal Declaration of Human Rights*, 10 December 1948, 217 A (III).
2. Recommendation concerning HIV and AIDS and the World of Work, 2010 (no. 200).

Chapter 3

Making a Change

Discrimination and Stigma against People Living with HIV or AIDS

Susan Timberlake

Senior Human Rights and Law Adviser, UNAIDS Secretariat

The Caribbean remains the region with the second highest rate of HIV prevalence in the world, after sub-Saharan Africa.[1] This was a driving force behind the 2010 Symposium on HIV and Human Rights, which tackled some of the most challenging aspects of the HIV epidemic in the Caribbean. Among other things, these challenges include high levels of HIV-related stigma and discrimination based on HIV status, widespread gender-based violence and inequality, pervasive homophobia, and punitive laws and law enforcement that impact some key populations[2] at risk of HIV infection – all major obstacles to effective national responses to HIV. These human rights–related challenges are not easy ones. They result from and raise extremely sensitive and complex issues, and they demonstrate the still corrosive power of the AIDS epidemic.

The symposium was held in one year before the thirty-year anniversary of the recognition of the HIV virus in June 1981. The symposium recognized that during the thirty years we have struggled against HIV, it has become ever more apparent that human rights are central to any effective response to HIV. In these thirty years, we have made significant progress, as new infections peaked worldwide in 1996 and have since declined,[3] although thirty-four million people are still living with HIV.[4] However, we cannot yet claim that we have "halted and begun to reverse the spread of HIV/AIDS", as called for under the UN Millennium Development Goal,[5] and we will not be able to do so unless we address the long-standing human rights issues that surround the HIV epidemic.

HIV and AIDS have spawned some of the worst stigma and discrimination ever seen in history. Many at risk for HIV infection are people who engage in behaviours that are subject to moral condemnation or criminalized by the law: same-sex sexual relations, drug use and sex work. Largely because of their criminalized status, they live at the margins of society and already experience barriers to accessible health care. Their association with HIV infection has in some places marginalized them even further, as they are now also associated with a stigmatized health condition. Due to these associations, people living with HIV are now often associated with these illegal or "immoral" activities, and this belief perpetuates the stigma they suffer not only from ignorance and fear of HIV but also from moral disapproval. This stigma and discrimination create major human rights and health challenges in the AIDS response. Additionally, women have become infected over time to a greater degree than men globally, and, in some communities, it has become apparent that it is not only their increased biological vulnerability to HIV infection at fault but also the fact that they cannot control if, when and under which circumstances they have sex. This puts them at great risk of HIV due to gender-based violence and sexual coercion as well as gender inequality in the social, political and economic spheres.[6]

These are the major issues facing the fight for elimination of AIDS. Many governments and international organizations have recognized that HIV infection and illness due to AIDS are not merely health conditions. However, at the onset of the disease, not all parties accepted this. Jonathan Mann was one of the first to make the link between vulnerability to HIV infection and the impact of AIDS and human rights protections back in the 1980s.[7] Where the human rights of those most vulnerable to HIV and those living with HIV are protected, the vulnerability to infection and the impact of AIDS is reduced for society at large.[8] Over the years, governments, the UN system and civil society have embraced the link between HIV, human rights and effective responses. In particular, governments have embraced the link by making strong commitments related to human rights and the law, starting with the UN General Assembly Special Session on HIV in 2001. In the "Declaration of Commitment on HIV/ AIDS" proclaimed at this meeting, states affirmed the central importance of human rights to the HIV response and committed themselves to protecting the rights of those living with and vulnerable to HIV, as well as protecting women and girls by, among other things, promoting gender equality and freedom from violence.[9] The declaration also recognized the need for laws that protect the rights of those living with and vulnerable to HIV.[10]

Later, in the "2006 Political Declaration on HIV/AIDS", states made the groundbreaking pledge to work towards achieving *universal access* to HIV prevention, treatment, care and support. They also made very specific commitments to human rights objectives as well as to those involving the legal environment relevant to HIV. In particular, they committed to overcome legal barriers to HIV services and enact laws against discrimination. They also reaffirmed the pledge to eliminate gender inequality and violence against women.[11]

Finally, in the High Level Meeting on HIV/AIDS that occurred at the General Assembly in June 2011 (after the symposium), states issued the "Political Declaration on HIV/AIDS: Intensifying Our Efforts to Eliminate HIV/AIDS" and specifically pledged to "fulfil obligations to promote universal respect for and the observance and protection of all human rights and fundamental freedoms for all" in response to HIV.[12] They committed themselves to enabling legal environments for the HIV response and to scaling up key programmes to end discrimination and increase access to justice in the context of HIV.[13] For the first time in an internationally agreed document, they also named three key populations at risk of HIV infection: sex workers, people who use drugs and men who have sex with men.[14]

At the time of the symposium and today, over a year later, levels of stigma and discrimination related to HIV and gender-based violence remain persistently high across the globe, and the human rights pledges of the political declarations remain largely unfulfilled. With regard to laws that can act as obstacles to access to HIV services, some seventy-nine countries and territories criminalize same-sex sexual relations and six impose the death penalty for such behaviour.[15] At least 116 countries impose legal sanctions for various aspects of sex work;[16] forty-seven countries retain HIV-related restrictions on entry, stay and residence;[17] and finally, fifty-six countries have enacted laws specifically criminalizing HIV transmission,[18] the majority of which are in the developed world.[19]

Unfortunately, the 2001, 2006 and 2011 Declarations on HIV/AIDS did not create numerical targets or indicators related to human rights and law in the context of national responses to HIV. However, systems by which to measure the accountability of governments to their commitments (a key human rights principle) have been developed by the Joint United Nations Programme on HIV/AIDS (UNAIDS) and various nongovernmental organizations. With the agreement of governments, UNAIDS established what has been known as UN General Assembly Special Session (UNGASS) reporting, wherein states reported every two years the degree to which they were achieving the targets set in the "2001 Declaration of Commitment". UNGASS country reports contain detailed epidemiological information on specific national epidemics and the national response in terms of HIV prevention, treatment, care and support. Additionally, its reports included questions in the "National Composite Policy Index" to which states and civil society groups provided information as to whether certain laws, policies and programmes were in place to support human rights protections in the context of HIV.[20] For instance, nearly one-third of states have reported that they do not have laws against discrimination based on HIV status.[21] In contrast, over two-thirds of states have reported that their laws or policies do not specifically address discrimination against a person's AIDS status and that this impedes access to HIV services for vulnerable populations.[22] These laws relate to criminalization for transmitting AIDS and travel restrictions determinant on status.

Various nongovernmental organizations have also monitored the human rights situation in the context of HIV. The Global Network of People Living with HIV (GNP+) has implemented "Human Rights Count", a project that documents human rights abuses against people living with HIV. Under this project, GNP+ developed a questionnaire to help elicit qualitative and quantitative data regarding human rights violations. The responses to these questionnaires are collected through regional focal points, where they are in turn used to inform advocacy campaigns to promote rights-based responses for people living with HIV. Through its "Global Criminalization Scan", GNP+ also monitors the countries that criminalize people living with HIV by prosecuting them for HIV nondisclosure, exposure and transmission.[23]

Housed at the International AIDS Society, the "HIV Travel Restrictions Database" lists countries that restrict entry, residence and stay based on positive HIV status.[24] Two longtime AIDS activists maintain this database.[25] Since the 1980s, experts have characterized such restrictions as discriminatory and without public health benefit.[26] The International Lesbian and Gay Association (ILGA) maintain the "ILGA List of Countries that Criminalize the Conduct of Sexual Minorities", which documents those countries that impose sanctions on same-sex sexual conduct.[27] Such laws are discriminatory and also act as obstacles to the roll-out and uptake of HIV prevention, treatment and care services for men who have sex with men and transgender people.

In the last few years, the focus on human rights and legal responses in the context of HIV has deepened. The UNAIDS 2011–15 strategy "Getting to Zero" challenges the world to move forward and improve the AIDS response, with the latest tools and information on what works at global, regional and country levels. It posits a vision of "zero new HIV infections, zero AIDS-related deaths and zero discrimination". The strategy also describes three strategic directions for global, regional and national responses to HIV: "revolutionizing HIV prevention; catalysing the next generation of treatment, care and support; and advancing human rights and gender equality for the HIV response".[28] As can be seen, for the first time, human rights and gender equality have been put at the same level of importance to AIDS responses as HIV prevention and treatment. This underlines that a higher level of political and programmatic attention should be paid to human rights and gender equality in relation to HIV or AIDS. Among other things, the strategy of 2011–15 has committed the United Nations to addressing the specific needs of women and girls in national HIV responses, as well as to cutting in half the number of countries that have punitive laws related to HIV and key populations.[29] It is in this context of concrete objectives and structure for UN, government and civil society accountability that the results of the symposium will move forward.

At the time of the symposium, groundwork for the developments in the UNAIDS strategy and the commitments on human rights and law in the "2011 Political Declaration" had already been laid. The response to HIV and AIDS has changed dramatically in the last five years: there is greater recognition of the importance of a rights-based approach to HIV and AIDS, renewed attention to people living with HIV as being at the heart of any response, a new focus on legal environments and their relevance to HIV, and, finally, a new focus on the need to expand specific programmes to reduce stigma and increase access to justice in the context of HIV.

The call for "universal access to HIV prevention, treatment, care and support", combined with the call to "know your epidemic and response", perhaps made it clearer than ever that a *rights-based response* to HIV and AIDS is required. One can only reach universal access if the response finds and provides for all those in need of HIV prevention, treatment, care and support, including the criminalized and most marginalized. A rights-based approach to HIV builds on the conceptual framework laid out in "Human Rights Based Approach to Development Cooperation: Towards a Common Understanding among UN Agencies".[30] It requires that (1) the needs of the most vulnerable to and most affected by HIV are addressed and their meaningful participation in the response is secured; (2) human rights goals are furthered through policy, funding and programming; (3) there are specific programmes to empower those living with and affected by HIV to succeed in a world with HIV; and (4) there are ever-improving accountability mechanisms, including increasingly disaggregated data, not only by sex and age but also by marital status, rural/urban classification, economic status, ethnicity and participation. A rights-based approach puts a UN programme like UNAIDS squarely between government and civil society to support (and push) governments to realize and protect human rights in the context of HIV and to support civil society to know and claim their rights in the context of HIV.

Participants of the symposium discussed what human rights are relevant in the context of HIV and AIDS: broadly speaking, the "right to HIV prevention" and the "right to HIV treatment". The "right to HIV prevention" comprises all the human rights necessary for people to be able to avoid HIV infection: the rights to education and information (on HIV, sexuality, life skills and human rights), health (HIV prevention services/commodities, prevention of mother to child transmission), privacy (noninterference and confidentiality of private matters including HIV status), liberty (autonomy and informed consent regarding health decisions and sexuality), nondiscrimination (including protection from discrimination based on health, legal status and sexual orientation), freedom from cruel and inhuman treatment (denial of health care in prison), freedom from gender-based and sexual violence, and security and due process.

The "right to HIV treatment, care and support" comprises all the human rights necessary to live successfully with HIV. These principally involve the right to nondiscrimination in major life activities (employment, education, social protection), health (antiretroviral therapy, palliative care, treatment for tuberculosis and drug dependency), privacy (confidentiality, prohibition of unlawful disclosure of HIV status), liberty (autonomy and informed consent in health decisions), sexual and reproductive rights for people living with HIV, and security and freedom from violence.

Again, the rights of the uninfected should not be pitted against the rights of those living with HIV. This is a false and unhelpful dichotomy. Only when *all* people know how HIV is and is not transmitted, have access to the commodities that prevent HIV transmission, and have the autonomy and support to use them will people be protected from infection. Though people living with HIV have responsibility to prevent the onward transmission of HIV, uninfected people cannot depend on them to do so, especially because over half of those living with HIV do not know they are infected. Thus responsibility for sexual health must be shared. We should recognize that people living with HIV and support for them must be at the heart of the AIDS response.

Increasingly, over the years of the epidemic, the dichotomy of HIV prevention and HIV treatment has broken down. The fact that "treatment equals prevention" has long been known by people living with HIV who are on treatment and by pregnant, HIV-positive women who receive, with their newborn infants, antiretroviral treatment to prevent vertical transmission. In both cases, the treatment, through antiretroviral drugs, reduces viral load to such low levels that the person living with HIV being treated is hardly infectious. Before the symposium, this was recognized in the so-called Swiss Statement of January 2008, in which Swiss HIV experts concluded that HIV-positive individuals who were on antiretroviral treatment and were free of STIs were sexually noninfectious.[31] After the symposium, the HIV Prevention Trials Network study, "A Randomized Trial to Evaluate the Effectiveness of Antiretroviral Therapy Plus HIV Primary Care versus HIV Primary Care Alone to Prevent the Sexual Transmission of HIV-1 in Serodiscordant Couples",[32] confirmed

that, at least among discordant couples, treatment with antiretrovirals reduces transmission to others by 96 per cent.[33] Thus by increasing access to
treatment (a fundamental tenet of universal access), there will eventually be a
population-level impact on new infections.

These incredible developments coincide with a new movement among people living with HIV called "Policy, Health, Dignity and Prevention" (PHDP).
It links together the social, legal, health and prevention needs of individuals
living with HIV within a holistic and human rights framework of support.
Among other things, this support ensures that people living with HIV acquire
complex skills for communication and decision-making about HIV transmission risk: namely, that they are willing and able to practise HIV prevention and
disclose their positive status without fear and without experiencing discrimination and stigma. In this context, they know how to practise safe sex and use
and have access to condoms, and they are supported to stay on treatment to
both protect their own health and to reduce infectiousness.[34] This paradigm
calls for HIV to be recognized for what it is – a chronic health condition that
does not stop people living with HIV from living long, productive lives without posing a risk to others. Such an approach brings HIV out of secrecy and
shame and engenders an atmosphere where uninfected and infected alike can
access information, education and services and act on them to protect themselves both from infection and from discrimination.[35]

However, the PHDP framework relies on the establishment of a positive
social environment in which stigma surrounding HIV is dramatically reduced.
Thus another new focus of the HIV response relates to the social and legal
environments that enable or disable national AIDS responses. There is clear
evidence that stigma (an attitude) and discrimination (an act prohibited by
human rights law) impedes individual uptake of HIV prevention and treatment.[36] It also discourages disclosure of positive HIV status.[37] UNAIDS has
therefore worked hard to assist in the development of tools that measure
stigma and promote programmes to reduce stigma towards people living with
HIV as well as other key populations that are vulnerable to infection, including sex workers, men who have sex with men and people who use drugs.[38]
With regard to these populations, it also appears that a combination of stigma
against them, denial of their existence (in some countries) and their criminalized status blocks governments from funding and programming HIV prevention and treatment on their behalf.

A key tool by which to measure HIV-related stigma is the "Stigma Index
for and by People Living with HIV".[39] This tool is the product of a joint effort
among many partners but benefiting from the leadership of people living with
HIV. It was meant to address two challenges: First, it enables people living

with HIV to be the actors, not just the subjects, in research done about their experience. Second, it created a robust research tool, with resulting data on the experience with stigma by people living with HIV. These data can and should be used to inform priorities and programming in national responses. The data can also be triangulated with other measurements of HIV-related stigma that often take place, primarily in the community at large and in health care settings – both places where people living with HIV continue to experience very pervasive stigma. The index not only seeks to measure the experience of stigma among people living with HIV but also empowers those who interact with the tool to learn about their human rights, voice their experience and mobilize for change to become leaders in the response to HIV, not "victims".[40] As of November 2011, some fourteen countries have conducted the index and issued a report. Some thirty-six countries are still in the process of rolling it out. In the Caribbean region, the index has been rolled out in the Dominican Republic, and fieldwork is being conducted in Jamaica.[41]

In addition to supporting the use of the index, the UNAIDS Secretariat has been working with partners to develop and field test new indicators of community-based stigma.[42] It is also working to develop improved indicators for stigma in health care settings.

While it is important to measure stigma, it is even more important to *do something about it*. Increasingly, there are programmes which have been evaluated as effective in reducing stigma. These address the "actionable causes of stigma": failure to understand the harm of stigma, continuing irrational fears of infection and moral judgements against people living with HIV.[43] However, there is still insufficient investment in stigma-reduction programmes. Those programmes that have been implemented appear to be at project level and of insufficient scale to have serious impact.[44]

The "investment framework"[45] seeks to guide countries to retool the programming in their AIDS responses to those "basic programmes" that have been proven effective against HIV and "critical enablers" – that is, programmes that are critical to enable the basic programmes to be taken up and used. For instance, widespread stigma in health care settings discourages those living with or vulnerable to HIV from coming forward, discussing their health needs openly and getting medical help. In many parts of the world, stigma is so bad that people wait until they are so ill that their life is threatened – the phenomenon of "late reporting". In such cases, they are willing to risk their lives rather than face the stigma that may come down on them for being HIV positive. Thus stigma reduction is a critical enabler and must take on new prominence if we are to reach universal access to HIV prevention, treatment, care and support.

In addition to stigma, another new focus in the AIDS response is on the legal environment – particularly whether the legal environment enables or disables rights-based and effective responses to HIV. UNAIDS defines the legal environment as comprising three components: law, law enforcement and access to justice – all critically important to the AIDS response.[46] In terms of law, UNAIDS promotes protective laws that protect people living with HIV from discrimination, protect their confidentiality and informed consent, provide for access to HIV prevention and treatment, protect women from violence and gender inequality that increase vulnerability to infection and impact, and provide children (orphaned or affected by HIV) as well as their caregivers with social and legal protection. On the other hand, punitive laws that can act as obstacles to universal access include overly broad laws that criminalize HIV nondisclosure, exposure and transmission; laws that criminalize sex work, drug dependency and homosexuality; HIV-related restrictions on entry, stay and residence; and laws that prevent the use of The Agreement on Trade Related Aspects of Intellectual Property Rights (TRIPS) flexibilities to keep the prices of HIV treatment and medicines as low as possible. The UNAIDS strategy calls for the removal of punitive laws that affect sex workers, people who use drugs and men who have sex with men in half of the countries that have them by 2015; the removal of HIV-related restrictions on entry stay and residence in half of the countries that have such restrictions; and zero tolerance for gender-based violence.

Although 71 per cent of countries claim to have laws prohibiting discrimination against people living with HIV,[47] unfortunately there appears to be insufficient enforcement of such laws. Furthermore, stigma, discrimination and criminalization regarding key populations at risk of HIV infection also appear to go hand in hand with widespread abuse by police. This police abuse can and does take the forms of harassment, extortion, arbitrary arrest and detention, violence, and rape against sex workers, people who use drugs and men who have sex with men. Such police abuse is not only a fundamental matter of governance and justice but also a serious obstacle for health, outreach and mobile services related to HIV.

In July 2010, the UN Development Programme (UNDP) and the UNAIDS Secretariat launched the Global Commission on HIV and the Law which has focused on the impact of the law in the context of HIV. The UNDP-supported commission has met three times, held regional dialogues in seven regions, and has received and reviewed hundreds of submissions from countries on the impact of the law on national HIV responses and key populations. Early 2012, the commission issued its report with findings and recommendations concerning how the law can better support human rights and public health in the context of HIV.[48]

Though law is critically important, it is not necessarily the solution. In some countries, there are very good laws relating to HIV, but there is little enforcement of these laws. Furthermore, few people living with or vulnerable to HIV infection, particularly in developing countries, have access to the national justice system so to bring complaints to a court of law or other tribunal regarding discrimination and mistreatment in the context of HIV. For these reasons, UNAIDS promotes seven key programmes which, among other things, put into the hands of those affected by HIV the knowledge and ability to create change in their own legal and social contexts. These include the aforementioned programmes to reduce stigma and discrimination. Other key programmes include (1) programmes to reform and monitor laws relevant to HIV; (2) programmes to train police on nondiscrimination, support to HIV outreach services, nonharassment of key populations, and so on; (3) programmes to train health care workers on nondiscrimination, informed consent, confidentiality, duty to treat, and infection control in the context of HIV; (4) legal services; (5) legal literacy (know your rights and laws campaigns); and (6) programmes to reduce harmful gender norms and violence against women.[49] These programmes include more of the programmes necessary to critically enable the biomedical and behavioural responses to HIV.[50] Without them, those affected by HIV will continue to be burdened by layers of stigma, shame and silence. These programmes help to empower those affected to control their own fate and call for the social and legal changes that will protect their health and that of others.

The new focus in the AIDS response that has been described in this chapter adds up to an approach to HIV that identifies vulnerabilities and responds to them in terms of identifying (1) those who are most vulnerable to or affected by HIV; (2) the programmes that will reduce that vulnerability; and (3) those partners who are critical to engage to carry them out – again, knowing your epidemic and responding to it. It could be said that in the last thirty years the "easy stuff" has been accomplished in the AIDS response. Millions of people know how HIV is transmitted and know the basics of how to avoid HIV infection. And yet as recently as 2009, 2.6 million people were infected with HIV, and 1.8 million died as a result of AIDS.[51] To respond to HIV in the future, it will be necessary to do the "hard stuff", and that is where human rights become a factor. This new response requires three major shifts in the response, all stemming from a rights-based response to HIV.

The first is a shift in *coverage* of HIV programming. Fewer programmes should be directed to those at little risk of HIV infection, and more should be directed to those at higher risk. In rights-based language, this means more expenditure and programmes for those most heavily affected by or vulnerable to HIV. This means shifting coverage of programmes to women where they are heavily affected; to discordant couples where one partner is infected and one is not; to young people who have, in many countries, the highest rate of infection; and in concentrated epidemics, to men who have sex with men, sex workers and people who use drugs. Caribbean countries have concentrated epidemics and need to shift their focus to their most vulnerable populations, difficult as it may be.

The second shift is a shift in the *content* of programming. Where social and legal environments increase vulnerability to HIV infection and do not support people to take up HIV information, services and commodities, there must be a shift in the content of programmes beyond biomedical and behavioural programmes to programmes that empower and address legal and social vulnerabilities and other structural issues. In the 2006 "Political Declaration on HIV/AIDS", governments committed to create a "social and legal environment that is supportive of and safe for voluntary disclosure of HIV status".[52] HIV programming must do much more to create this sort of environment.

Finally, there must be a shift in *partners* in the response to those who can change the social and legal environments that impact HIV. For too long the response has depended almost entirely on the hard work of ministries of health. Now there is need to engage, in a much more effective way, with ministries of interior, gender and justice; parliaments; the judiciary; human rights groups, justice reform groups, migrant groups and labour unions; human rights defenders networks; and so on. These partners, whether working on HIV alone or integrating HIV issues into larger social and justice challenges, are the ones that can bring a rights-based approach to HIV into being. In some parts of the world, national AIDS responses include national working groups on human rights and law which bring together these partners to identify and work to overcome the legal and social blocks to effective responses.

Based on these new foci in the global AIDS response, what should be some priorities for investment and expansion in the Caribbean? The first priority would seem to be reducing HIV-related stigma and discrimination in communities and in health care settings. The second would be building the human rights and legal literacy/capacity of people living with HIV in the Caribbean, including women living with HIV. These actions, coupled with HIV-relevant legal services (integrated into existing legal aid and redress mechanisms), would enable people living with HIV to move out from under the heavy burden of stigma and take up productive and dignified lives. Third, it would seem important to work with police to open spaces and get protection for key populations that are criminalized in the region, such as sex workers, men who have sex with men and transgender people, and

people who use drugs. This could presage longer-term efforts to decriminalize these populations so that they too can live free of fear of police abuse,
arrest and incarceration (where, among other things, vulnerability to HIV
infection is high). The police should also be supported to do the right thing
in terms of enforcing the laws against gender-based and domestic violence.
Finally, the Inter-American system of human rights, as well as national strategic litigation, must provide opportunities to not only increase access to
justice but also open greater social and legal debate on what sort of societies the Caribbean people want to create in face of the challenges posed by a
world with HIV. The Caribbean nations have risen from political oppression,
slavery and racism. To have overcome these major human rights violations
is their human rights legacy. Now it is time to ensure that in the context of
disease and marginalization, Caribbean people embrace this human rights
legacy to create societies where all can access health care and avoid disease,
where all are included, all can be free of discrimination and all can live full
and dignified lives.

Notes

1. In 2000, approximately 240,000 people lived with AIDS in the Caribbean,
   and women accounted for more than 53 per cent of cases. UNAIDS, "Global
   Report Fact Sheet (2010)", http://www.unaids.org/documents/20101123_FS
   _carib_em_en.pdf.
2. "Key populations, or key populations at higher risk, are groups of people who
   are more likely to be exposed to HIV or to transmit it and whose engagement
   is critical to a successful HIV response. In all countries, key populations include people living with HIV. In most settings, men who have sex with men,
   transgender people, people who inject drugs and sex workers and their clients
   are at a higher risk of exposure to HIV than other groups. However, each country should define the specific populations that are key to their epidemic and
   response based on the epidemiological and social context." UNAIDS, "Getting to Zero, UNAIDS 2011–2015 Strategy" (December 2010), 62, http://www
   .unaids.org/en/media/unaids/contentassets/documents/unaidspublication/
   2010/JC2034_UNAIDS_Strategy_en.pdf.
3. In recent years, there has been a slight decline in new HIV infections in the
   region, from 20,000 (17,000–23,000) in 2001 to 17,000 (13,000–21,000) in
   2009. UNAIDS, "Global Report Fact Sheet" (2010), http://www.unaids.org/
   documents/20101123_FS_carib_em_en.pdf.
4. UNAIDS, "Global Summary of AIDS Epidemic", http://www.who.int/HIV/
   data/2011_epi_core_en.png.

5. United Nations, "The Millennium Development Goals Report (2010)", http://www.un.org/millenniumgoals/pdf/MDG%20Report%202010%20En%20r15%20-low%20res%2020100615%20-.pdf.

6. George Lerner, "Rape a Weapon of War in Congo, Activists Say", *CNN World*, 16 October 2009, http://articles.cnn.com/2009-10-16/world/amanpour.congo.rape.documentary_1_anneke-van-woudenberg-eastern-congo-congolese-army?_s=PM:WORLD.

7. Mann is the former head of WHO's global AIDS programme.

8. This has been called the "AIDS paradox". See Jonathan M. Mann, Sofia Gruskin, Michael A. Grodin and George J. Annas, *Health and Human Rights: A Reader* (New York: Routledge, 1999).

9. United Nations, "Declaration of Commitment on HIV/AIDS, Global Crisis" (global action declaration adopted by the General Assembly on 27 June 2001), paragraph 16, http://www.un.org/ga/aids/coverage/FinalDeclaration HIVAIDS.html.

10. Ibid., paragraph 58.

11. United Nations, "Political Declaration on HIV/AIDS" (resolution adopted by the General Assembly on 15 June 2006), paragraphs 7, 11, 12, http://data.unaids.org/pub/Report/2006/20060615_hlm_politicaldeclaration_ares60262_en.pdf.

12. United Nations, "Political Declaration on HIV/AIDS: Intensifying Our Efforts to Eliminate HIV/AIDS" (resolution adopted by the General Assembly on 10 June 2011), paragraph 38, http://www.unaids.org/en/media/unaids/contentassets/documents/document/2011/06/20110610_UN_A-RES-65-277_en.pdf.

13. Ibid., paragraph 39.

14. Ibid., paragraph 29.

15. International Lesbian, Gay, Bisexual, Trans and Intersex Association, "State-Sponsored Homophobia: A World Survey of Laws Prohibiting Same Sex Activities between Consenting Adults" (2010), http://old.ilga.org/Statehomophobia/ILGA_State_Sponsored_Homophobia_2011.pdf.

16. United States Department of State, Bureau of Democracy, "2009 Country Reports on Human Rights Practices".

17. UNAIDS, "Mapping of Restrictions on Entry, Stay and Residence of People Living with HIV" (first published in May 2009 and revised in July 2010), http://www.unaids.org/en/media/unaids/.../pub/.../jc1727_mapping_en.pdf.

18. Global Network of People Living with HIV (GNP+), "Global Criminalisation Scan (GCS)", http://www.gnpplus.net/criminalisation. Primary legal text is obtained from official law databases whenever possible.

19. Ibid.

20. For a country-by-country breakdown of reports under the National Composite Policy Index, see http://www.unaids.org/en/dataanalysis/monitoring countryprogress/2010nationalcompositepolicyindexncpireports-countries. See also UNAIDS, "Guidelines on Construction of Core Indicators 2010 Reporting, UNAIDS/09.10E/JC1676E" (2009), http://www.unaids.org/en/ media/unaids/contentassets/dataimport/pub/manual/2009/jc1676_core _indicators_2009_en.pdf. For the latest reporting guidelines by which to monitor the 2011 Political Declaration, see UNAIDS, "Global AIDS Response Progress Reporting 2012, UNAIDS/JC 2215E" (October 2011), http:// www.unaids.org/en/dataanalysis/monitoringcountryprogress/ 2010nationalcompositepolicyindexncpireports-countries.

21. UNAIDS, "Non-Discrimination in HIV Responses UNAIDS/PCB[26]/10.3" (3 May 2010), http://www.unaids.org/en/media/unaids/contentassets/documents/ priorities/20100526_non_discrimination_in_HIV_en.pdf.

22. Ibid.

23. Global Network of People Living with HIV, "Global Criminalisation Scan", http://www.gnpplus.net/criminalisation.

24. "The Global Database on HIV Specific Travel and Residence Restrictions", http://HIVtravel.org/Default.aspx?pageId=150.

25. Peter Wiessner (European Aids Treatment Group [EATG], coauthor), David H.U. Haerry (EATG, online edition) and Karl Lemmen (database editor), "Bundesgeschäftstelle der Deutschen AIDS-Hilfe e.V" (German AIDS Federation).

26. For a full discussion of this issue and its history, see UNAIDS, "Report of the International Task Team on HIV-Related Travel Restriction" (December 2008), http://www.unaids.org/en/media/unaids/contentassets/dataimport/pub/ report/2009/jc1715_report_inter_task_team_HIV_en.pdf.

27. International Lesbian, Gay, Bisexual, Trans and Intersex Association, "Homophobia Report" (14 March 2008), http://ilga.org/ilga/en/article/1165.

28. UNAIDS, "Getting to Zero", 10, http://www.unaids.org/en/media/unaids/ contentassets/documents/unaidspublication/2010/JC2034_UNAIDS _Strategy_en.pdf.

29. UNAIDS, "Getting to Zero", http://www.unaids.org/en/media/unaids/ contentassets/documents/unaidspublication/2010/JC2034_UNAIDS _Strategy_en.pdf.

30. See United Nations, "The Human Rights Based Approach to Development Cooperation: Towards a Common Understanding among UN Agencies", http://www .unescobkk.org/fileadmin/user_upload/appeal/human_rights/UN_Common _understanding_RBA.pdf. See also United Nations Development Programme, "Applying a Human Rights-Based Approach to Development Cooperation and

Programming" (September 2006), http://hurilink.org/tools/Applying_a_HR _approach_to_UNDP_Technical_Cooperation--unr_revision.pdf.

31. P. Vernazza, Bernard Hirschel, Enos Bernasconi and Markus Flepp, "Les personnes séropositives ne souffrant d'aucune autre MST et suivant un traitement antirétroviral efficace ne transmettent pas le VIH par voie sexuelle", *Bulletin des Médecins Suisses* 89, no. 5 (2008).

32. For more information, see the "HIV Prevention Trials Network", http://www .hptn.org/research_studies/hptn052.asp.

33. National Institute of Allergy and Infectious Diseases, "Treating HIV-Infected People with Antiretrovirals Protects Partners from Infection" (12 May 2011), http://www.niaid.nih.gov/news/newsreleases/2011/Pages/HPTN052.aspx.

34. UNAIDS and GNP+, "Policy, Health, Dignity and Prevention: A Policy Framework", http://www.gnpplus.net/images/stories/PHDP/GNP_PHDP _ENG_V4ia_2.pdf.

35. See AIDS Support and Technical Assistance Resources, Sector I, Task Order 1 (AIDSTAR-One), "HIV Prevention Knowledge Database", http://www.aidstar -one.com/focus_areas/prevention/pkb/combination_approaches/positive _health_dignity_and_prevention_phdp.

36. See, for instance, William Sambisa, "AIDS Stigma and Uptake of HIV Testing in Zimbabwe" (working paper, Demographic Health and Research, Marco International, August 2008).

37. See, for instance, J.M. Serovich, "A Test of Two HIV Disclosure Theories", *AIDS Education and Prevention* 13, no. 4 (2001): 355–64.

38. See UNAIDS, "Reducing HIV Stigma and Discrimination: A Critical Part of National AIDS Programmes" (report published in 2008), http://data.unaids .org/pub/Report/2008/jc1521_stigmatisation_en.pdf.

39. UNAIDS, "The People Living with HIV Stigma Index: User Guide" (2008), http://www.stigmaindex.org/download.php?id=12.

40. Ibid.

41. As part of the People Living with HIV Stigma Index International Partnership, UNAIDS is tracking and supporting the uptake of the Stigma Index; contact the author for further details. See http://www.stigmaindex.org/106/ international-partners/unaids.html.

42. Since 2009, UNAIDS and its partners have identified several possible indicators to measure HIV-related stigma at community level. These indicators were field tested in spring 2011. See UNAIDS, "Technical Meeting to Consolidate HIV Stigma Measures and Measurement Tools November 23–25, 2009 Washington DC", http://www.stigmaactionnetwork.org/atomicDocuments/ SANDocuments/20110509195701-Microsoft%20Word%20-%20Stigma%20 Measurement%20Meeting%20Summary_12.17.09.pdf.

43. UNAIDS, "Reducing HIV Stigma and Discrimination", 5, http://data.unaids .org/pub/Report/2008/jc1521_stigmatisation_en.pdf.
44. For example, see Mandeep Dhaliwal et al., "Analysis of Key Human Rights Programmes in Global Fund-Supported HIV Programmes", http://content.undp .org/go/cms-service/download/publication/?version=live&id=3107370.
45. See Bernhard Schwartländer, J. Stover, T. Hallett, R. Atun, C. Avila, E. Gouws, M. Ghys, P.D. Bartos, M. Opuni, D. Barr, R. Alsallaq, L. Bollinger, M. de Freitas, G. Garnett, C. Holmes, K. Legins, Y. Pillay, A.E. Stanciole, C. McClure, G. Hirnschall, M. Laga and N. Padian, "Towards an Improved Investment Approach for an Effective Response to HIV/AIDS", *Lancet* 377, no. 9782 (June 2011).
46. For a full discussion, see UNAIDS, "Thematic Segment: HIV and Enabling Legal Environments, UNAIDS/PCB(29)/11.27" (21 December 2011), http:// unaidspcbngo.org/?p=16090&article2pdf=1.
47. See UNAIDS, "Reducing HIV Stigma and Discrimination", http://data.unaids .org/pub/Report/2008/jc1521_stigmatisation_en.pdf.
48. See the Global Commission on HIV and the Law website: http://www .HIVlawcommission.org.
49. The UNAIDS Secretariat has developed a costing tool for these programmes, which will be released by end 2011, and is in the process of developing guidance on the content of these programmes. For a full discussion of legal services in the context of HIV, see UNAIDS, "Toolkit: Scaling Up HIV-Related Legal Services", http://data.unaids.org/pub/Manual/2010/ 20100308revisedHIVrelatedlegalservicetoolkitwebversion_en.pdf.
50. B. Schwartländer, "Towards an Improved Investment Approach for an Effective Response to HIV/AIDS".
51. UNAIDS, "Report on the Global AIDS Epidemic" (2010), 19, http://www .unaids.org/globalreport/global_report.htm.
52. United Nations, "Political Declaration on HIV/AIDS" (resolution adopted by the General Assembly on 15 June 2006), paragraph 25, http://data.unaids.org/ pub/Report/2006/20060615_hlm_politicaldeclaration_ares60262_en.pdf.

Chapter 4

Human Rights and the Caribbean Constitution

Simeon C.R. McIntosh

Faculty of Law, University of the West Indies, Cave Hill

The member states of the Caribbean Community, including the British territories, stand in the tradition of written, democratic constitutionalism: they have embraced the idea of a democratic polity constituted and regulated by a written fundamental law founded on the principle of the separation of powers and containing a set of basic human rights which constrain the exercise of legitimate governmental powers by the agencies of the state. These rights are legally enforceable in favour of the citizen through the practice of judicial review by an independent judiciary. It is for this reason that the typical Caribbean constitution may be dubbed a *constitution of rights*, and the community which that constitution constitutes may be dubbed a *community of rights*.

But these rights referred to are not the legal or political enactments of any particular institution; rather, these rights are universally recognized as products of our "higher" or moral reason, and they are claimed as moral entitlements of persons anywhere in the world, irrespective of citizenship, residence, race, class, caste or community.[1] They are more commonly acknowledged as the subject of Universal Declarations such as the UN Declaration on Human Rights. It means, then, that the rights articulated in the Caribbean Constitution represent a particular political instantiation of some of the rights imbedded in the universal declarations and international human rights conventions.

This idea of human rights – rights which we have simply in virtue of the fact that we are human beings and which may have been the secularized notion of the idea of natural rights – has been challenged by some to be without any reasoned foundation and deemed nonexistent. A related view is that there is no universal validity to the idea, but it is rather the product of a Western cultural, intellectual and philosophical tradition that traces its provenance from Plato and Aristotle, through Rousseau, Kant and Hegel, to John Rawls, Dworkin, and others. Instead, some believe that the rights which people have are "contingent on specific qualifications such as citizenship, related to provisions in actual legislation or in the accepted 'common law'".[2]

These views notwithstanding, today it is an incontrovertible fact that the language of human rights constitutes the core of a universal discourse by which we make critical assessments of the moral legitimacy of states and their treatment of their citizens. This language helps us to determine the grounds for international intervention into certain situations in order to rescue some citizens or groups of certain states from torture, hunger, starvation and so on. Put differently, human rights norms establish the moral ground for action, where such action is imperative to save the lives of other human beings.

The incorporation of these rights in a constitution founded on the principle of the separation of powers may therefore be viewed as the institutional embodiment of a conviction that there are certain human interests of such transcendental importance that they ought to be affirmed and protected by such a formal declaration of moral claims. It is now widely understood that the *separation of powers* principle is an indispensable principle of the just constitution, in that it helps establish an independent judiciary as one of the principal means of protecting the citizenry from the tyranny of government. And this is accomplished mainly through the practice of judicial review, whereby the courts, among other things, pronounce on the compatibility of legislation and executive decrees with the rights provisions of the constitution. In sum, then, the separation of powers principle and the rights provisions of the Caribbean Constitution unequivocally establish the normative foundations of that constitution. There is the near-universal conclusion that the human rights articulated in a constitutional text have become the principal means for determining the moral legitimacy of law and the state. An independent judiciary through which these rights are judicially enforced is a common feature of democratic constitutions. It remains, therefore, for us to consider the rights and liberties articulated in the Caribbean Constitution.

As noted previously, the rights and freedoms articulated in the constitution are particular instantiations of some of the basic human rights declared in universal declarations and international conventions. Jurists, philosophers and legal theorists all agree that the fundamental value affirmed by such a constitution and, in particular, the rights provisions, is the value of human dignity: the moral status of all human beings. To paraphrase the late Justice William Brennan, "these rights are a sublime oration on the dignity of *man*".[3]

These constitutional rights in question are therefore regarded as basic human rights, in the sense that they predate – historically, logically, morally or politically – the institutions of the modern state and, therefore, on some fundamental level, are said to pre-empt the powers of government. Their claim of fundamentality speaks to the crucial human interests they are deemed to protect – the defining essence of such interests being the value of human dignity.

The moral philosopher Alan Gewirth states unequivocally that human dignity is the basis of human rights. He sees human rights as being based on or derived from human dignity. In this sense, the rights which we claim to be fundamental are the products of our moral reason. Their claim to universality rests on the ascription of the distinctively moral status of dignity to all human beings, which secures all human beings against torture, cruelty or any form of arbitrary contempt.

With this view, our constitutional rights are moral rights which function as a basic and indispensable constraint on the legislative process, executive decisions and judicial determinations. For example, the rights of free speech, due process, and equal protection and the proscription of cruel, inhuman, and degrading punishment or treatment, among others, protect human dignity. The right of due process forbids injustice in the form of capricious legislative deprivation of life, liberty or property, and the equal protection principle prohibits injustice in the form of capricious legislative classifications.

However, it bears emphasis that in addition to those rights, such as the ones mentioned previously, which are expressly stated in the constitution as constitutional rights, are the ones which are implicitly guaranteed – that is to say, rights that follow from a reasonable or defensible philosophical interpretation of the language in which the constitutional rights are expressed. For example, the moral status of human dignity, which may be seen as embracing the rights of privacy and self-determination, is said to be understood as following from a reasonable, philosophical interpretation of the language of rights.[4]

But the question still beckons, what exactly should we count as a human right? What does it mean to identify a right as a *human right*? Tom Campbell reminds us that although human rights now have a positive and concrete manifestation in international and domestic instruments, we should recognize that human rights remain first and foremost a type of moral discourse and cannot be equated, except contingently, with any part of positive law. The identification of any right as being a human right must therefore be a matter of moral judgement.[5] He argues that, in a fundamental sense, human rights do not literally exist. In other words, "Human rights are not out there to be discovered by experience or observation. . . . They are not the conclusions of rational deduction from matters of fact. They are not the subject matter of cognitive intuitions that can be regarded as either true or false. Their nature, content, and function cannot be revealed to us by any external authority."[6]

But what, then, is the ontological basis for human rights? Is there any solid foundation on which they can be supported, or are there any grounds for accepting them as starting points of political morality in and of themselves? These questions are compelling; it is a fact that, today, moral and political debate is conducted in the language of rights. As James Allan puts it, "The doctrine of human rights has become the prime philosophical inspiration of political and social reform."[7] In other words, human rights discourse is an essential part of a broader discourse on justice, which proceeds with the assumption that "such rights are non-positivistic, principled, legal limits to what States, state actors, and state agents can do to their citizens".[8] They are through and through moral in content. They are, as we have noted, not legislated by the constitutional texts in which they are embodied but are rather "the transcendental-logical deductions of higher reason" that are applied against political branches. "As such, they are a fundamental, constitutive part, not just of the positive law, but also of the rule of law. They constrain the State from taking certain sorts of action at odds with human freedom, They may, however, be interpreted to spur the State to take positive actions to promote the well-being of citizens, consistent with the view of positive rights at the heart of international human rights discourse."[9]

On the question of the ontological basis of human rights, there are varied and competing responses. William Talbott, for example, suggests that the basis for human rights is "the capacity for making reliable judgments about one's own good. All normal human beings have this capacity; and basic human rights provide the background conditions that enable them to develop and exercise it."[10]

On the other hand, James Griffin suggests that human rights should "be seen as protections of our human standing or, our personhood"; "personhood" being an interpretation of the idea of human dignity.[11] With this view, "human rights are supposed to be 'universal' not only in their reach but also in the character of the associated obligations. That is to say, the idea of universal rights imports the idea of universal obligations; meaning, obligations to respect someone's human rights are, in principle, held not only by members of that person's own society or by its government, but also by the international community."[12]

For Talbott, "the fundamental idea behind basic human rights is that all adult human beings with normal cognitive, emotional, and behavioural capacities should be guaranteed what is necessary to be able to make their own judgements in living their lives, and to be able to have an effective voice in the determination of the legal framework in which they live their lives".[13] In other words, "rights are guarantees of what is necessary for individual autonomy. Rights to religious freedom protect individuals from coercion based on someone else's opinion about how best to secure salvation or avoid damnation."[14] Autonomy is therefore absolutely essential to human well-being since it entails the freedom and the ability to make important, intimate and personal choices about one's own life. He lists eight rights which he maintains constitute the social basis of autonomy. They are a right to physical security; a right to physical subsistence; children's rights to that which is necessary for their normal physical, cognitive, emotional and behavioural development; a right to education; a right to freedom of the press; a right to freedom of thought and expression; a right to freedom of association; and a right to freedom from paternalistic interference.[15] These are a reminder that autonomy itself is a social achievement, and it is the capacity for autonomy, which entails the capacity for good moral judgement and the capacity for self-determination, that grounds human rights.

It would seem evident that, generally, moral philosophers are all agreed that human rights are protections of our human dignity and are therefore conceived as having connections with familiar philosophical concerns about respect for persons, the inviolability of the person, and limits on the pursuit of the common good.[16] Put differently, the dignity of the human person is conceived as the foundation for human rights.

But if personhood, conceived in terms of human dignity, is the foundation for human rights, then the question remains as to the set of rights that may genuinely be said to be human rights, constituting the moral status of human personhood. Griffin considers that there are three basic human rights: life, autonomy and liberty.[17] The right to life extends beyond the mere prohibition of murder. It justifies certain positive rights, such as the right to rescue, if one is in great danger; food, if one is starving; medicine, if one is dangerously ill; and education. In sum, it is the right to basic welfare provisions and to a fully flourishing life.[18] The related right of autonomy involves deliberation and decision; it has to do with the capacity to decide for oneself and make critical decisions about one's own life. Liberty involves action; it concerns pursuing one's aims without interference.[19] In sum, we each have a conception of ourselves, our past, our future and the form of life we want, and it is therefore critical that we should have the means and the liberty to pursue that form of life.[20]

So, for Griffin, it is this notion of personhood that generates most of the conventional list of human rights. The right to life, we have noted, is indispensable to our human standing; for, without life, personhood is impossible.[21] A similar argument can be made for security of person as a human right and for the right to not be tortured or treated inhumanely. We therefore need a right to the due process of the law and to be treated as equals under the protection of the law. Then we need freedom of thought and expression and a voice in political decision, among other things, in addition to freedom of worship and religion and the right to a basic education and the minimum provision needed for existence befitting a human person.[22] To repeat, then, human rights are grounded in the substantive values of personhood. Therefore, for Griffin, the essential value of human rights is not the promotion of human good or flourishing but simply what is needed for or constitutive of our human status.[23] In a word, human rights are "protections of that somewhat austere state, a characteristically human life, [and] not a good or happy or perfected or flourishing life".[24] What we attach value to, what we regard as giving dignity to human life, is our capacity to choose and to pursue our perception of a worthwhile life – in a word, our normative agency.[25]

Thus, according to the personhood account of human rights, human rights are the protections of our normative agency, and the constitutive elements of personhood are autonomy, liberty and minimal welfare provisions.[26] Further determinations of human rights can be seen as falling under one of these three headings.[27] As we have seen, autonomy, as a particular moral and political value, is deemed to be the basis of a human right because it is indispensable for the exercise of our human capacity to make moral judgements and also critical choices about our lives. Autonomy, we have earlier intimated, is a constituent of the dignity of the human person. It requires the individual to be the final arbiter of his or her conception of a worthwhile life.[28]

Autonomy requires liberty so that one may be free to act on or pursue one's conception of a worthwhile life. Under liberty would therefore fall certain universally recognized freedoms, such as freedom of thought and expression, freedom of conscience and religion, freedom of association and assembly, and so on.[29] Liberty is, however, subject to the formal constraint that one's liberty must be compatible with a like liberty for all. Therefore, no one's freedom of religion, for example, extends to denying the basic rights of autonomy and liberty to others: some examples would include a religious sect denying women's rights or the state denying some individuals the basic rights of autonomy and liberty through the criminalization of same-sex relations among consenting adults in private.

But the pursuit of a conception of a worthwhile life may sometimes require that the society assists in providing, at least, the minimum conditions for that purpose, such as education, basic health, minimum material provisions, and so on, where one is unable to provide those conditions for oneself. In other words, it is agreed that certain "welfare rights" fall into the category of human rights, since they are indispensable for securing the basic values of autonomy and liberty. They are protections of our human standing: "our autonomously choosing or freely pursuing our conception of a worthwhile life".[30] However, in order that we may live a life that is autonomous and free, there should be available to us the minimum welfare conditions that would sustain that form of life. These conditions include education, health care and material sustenance. Human rights to welfare only involve the minimum material resources that are necessary for one to pursue a worthwhile form of life.[31]

An International Perspective

From an international perspective, human rights norms may be said to specify standards of transnational justice, comprising the minimum conditions that a just international order would require every state to meet in its treatment of human beings, both domestically and abroad.[32] Human rights norms are based on the premise that there are certain characteristics shared by all human beings and that a proper recognition of the moral significance of these characteristics requires that they be treated in certain ways.[33] The rights against torture and cruel treatment are a case in point; they point to the fact that the interests of personhood which they protect are common to all human beings.

Put differently, the idea of human rights might be read as an expression of our commitment to the principle of the moral equality of persons. Therefore, the norms that constitute the basis of our assessments of the legitimacy of states and the international legal order are, in fact, human rights norms, meaning norms that identify rights that all human individuals have, irrespective of whether their own governments acknowledge them.[34] As Allen Buchanan puts it, "Only such universal rights could justify the kinds of restraints on sovereignty and even on the self-determination of democratic peoples that the international legal order now attempts to impose."[35] In other words, the ideal that all persons are to be treated as moral equals might be the only ground for meeting the challenge from some quarters that human rights are not in fact universal but instead merely reflect "an arbitrarily restricted set of moral values; or, an arbitrary ranking of certain moral values of a particular culture or type of society".[36] In essence, the very idea of human rights suffers from the failure to appreciate different but equally valid perspectives about how states may treat their citizens. Thus it must be conceded that, among other things, there would be an absence of any authoritative view as to the grounds of human rights norms and a variety of the paradigms of political action that might be understood as justified in response to infringements of these norms.[37]

From this viewpoint, it may be argued that democratic governance or constitutional democracy is not the only form of political rule compatible with
a rigorous protection of human rights. There is also no fundamental right
to democratic governance that all human societies ought, in principle, to respect. Still, the question remains whether the epistemic virtues of democratic
governance are not in fact more conducive to the protection of human rights.
Starting with the basic premise of constitutional democracy that people, as
free and equal, have the collective moral right of political self-determination
to choose for themselves the form of political rule for the own governance, we
are inevitably led to the conclusion that even voting or otherwise participating in governance may not be a constituent of a minimally good life for all
human beings. Still, it is widely accepted that democratic governance provides
the most reliable protection for human rights.[38] This is because democracy
not only requires protection of certain fundamental rights, known as human
rights, but also prescribes a particular kind of institutional mechanism for
that purpose.[39] For example, it is noted that in Western democracies, generally, an essential means of guaranteeing the protection of human rights is by
declaring them in a written constitution and making that constitution enforceable against the state in the courts through the process of constitutional
judicial review.[40]

As Richard Kay surmises, the most prominently recognized potential violator of human rights is the state – that is to say, all state agents and competences, such as the legislature, the executive, the judiciary, in addition to those
indispensable administrative and extractive agencies responsible for carrying
out the policies of the state. "It is therefore implausible to see the legislature
as possessing the power to make and unmake the rules that define rights. For,
it is something of a contradiction in terms to claim certain rights against the
State but vest in the State the power to say what those rights are."[41] The practice
of constitutional judicial review of legislation (and of executive decrees) thus
appears to be built into the very idea of entrenching human rights in fundamental rules of law. However, in the final analysis, these fundamental rules of
law of constitutional democracy entrench two abstract rights at the centre of
normative agency: autonomy and liberty, which serve as the moral grounds
for democracy.

And if, as we have intimated, human rights are "universal", both in their
reach and in the character of the associated obligations, then this imports
the idea of universal obligations. The obligations to respect someone's
human rights are, in principle, held not only by members of one's own society or by its government but also by the international community. In reality,
however, it is a person's society and government that would bear primary

responsibility for the obligation to respect that person's human rights. A legislature is therefore required to honour its moral and political obligation in the protection of the human rights of the citizenry by taking the affirmative steps, beyond the mere avoidance of hostile and discriminatory legislation, to secure the civic and social conditions for the peaceful enjoyment of fundamental rights without fear.[42] These civic and social conditions may imply certain minimum welfare rights such as a basic education, health care, food and shelter. And a state's satisfactory protection of the fundamental rights of its citizens might well depend on the level of the social and economic development of the society. Does the international community now have the moral obligation to help a poor developing state fulfil its human rights obligations to its citizens?

The West Indian Constitution

It is in this context that we may attempt a more fulsome discussion of the West Indian Constitution. This constitution, as we have noted in the beginning, is in the tradition of written, democratic constitutionalism and therefore shares with Western constitutions, generally, the embodiment of the principle of the separation of powers, in particular an independent judiciary, and a set of basic and fundamental human rights which are judicially enforceable against the state through the process of constitutional judicial review.

The West Indian Constitution, in concert with its Western counterparts, is therefore part of the redefinition of democratic governance in modern political theory. For the very idea of a constitution entrenching a set of basic moral rights of the individual citizen, enforceable through the practice of constitutional judicial review of legislation, unmistakably puts the understanding of democratic governance beyond the mere implementation of the majority will – whether or not that will is directly expressed in a popular vote or through executive and legislative decrees. Therefore, although the majoritarian principle will forever remain an essential principle of democratic rule, it is now the common understanding that majority rule must be made compatible with respect for the fundamental rights and interests of the minorities in the society. And this is especially apropos in the context of the West Indian political order, where the cabinet and the legislature are institutionally joined. The institutional separation of the judiciary from the other two political branches of government is therefore of compelling importance. In the event of the excesses of the cabinet-executive and the legislature, the judiciary, as the third institution of democratic governance, virtually stands in the breech to protect the citizenry against arbitrary and capricious rule.

In summary, the West Indian Constitution is a fundamental part of our democratic governance. And although, in the majority of cases, our constitutions were not of our making, they have nonetheless been tacitly accepted by the bulk of the populace; they can be said to have been sanctified on an overwhelming "popular vote". The democratic nature of the West Indian Constitution has been further underscored by the constitutional entrenchment of certain democratic rights, such as the right to vote, freedom of thought and expression and freedom of association and assembly, among others. Then there is an independent judiciary as a fundamental requirement of democratic governance, given that it is the principal institution for the legal enforcement of the democratic constitution. All the institutions and offices of the state are democratic institutions in the sense that the principal nature of their office is the implementation of the democratic constitution.

But the West Indian Constitution contains a peculiarity: a savings law clause which purports to protect certain laws in existence before "the coming into force" of the independence constitution from being declared unconstitutional in violation of the fundamental rights provisions of the constitution. For example, a savings law clause protects hanging as a method of execution and the mandatory death penalty on conviction for murder. A savings law clause also criminalizes same-sex relations among consenting adults in private, to name a few. This means that where an existing law might well be in violation of the fundamental rights provisions of the constitution, that law must nonetheless be ruled as being constitutionally valid. The savings law clause is therefore a contradiction within the constitutional text and has seriously compromised the hermeneutic reading of the constitution.

Let us take the law against same-sex relations in private as an example. Now this law is common to virtually every West Indian jurisdiction, and it pre-exists the independence constitutions. The fact that this law may be saved by a savings law clause, according to the general attitude of our courts to such clauses, means that the criminalization of homosexual relations among consenting adults in private will not likely be ruled unconstitutional in violation of the individual's right to privacy and intimate relations with others.

And this is further underscored by what seems to be a widespread and overwhelming opposition throughout the Caribbean towards decriminalizing homosexual relations among consenting adults in private. Legislatures in the Caribbean are therefore hardly likely to take an affirmative step to decriminalize such behaviour. Former Barbados attorney-general Mia Mottley suggested that Barbados might have to consider repealing the legislation in question in order to distribute condoms in the prisons to stop the spread of AIDS. Not only was there a very strong opposition to Mottley's statement, but one Anglican cleric has gone so far as to suggest that before parliament can pass new law to decriminalize same-sex relations, the people of Barbados must have their say in a public referendum. Of course, this cleric is quite aware that the majority of the church in Barbados and the populace, as a whole, would more likely than not vote against decriminalization. Added to all this is the pronouncement of Prime Minister Bruce Golding that he would not countenance the presence of any homosexual in his cabinet. He also said that as long as he is a member of the Jamaican parliament, there would be no legislation decriminalizing same-sex relations among consenting adults in private. Golding has specifically stated that he will not acknowledge "homosexual rights" and, of course, the Jamaican clergy and perhaps the majority of the Jamaican populace stand behind him.

Oftentimes, our attitude towards same-sex relations may frustrate our very efforts to develop policies to address the AIDS pandemic. The widespread antipathy to same-sex relations may directly influence our state legislatures on the question of decriminalizing homosexual relations, and our courts, in their reading of our fundamental laws, would likely be reluctant to confront the savings law clause in the absence of legislative repeal of the existing law. In this event, we therefore need to address how the West Indian Constitution ought to be read, paying particular attention to the savings law clause.

Reading the Constitution

It bears repeating that the West Indian Constitution is a fundamental part of our democratic governance. It is a constitution that embodies a set of basic human rights, enforceable by an independent judiciary through the process of constitutional judicial review. An independent judiciary, as the required institutional condition for the protection of the citizenry's fundamental rights, would therefore seem to be built into the very idea of entrenching human rights in our fundamental rules of governance.[43] As it has been stated, "Rights underpin the institutional structure of constitutional democracy. Basic rights . . . become constitutive of democratic will-formation. [They] provide the basic building blocks of the political structure and give expression to the idea of democracy. Properly understood, rights and democracy do not conflict. They are rather two sides of the same coin."[44]

And given that the state, through its legislative, executive and administrative offices, is the most prominently recognized potential violator of the human rights of its citizens, it is widely conceded that the arm of government best positioned to interpret and enforce human rights guarantees is the judiciary. In sum, then, a judicially enforceable instrument for the protection of human rights is considered an essential part of a true democracy. And this is underscored by the fact that both the international instruments on civil and political rights and our constitutions highlight the dependency of democracy on human rights. As we would have intimated earlier, the most fundamental democratic human right of any people is their collective moral right of self-determination: their right to determine their own political status for themselves. And this right includes, in addition to the framing of their own fundamental rule of governance, the right to free, fair and open participation in the democratic processes of government, such as freedom of thought and expression, the right to vote, and the right to stand for and hold public office.[45] As Julie Debeljak puts it, "Freedom of expression and of assembly and association create the conditions for debate that are necessary to a democratic order. Individuals could not participate effectively in a democracy without the right to liberty, physical integrity, and due process."[46] In addition, economic, social and cultural rights promote effective democracy; for, without education, housing, food and shelter, individuals cannot exercise their civil and political rights effectively.[47]

The question, then, as to how these fundamental rights in the West Indian Constitution are to be read must begin with the fact that they are through and through moral in their content and, equally important, not the enactments of the fundamental laws in which they are incorporated. In essence, these fundamental laws cannot determine and fix, once and for all, the meanings of these human rights norms. More important, these rights express a certain conception of the human person as a bearer of rights and define how that being ought to be treated by the state. These rights therefore delimit the exercise of state authority regarding how the state may treat the individual citizen.

But, above all else, these constitutional rights, as human rights, are held by all citizens equally. Therefore, they cannot be interpreted in a manner that accords deferential preference to the views or interests of certain groups in the society – whether or not those groups are in the majority or the minority. Some of these rights, such as freedom of conscience, religion, thought and expression, and due process and the equal protection of the law, expressly address the moral autonomy and liberty of the individual. They define the moral and political independence of the individual citizen, and the exercise of these rights may only be delimited as is required in a democratic polity to protect the rights and interests of others or to defend the state from imminent danger.

The question remains as to the rights entailed in a couple's intimate relations with each other and the circumstances in which the exercise of those rights may be legitimately limited. It is submitted that the rights in question are pre-eminently the basic human rights of autonomy and liberty, from which we generate so many of the human rights specified in the international instruments and in our constitutions. As we have noted earlier, the basic human rights of autonomy protect our human capacity to make reliable and critical judgements about our good – the freedom to formulate for oneself one's plan of life and to decide for oneself when, with whom, and under what circumstances one may choose to be intimate with another person. Liberty, as the companion basic human right, protects our freedom to pursue our plan of life without hindrance or arbitrary restraint from the state.

Again, it must be emphasized that the basic human rights of autonomy and liberty are rights which we all hold equally, simply in virtue of the fact that we are human beings. Therefore, in the context of constitutional law, they are the rights of equal citizenship. This means that the state must advance compelling moral justification for denying to one group of citizens the legitimate exercise of these two basic human rights while it steadfastly protects the other group in the exercise and enjoyment of the same rights. Put differently, the issue may be posed in terms of the constitutional authority of the state to criminalize same-sex relations among consenting adults in private. Such authority must derive from the state's authority to criminalize certain forms of behaviour that threaten and violate the basic human rights of others. For example, murder and rape are legitimately classic crimes because they entail a violent breach of the basic human rights of a person's right to life and bodily integrity and the right of self-determination, among others. In a word, recognition of these as fundamental interests of the human person is the justificatory predicate for criminalizing the forms of behaviour that constitute a violent breach of those interests. Might similar arguments be advanced in justification of the criminalization of homosexual relations among consenting adults in private?

What the foregoing discussion has established is that the constitution not only establishes the political authority of the state to criminalize certain forms of behaviour for the "peace, order and good governance" of the society but also provides the compelling moral justification for the state's doing so. By the same token, however, the constitution constrains the state as to the forms of behaviour it may or may not legitimately criminalize. For example, if the state is constitutionally bound to offer compelling moral justification for criminalizing any form of behaviour, then the state is equally barred from criminalizing a form of behaviour that is protected by the fundamental rights provisions of the constitution.

In light of this, we may wish to consider some of the arguments broadly advanced in favour of the criminalization of homosexual relations among consenting adults in private. Maybe the most compelling argument favouring criminalization is that our scriptural texts describe homosexual sodomy to be a sin and an abomination in the face of God. Closely connected is the view that the practice is unnatural and is therefore morally and socially disgusting. Then, because of the causal connection drawn between homosexual sodomy and HIV and AIDS, we feel justified in continuing the practice of criminalization.

It is, however, submitted that a constitutionalist state, bounded by a written fundamental law embodying a set of basic human rights, cannot so easily justify the criminalization of a social practice by pointing to the fact that the practice is contrary to the religiously held beliefs of the overwhelming majority of the society. Nor can the state advance the unnatural and disgusting nature of the practice as the moral ground for criminalizing it. Rather, as we have noted earlier, the state must advance justificatory reasons similar to those for the criminalization of murder and rape. Philosophers like John Rawls and Martha Nussbaum recognize that the religious condemnations of homosexuality are, for many citizens, "not trivial concerns but profound and deep convictions accepted as ethical and moral principles to which they aspire and which thus determine the course of their lives".[48] Still, in the pluralistic democratic society, "the issue is whether the majority may use the power of the [constitutionalist] State to enforce these views on the whole society through the operation of the criminal law".[49] Thus, whereas we cannot discount the critical value of religion and religious beliefs in human life, these cannot be the sole ground for subjecting private, intimate acts by adults to criminal sanction.

Equally important is the fact that all members of society equally hold true the fundamental rights stated in the constitutional text; these rights do not belong only to those groups in the society of whose intimacies we approve. These rights define the moral and political independence of all persons. There are basic moral rights and freedoms, such as freedom of thought, conscience, and intimate association, and the rights of privacy, autonomy, and self-determination. These rights and freedoms secure one's choice as to the forms of intimacy one chooses. They protect heterosexual behaviour among consenting adults in private and should equally protect homosexual intimacy among consenting adults in private. It bears remarking that our fundamental rights of free speech, conscience and religious beliefs protect the theological debate over the sinfulness and immorality of homosexuality. The debate is an essential part of a moral discourse, open to all conscientious citizens in the democratic polity, as to the kind of society they should wish for themselves and their posterity. That moral discourse may be reflected in legislation, duly enacted. However, that very moral discourse enjoins the courts in a democratic polity to repudiate statutes in defence of legal rights or interests that, though officially acknowledged in the constitutional text and widely accepted in principle, are largely overlooked or even consciously and unjustifiably denied in practice to certain groups in the society. Put differently, the fundamental premise that persons in the democratic society be treated as equals, or with equal respect and concern, amounts to a requirement of justification, whereby the legality of a person's treatment at the hands of the state depends on its being shown to be morally justified. Government regulations or legislation, even when enacted by established democratic procedures, must conform to certain standards of justice to which we have committed ourselves – standards that are themselves intrinsic to the idea of law as a means of governance in the constitutional democratic polity.

In sum, then, the ideal of law embodying a concept of the moral equality of persons enjoins in particular the infliction of penalties on unpopular persons or groups without compelling moral justification. As one commentator puts it, "The rule of law entails a requirement of *equal citizenship*, obliging government to justify the distinctions between persons on which it relies; and that obligation is not merely one of political wisdom or expediency, dependent for its efficacy on the vigilance of politicians or the force of public opinion [even when that opinion is formally expressed in a public referendum], but has legal force, regulating the validity of laws and administrative orders and decision's, in virtue of its rightfulness."[50]

The question still remains as to how the fundamental rights provisions of the West Indian Constitution may be read in the face of a savings law clause which bars pre-existing laws from being declared inconsistent with these constitutional rights. As we have earlier intimated, such a savings law clause creates a contradiction within the constitution and allows what is otherwise ordinary legislation to trump the fundamental rights provisions of the constitution. The question is also one of the adjudicative authority of the courts in a constitutional democracy to resolve this contradiction in the determination of cases.

My position is that fidelity to the constitution and to the moral principles underlying the constitutional order obliges the courts, in particular the highest appellate court, to interpret the constitution in a manner that makes it an instrument of justice rather than one of arbitrary discrimination. Therefore, unless the state can advance compelling moral justification for criminalizing same-sex relations among consenting adults in private, then the courts, in this instance, ought to resolve the contradiction against the continuing criminalization. The choice then facing a court is if it should declare the law criminalizing same-sex relations unconstitutional, notwithstanding the savings law clause, or if it should honour the savings law clause but nonetheless refuse to enforce it, since this would amount to holding a person criminally liable on the authority of a law that is deemed to be in violation of the fundamental rights provisions of the constitution. As we have already intimated, a court's determination in this instance does not depend on the weight of majority opinion against same-sex relations – for the minority in a constitutional democracy do not hold their fundamental human rights at the sufferance of the majority. Therefore, Caribbean governments are empowered by our constitutions to adopt whatever policies are reasonably required, consistent with a free and democratic society, to counter the AIDS pandemic and to protect those persons infected with HIV and those suffering from AIDS from discriminatory practices.

We may now return to the question of the moral obligation of the international community to intervene in the Caribbean and in other developing countries to assist in fighting the AIDS pandemic. The Caribbean jurisdictions are relatively poor and are therefore unable to meet the cost of the pandemic. In the circumstances, is the international community under a moral obligation to assist?

On the understanding of human rights as protections of our human personhood, universal in their reach and also in the character of their associated obligations, we concede that, in reality, human rights apply in the first instance to the political institutions of the states, including their constitutions, laws and public policies: "They impose upon state institutions the obligation to respect and protect the underlying interests against threats from non-state agents subject to the State's jurisdiction and control, and to aid those who are non-voluntarily victims of deprivation."[51]

But human rights are matters of international concern. Therefore, the international community, through its political institutions, may hold states accountable for carrying out their human rights responsibilities to their citizens and to persons within their borders.[52] Other states and nonstate agents with the means to act effectively have the moral obligation to assist an individual state to satisfy human rights standards in cases in which the state itself lacks the capacity to do so. They can intervene to protect the human rights of persons or groups in cases in which the state fails through lack of will to do so.[53]

However, it must be emphasized that this obligation does not have the force of law in the sense in which a state has an obligation to its citizens. The obligation is rather one of a moral imperative to act where the international community is in a position to assist without incurring any serious disadvantage. But international intervention is more easily facilitated where a state's constitution rests on the very moral principles that are declared in the universal declarations and international conventions.

It is therefore of profound importance that the West Indian constitutional order is founded on a set of moral principles that correlate with the principles of the universal declarations. It remains for us to read our constitutions in a way that makes them the best instruments for the protection of our human rights. True, the articulation of a set of basic, fundamental human rights in the West Indian Constitution represents our acceptance that these rights will, and should, serve as constraints on state actions. However, this does not absolve our parliaments of the responsibility to take full account of the basic principles and values underlying the constitution's fundamental rights provisions and the need to respect these rights in their formulation of legislative policies, even in the face of overwhelming majoritarian preferences to the contrary. This argues that our parliaments have the capacity to come to well-reasoned judgements that certain established practices, sanctioned by pre-existing laws, now saved, may constitute a violation of the citizen's fundamental rights and, on the authority of the very constitution, may take affirmative steps to repeal the offending laws. The fact that the overwhelming majority of West Indian citizens may believe that the laws criminalizing same-sex relations among consenting adults in private should not be repealed is hardly the normative criterion for determining whether our parliaments are morally and constitutionally justified in repealing such legislation – particularly where these pre-existing laws stand in the way of parliament's adoption of compelling and justifiable policies designed to address the AIDS pandemic.

However, in the face of our parliament's failure to act, the courts – in particular, our highest court, the Caribbean Court of Justice – have the constitutional authority, in the event of a legal challenge to the constitutionality of such pre-existing laws, to resolve any conflicts in favour of a reading of the constitution that respects the basic principles and values underlying the fundamental rights provisions. This means that the courts cannot hide behind the savings law clauses and hold laws to be constitutionally valid that, on a plausible reading of the constitutional text, violate the citizen's fundamental rights. The courts, as indispensable institutions of democratic governance and on the authority of their oath of fidelity to the constitution, are best positioned to protect the fundamental rights of the citizenry in the event of the failure of parliament to do so.

Notes

1. Amartya Sen, *The Idea of Justice* (Cambridge: Harvard University Press, 2009), 355.
2. Ibid., 356.

3. William A. Parent, "Constitutional Values and Human Dignity", in *The Constitution of Rights: Human Dignity and American Values*, ed. Michael J. Meyer and William A. Parent (Ithaca: Cornell University Press, 1992), 65.
4. Ibid.
5. Tom Campbell, "Human Rights: The Shifting Boundaries", in *Protecting Human Rights: Instruments and Institutions*, ed. Tom Campbell, Jeffrey Goldsworthy and Adrienne Stone (New York: Oxford University Press, 2003), 24.
6. Ibid., 25.
7. James Allan, "A Defence of the Status Quo", in *Protecting Human Rights: Instruments and Institutions*, ed. Tom Campbell, Jeffrey Goldsworthy and Adrienne Stone (New York: Oxford University Press, 2003), 184.
8. Robin West, "Human Rights, the Rule of Law, and American Constitutionalism", in *Protecting Human Rights: Instruments and Institutions*, ed. Tom Campbell, Jeffrey Goldsworthy and Adrienne Stone (New York: Oxford University Press, 2003), 93.
9. Ibid., 95.
10. William J. Talbott, *Which Rights Should Be Universal?* (New York: Oxford University Press, 2005), 17.
11. James Griffin, *On Human Rights* (New York: Oxford University Press, 2008), 118.
12. Ibid.
13. Talbott, *Which Rights Should Be Universal?*, 11n10.
14. Ibid.
15. Ibid., 137.
16. Griffin, *On Human Rights*, 3n11.
17. Ibid., 212.
18. Ibid.
19. Ibid., 226.
20. Ibid.
21. Ibid., 33.
22. Ibid.
23. Ibid., 34.
24. Ibid.
25. Ibid.
26. Ibid., 159.
27. Ibid.
28. Ibid., 150.
29. Ibid., 170.
30. Ibid., 179.
31. Ibid.

32. Allen Buchanan, *Human Rights, Legitimacy, and the Use of Force* (New York: Oxford University Press, 2010), 52.
33. Ibid., 53.
34. Ibid., 72.
35. Ibid.
36. Ibid.
37. Charles R. Beitz, *The Idea of Human Rights* (New York: Oxford University Press, 2009), 44.
38. Buchanan, *Human Rights*, 54n32.
39. Beitz, *Idea of Human Rights*, 174n37.
40. Richard S. Kay, "Rights, Rules, and Democracy", in *Protecting Human Rights: Instruments and Institutions*, ed. Tom Campbell, Jeffrey Goldsworthy and Adrienne Stone (Oxford: Oxford University Press, 2003), 117.
41. Ibid., 119.
42. Ibid., 123.
43. Buchanan, *Human Rights*, 243n32.
44. Kay, "Rights, Rules, and Democracy", 119n40.
45. Ibid., 123.
46. Julie Debeljak, "Rights and Democracy: A Reconciliation of the Institutional Debate", in *Protecting Human Rights; Instruments and Institutions*, ed. Tom Campbell, Jeffrey Goldsworthy and Adrienne Stone (New York: Oxford University Press, 2003), 149.
47. Ibid.
48. Ibid.
49. See Martha C. Nussbaum, *Hiding from Humanity: Shame, Disgust, and the Law* (Princeton: Princeton University Press, 2004).
50. Ibid.
51. Beitz, *Idea of Human Rights*, 114n37.
52. Ibid., 121.
53. Ibid.

Chapter 5

The Responsibility of Parliamentarians in Shaping and Promoting the Human Rights Agenda on HIV and AIDS

Promoting Human Rights for All

Anne Peters

Minister of Health, Grenada

Juliette Bynoe-Sutherland

Head, Policy Analysis Division, PANCAP Coordinating Unit, Guyana

The role of parliamentarians in the HIV response has been underappreciated and therefore underresourced in the regional response to HIV and AIDS. Advocates often expect parliamentarians to have an unrealistic level of understanding and awareness of the issues and then place blame on the political directorate for failure to advance the human rights agenda.

The advocacy agenda continues to be advanced without a full appreciation of the political dynamics and the space in which policy is made. Human rights discussions often centre on the rights of the individual to self-determination in a number of ways. When these individual rights conflict with the primacy of the status quo, they are often set aside and not promoted by the political directorate. However, parliamentarians cannot proceed on the basis that the needs of some individuals in the community are less important than others.

This chapter makes a case for supporting capacity building for regional parliamentarians to advance the human rights agenda and allow human rights advocates to more effectively engage with parliamentarians. The chapter argues that parliamentarians have a special calling to give voice to the voiceless and seek social justice for all. It suggests that parliamentarians also have a responsibility to promote a broad and inclusive human rights agenda in which the needs of groups such as people living with HIV or AIDS (PLWHA), the disabled, and youth are met regardless of race, ethnicity, sexual orientation, gender and age. Parliamentarians could support the use of public health measures to target groups engaged in illegal or unlawful activities, address the vulnerabilities around sex work fuelling the epidemic and seek to stamp out the abuse of state authority by the police or other public officials that increase the vulnerability of socially and economically marginalized groups through human rights violations.

This chapter further calls for a more effective and sophisticated engagement of parliamentarians by advocates, for interest groups to coalesce and seek joint advocacy around areas of common interest and for investments to be made in capacity building at the parliamentary level by governments and the international development agencies.

Human rights as a concept is value laden and has historically occupied a strange place in the political discourse of the region. In the post-independence era, parliamentarians have been historically engaged on important human rights issues around the rights of children, the disabled, and women, and some progress has been made, though in many instances this progress is less satisfactory than would have been hoped by interest groups.

The concept of "individual rights" does not appear to occupy the same space and priority as seeing to the broad concept of "public interest". Much of public planning and policy in the region has sought to use human, material and financial resources in the best interest of delivering public goods such as education, health and housing to the population at large; specialized individual needs are often at the margin.

More recently, the advent of the HIV epidemic and the need to make targeted outreach to vulnerable communities have given impetus to the human rights agenda around the gay community and commercial sex workers.[1] The general public discourse has been extremely antagonistic to the interests of these communities, fuelled by prevailing social values and religious moral precepts.[2] "Human rights" has become politically stigmatized as equating to gay rights in some quarters. This is compounded by the strength and visibility of the gay rights agenda in the international arena and the pressures on regional governments by donors and development agencies to adjust their laws and policies to comply with international commitments. In this environment of polarization, some parliamentarians have been loath to take leadership on the human rights agenda, making political calculations around the risk of losing their seat or government in advancing the human rights agenda. As parliamentarians, we often search for political cover and find none.

At the national level and in the regional fora, human rights and its varying institutional supports are not seen as political priorities, particularly in times of economic scarcity and social dislocation. There is very limited discourse around independent human rights commissions, and the judiciary is not pushing the agenda with progressive human rights judicial decisions. Human rights advocacy is fragmented, with various groups deeply entrenched in their own agenda with little reference to other similarly affected groups. Countries with effective human rights frameworks are hard to locate, and there appears to be no groundswell impetus for a more increased emphasis on individual rights or human rights. So, from a political perspective, we as a Caribbean community have caused human rights to become a political back-burner issue.

Notwithstanding this, as parliamentarians we are called to lead, and as a female parliamentarian, I have a special responsibility to bring added value on issues that are less than popular and affect the vulnerable and marginalized, regardless of their age, race, ethnicity, gender, sexual orientation or HIV status. As parliamentarians, we are supposed to represent all the people in our constituencies.

In the sections that follow, I identify a few areas where the role and responsibility of parliamentarians can be used to promote the human rights agenda.

Support a Broad Human Rights Agenda, Not Narrow Interests

If the human rights agenda is to be advanced at the national level, it must be done holistically, as the investment in policy discourse, legislation and institutional building should be in the interest of not one or two groups but all individuals. For example, the needs of PLWHA not to be discriminated against because of their health status also correlates with the historical advocacy of the disabled community for the right to work, have decent accommodation and access to services.

Advocate for the Use of Public Health Measures to Target Risk Groups

We need to return to the basic principles of the public health approach, which dictate that all persons (including vulnerable communities, men who have sex with men [MSM], sex workers, prisoners, children and youth, and PLWHA) have a right to accessible treatment. Public health authorities are within their rights to target all segments of the community, whether they are engaging in legal or illegal activities, as the cost to the wider community of not providing access to prevention care and treatment is tremendous. Any impediments (social, institutional or legal) to treating vulnerable communities could be removed with this simple public health justification that is historically and empirically grounded. To do otherwise would unfairly stigmatize certain groups because of perceptions held by providers rather than legal restrictions. In Barbados, the Ministry of Health has directly reached out to commercial sex workers in collaboration with immigration and the police authority.

Do No Harm by Way of Legislation

In legislating, we must try not to inflict harm on already vulnerable persons. We may not be able in all territories to decriminalize sex work, but we can look at the approach of our law enforcement regimes to see to what extent we can empower women charged with soliciting and loitering. We know that criminalizing sex work creates an environment of fear, which reinforces the vulnerabilities that women and their clients experience. We can therefore safeguard against efforts to expand or further criminalize sex work if we agree that these efforts would not protect against the spread of HIV but instead increase the risk. We can look more closely at our social protection measures to provide women and men options other than sex work and, for those that choose sex work, seek to eliminate barriers to effective HIV and STI prevention measures, treatment, care and support.

Implement Zero Tolerance to Abuse of Vulnerable Communities by State Officials

We can have a zero tolerance to abuse of authority by police or other government authorities that violate the human rights and dignity of vulnerable and marginalized groups. By doing so, we weed out corrupt elements of our services that bring their ranks into disrepute.

Prevent the Marginalization of Women's Issues

Female parliamentarians can play a special role in bringing attention to the special vulnerabilities of women – particularly those that are HIV positive. We can significantly raise the profile of women and girls in discussions about vulnerabilities and social protection. We can insist that more resources be allocated to women's issues and that the human rights agenda of women is not marginalized in discussions about vulnerable groups. If the pandemic is being feminized, why should the solutions not be?

Increase the Visibility of Vulnerable Communities in the National Discourse around Social Protection

In our efforts, we must seek to increase the visibility of vulnerable groups so that their voices can be heard on a cross section of national issues. The absence of social protection (i.e., employment opportunities, good housing and education) is a driver of the epidemic, as persons often engage in transactional sex or multiple partnering for resources and are not able to effectively negotiate health sexual behaviours. Although significant headway has been made with the involvement of women, we must build on this by involving the disabled, youth, PLWHA and MSM at a high and visible level of our social discourse.

Conclusion

Although I have sought to make a few suggestions where I believe there would be consensus among parliamentarians, I must zero in on the point that as parliamentarians we cannot get away from the fact that it is our primary duty to speak out for human rights and social justice for persons whose voices often go unheard. We must be champions for change. This is the arena of personal responsibility and personal motivation which goes to the heart of an individual parliamentarian's reason for seeking office. For some, the 1990s brought the death of ideology, and we are required to be guided by personal goals and commitments, or else economic pragmatism will always win the day. As a consequence, the community of advocates needs to see value in engaging with us more effectively.

It must be appreciated that as parliamentarians we are not a homogeneous community and cannot be painted with one broad brush, as is the tendency. Some parliamentarians need evidence-based information to act. Many do not, as although we do not have strong cultures of data collection and analysis, our development patterns show strong progress in development planning across the region. Others, while appreciating the need for evidence, look to whether the advocate has acknowledged the political sensitivity of an issue and is empowering in proposing politically sensitive solutions. Some parliamentarians need to experience an issue to build their sensitivity. Still others are driven by political expediency, and timing therefore becomes very important. Advocacy with the political directorate must become more sophisticated, and efforts must be made to study the legislative behaviour and profile of individual parliamentarians. This is not all difficult, as most of what is done with policy exists in the public arena. However, interest groups are so often persuaded by the rightness and justness of their cause that they never consider that a lack of interest by a parliamentarian could be caused by their own advocacy style or approach. They fail to see when a parliamentarian has engaged effectively on another issue because it is not an issue that concerns them. Politicians are often very cynical when interest groups present themselves only at the stage when something is needed and fail to support the politician when he or she is experiencing challenges. There were no choruses of support for the few regional parliamentarians who have stood up for controversial human rights issues. It is important to build open noncompromising relationships with parliamentarians over time, and sensitizing them to an issue is one of the deepest and most sustainable forms of advocacy.

As parliamentarians, we must take some responsibility to equip ourselves to effectively persuade our parliamentary colleagues at the level of cabinet and wider parliament to move an issue onto the national agenda. This brings into focus the investment that needs to be made to engage parliamentarians. UNAIDS has produced a useful handbook for parliamentarians.[3] However, I am uncertain of the extent to which the UN agencies or other relevant bodies are effectively engaging parliamentarians. Indeed, it may be challenging with the perceived HIV burnout to get parliamentarians to a stand-alone HIV session, but sessions on policy development and implementation might be more useful, and HIV can be infused into the agenda. I am uncertain of the investment that has been made in education and capacity building of parliamentarians beyond one-off sessions or participation in a workshop at the country or regional level on particular topics. Where is the technical assistance to guide us in effective policy initiation, development and implementation around human rights? We invest in our community-based advocates and public servants (who are all critical), but we fail to build the capacity of our policymakers. Then we stand back and ponder why aspects of the regional policy agenda are stagnating.

Notes

1. Global Fund, "Information Note: Addressing Sex Work, MSM and Transgender People in the Context of the HIV Epidemic" (July 2011), 1, http://www.google .com/url?sa=t&rct=j&q=&esrc=s&source=web&cd=4&ved=0CEYQFjAD&url =http%3A%2F%2Fwww.theglobalfund.org%2Fdocuments%2Frounds%2F11 %2FR11_SOGI_InfoNote_en%2F&ei=ryd0T57aN4bt0gH0-tn_Ag&usg =AFQjCNFydrbbvLo7k0VX-SaxDaEhj3KOyg.

2. UNAIDS, "HIV-Related Stigma, Discrimination and Human Rights Violations: Case Studies of Successful Programmes", 2005, 69, http://www.unaids .org/en/media/unaids/contentassets/dataimport/publications/irc-pub06/ jc999-humrightsviol_en.pdf.

3. UNAIDS, "Taking Action against HIV/AIDS: A Handbook for Parliamentarians" (2007), http://www.ipu.org/PDF/publications/aids07-e.pdf.

Chapter 6

Pragmatic Approaches to HIV and Human Rights with Special Emphasis on Employment

Rose-Marie Belle Antoine

Professor of Labour Law and Offshore Financial Law,
University of the West Indies, Cave Hill

This chapter discusses the securing of human rights for persons living with HIV, particularly within the context of employment. Ultimately, the goal is to outline both the challenges and the prospects for referencing HIV within the context of a human rights agenda so that we may move forward to address accurately and effectively the several dimensions of HIV in the Commonwealth Caribbean region.

The chapter will first outline an appropriate jurisprudential framework for rights in the Commonwealth Caribbean as it relates to HIV. This will be followed by a discussion of specific aspects of employment law issues, examining how these can be viewed within the broader lens of rights.

Like many other countries, in the past two decades, the Commonwealth Caribbean has seen active engagement in countering the serious challenges presented by HIV. There has been considerable progress, particularly with respect to medical treatment, access to treatment and public education. However, the region continues to witness high and disproportionate levels of HIV, with a continuing negative impact on the population. The reasons for the continuing high prevalence of HIV in the Commonwealth Caribbean are various and complex, but there is an understanding that social and cultural mores contribute significantly to this malaise and prevent an effective HIV strategy. Many of the negative consequences of HIV are manifested in the workplace – hence the emphasis on this sector. However, the lessons learned in the workplace are broad enough to apply to other societal spheres where intervention is needed, such as in the schools, health care facilities, housing and other societal services.

There is a growing realization that one of the obstacles to an effective counterattack to HIV in the region is the lack of an effective legal infrastructure which can provide the impetus for meaningful change, helping to shape and define more positive social and cultural norms conducive to the "fight" against HIV. The absence of adequate laws and legal policy makes it difficult to suppress these harmful discriminatory practices manifested against persons living with HIV.

It is suggested that law is a direct and effective instrument of social change and an efficient tool for addressing many of the problems associated with HIV – in particular, practices of discrimination, which not only violate the dignity and rights of persons living with HIV but also perpetuate the "underground" nature of HIV. This, in turn, hinders the reach of effective treatment and places a wider pool of persons at risk. However, while there is a measure of consensus that an adequate legislative environment must be created, there is considerable discord with regard to the appropriate form of such legislation.

The Philosophical Framework for Promoting Human Rights in the Context of HIV

What has been labelled the "human rights approach" to HIV has been put forward as the mechanism to promote justice and, in particular, address the nondiscrimination agenda. However, there is a need to recognize that certain aspects of this approach are still controversial in the region, especially when we seek to promote rights under the rubric of "most vulnerable groups". Further, there are significant jurisprudential obstacles to the human rights approach to HIV which must be addressed.

One contingent issue is that there is considerable confusion as to what exactly is meant by a human rights approach. What do we understand to be the content of human rights when we refer to it? It is apparent that there are two dimensions to the concept *human rights*: On the one hand, *human rights* is a legalistic, juristic concept confined strictly to the constitutional mores of a particular jurisdiction as contained in a defined, written bill of rights. That juristic concept may extend, however uncertainly, to the international sphere in its reach to international human rights.

On the other hand, *human rights* is a populace concept that the average individual embraces as an entitlement, whether formally acknowledged in a jurisprudential sense or not. This dimension of the subject is indeed very important to persons living with HIV. People sense that they are entitled to certain rights and, quite understandably, demand them. For example, they may expect that their "right" to health be respected and demand access to medical treatment, but such a right may be entirely absent in the constitution or may be unenforceable.

Similarly, persons who belong to groups vulnerable to HIV, such as homosexuals,[1] may clamour for the recognition of their human rights in relation to their sexual orientation, but such rights inevitably do not exist under the constitutions which claim to protect rights described as "fundamental". In such circumstances, it is somewhat futile to speak of human rights, and the description may be quite counterproductive. It permits a court to too easily justify their exclusion by utilizing a constitutional tool ill-equipped to accommodate equity in the context of HIV.

It is in this sense that the notion of pragmatism is used in the title of the chapter. The pragmatic approach is an acknowledgement that there may be far more useful ways of securing fairness and justice for persons living with HIV than pursuing the formal human rights agenda – an agenda that often starts off with a presumption of illegality in the context of HIV.

There is, therefore, a need to outline a legislative policy that will be pragmatic and effective, outlawing discriminatory practices and creating new obligations and entitlements which are necessary to protect any society against the harms of HIV. The policy will also serve as an educational tool, providing the impetus for much-needed egalitarian norms in the various societies of the Commonwealth Caribbean. It is also necessary to dispel some of the myths surrounding the subject and to offer concrete proposals for enlarging the umbrella of "rights" that should attach to HIV.

Narrow and Narrow-Minded Constitutions Limit Human Rights

The unfortunate and inconvenient truth is that, although human rights seems an obvious route to obtaining just treatment in the context of HIV, from a legalistic point of view the human rights approach is severely deficient and fails to offer real justice to persons living with HIV because, in our legal system, human rights are located squarely within the written constitution. As such, the human rights approach is limited, simply because the constitution is limited in relation to making provision for rights in the context of HIV.

In fact, our constitutions are narrow and often narrow-minded law instruments, silent on important aspects of our rights expectations where HIV and related rights are concerned, such as protection against discrimination on certain grounds. Worse, our constitutions often mirror the most discriminatory and harmful attitudes of the society. They are ultimately far too often mere passive reflections of our societies and of ourselves. If we are a discriminatory society, then our constitutions, without more, will merely cement discrimination.

While at first blush this appears to be a harsh statement on our constitutions, consider that the freedom from discrimination is not adequately protected under our constitutions because of myopic interpretations of the antidiscriminatory clause. This clause requires a person alleging discrimination to prove bad faith or a deliberate intention to discriminate – a burden so high that it effectively aborts jurisprudence on discrimination.[2] It is only recently that the Trinidad and Tobago courts have begun to challenge this interpretation.[3]

Consider, too, that sexual orientation is not only absent as a ground of antidiscrimination in our bills of rights but, in ordinary legislation, specifically excluded on the grounds that sodomy is unlawful and that such unlawful and unjust laws are expressly preserved by our constitutions via the "savings law clause".[4] That exclusion has been a reason given by our highest court as to why the constitution could not be interpreted in favour of a discrimination challenge of sexual orientation. The case of *Surratt v. AG*[5] is instructive in this regard.

Reflect, too, on the fact that despite our awareness that the gender dimensions in HIV are very important in our understanding of the disease, both from a scientific point of view and in relation to hidden or subtle forms of discrimination, somewhat surprisingly, gender is absent as a ground of antidiscrimination in some constitutions in the region. That means that one could not bring a suit against discrimination on the basis of sex or gender.

In this vein, it should be reiterated that, despite popular misconception, there is no right to health in our bills of rights. Indeed, economic and social rights such as health, where they exist, whether in constitutions or international law instruments, have been treated as nonjusticiable (as mere ideals), given their cost implications.[6]

Further, our constitutions specifically permit the state to treat non-nationals differently, which will have implications for our need to protect immigrant populations in relation to HIV and, by extension, our domestic populations.

It goes without saying that nowhere in any constitution or bills of rights in the Commonwealth Caribbean is there any specific mention of HIV or AIDS.

These are some of the serious deficiencies which obstruct the efficacy of the human rights approach to HIV in the Commonwealth Caribbean. *Human rights* can thus be seen as both a restrictive and a liberating concept. Understanding its limitations enables us to plan more effectively for a strategy that can address the many issues that straddle the HIV phenomenon in the region.

Reimagining Our Constitutional Mores

It is for these reasons that I have gone on record as being very cautious about the so-called human rights approach, which too often has been an approach that does not truly understand the content and flavour of our existing human rights framework via our constitutions.[7]

My antagonism is not against human rights itself, but against a human rights approach which ignores the inadequacies of the legal infrastructure in which we operate. I suggest that while the rights approach is necessary, it is not sufficient in addressing HIV and AIDS and is certainly not a panacea for all ills. I prefer to emphasize basic principles of fairness and equity in law and practice generally. The so-called rights approach to HIV encourages a false sense of security about our constitutions instead of inviting us to think critically about them.

Thus, while rights are fundamental, indeed inalienable, the conundrum is explainable, since while fundamental human rights never fail us, human rights instruments often can and do. They are not always reflective of those fundamental rights or are not interpreted broadly enough to secure those inalienable rights. Rights are value-laden norms which are not necessarily grounded in our social environments. This, of course, also poses a challenge in relation to the need to educate our societies about the appropriate parameters of human rights.

While I warn of the pitfalls of the strict human rights approach, I continue to advocate for revolutionizing the way in which we view our constitutional instruments in order to invoke a more just, more relevant and more people-centred human rights agenda that will suit the needs of the HIV issue. In other words, we need to reimagine our constitutional and human rights mores and norms. This is the challenge which we face, but it presents exciting prospects. I have hope that these same constitutions can be rewired to serve our indigenous societies as we move forward and eliminate the scourge of discrimination on the ground of HIV status in all its forms. For our constitutions to truly serve us, we must reject the complacent interpretations of them and challenge the constitution to be more dynamic and relevant to present-day challenges and needs.

However, constitutional reform is a long-term, though necessary, strategy and cannot be the benchmark for the new approaches needed right now, if only because it is a slow and difficult process.[8] Yet with human rights instruments there are good prospects for expansion and liberation. International human rights norms have given us considerable enlightened food for thought and for the development of our constitutions.

Is a Rights Discourse Ill-Suited to the Private Law Sphere of Employment?

The language of *human rights*, a public law phenomenon, is ill suited to the private law sphere in which the world of work resides. Many other day-to-day activities in which persons living with HIV are discriminated against are also located in the private sphere. Such is the case, for example, when a landlord denies housing or a private school denies entry to a child who is HIV positive.

Most importantly, our constitutions and, by extension, our bills of rights apply only to actions of the state, not to those of private persons, so that persons in the private sphere will not be protected from human rights violations. If an employer discriminates against an HIV-positive person by firing him, for example, or a privately funded school refuses to accept a child who is HIV positive, these actions will not be protected by the rights clauses in the constitution and, in law, there will be no violation of rights. There is, therefore, a need for legislation separate from the constitutional rights framework to provide protection in such situations.

It is of course the case that where the employer is the state, or where the school is publicly funded or the hospital publicly owned, the constitution will still apply, but we have previously noted some limitations in constitutional interpretation even in this context.

Who Are the Legitimate Beneficiaries of Human Rights?

The subject of human rights under the umbrella of HIV also allows us to explore who is entitled to these rights. This is an important question, given that the HIV issue has been linked to notions of vulnerable communities. How do these subgroupings fit into our construct of human rights, which must apply to all and must also meet the challenges of HIV? Is our theoretical construct of human rights appropriately addressing the needs of these communities?

Part of the problem with our current human rights schema and, in particular, the nondiscrimination provisions, is that it has been interpreted as outlining rights only for some and not for all. It has been viewed as an exclusive human rights instrument when, arguably, it was meant to be inclusive. In this sense, the constitution is not an all-embracing document, since only certain designated grounds are protected from discrimination. Where there is silence or a lack of detail, it means that the excluded ground is not contemplated (e.g., health, sexual orientation and gender). This is a construct that appears fundamentally flawed and in discord with the true intent of our fundamental constitutional principles of equality and the rights to dignity, personhood, and life.

Consequently, our human rights agenda must now broaden its thinking and embrace all by being much more inclusive in its philosophy. It must be expansive in contextualizing the scope of each right and the constitution itself – offering to each person the broadest possible basket of rights. What should resonate is the preamble statements that are found in the various constitutions, notwithstanding that these preambles have been viewed as nonjusticiable but merely declaratory or idealistic. Typically, such statements read, "Whereas every person . . . is entitled to the fundamental rights and freedoms, that is to say, the right . . . to each and all the following, namely . . . life, liberty, security of the person, equality before the law and the protection of the law."[9] This, for me, sums up the essence of human rights. It speaks to the very basic, primeval notion of the dignity and worth of the individual.

If we were to treat each individual as deserving of dignity and as deserving of the life to which he or she has been given – and our laws and constitutions could be employed for this purpose – we would begin to arrive at the true intent of our constitutional principles.

There seems little justification, therefore, to break this down into the various categories, arguing for nondiscrimination on the basis of gender or sexual orientation and extending to rights for persons in vulnerable communities, since elemental rights transcend all boundaries; they are capable of bringing light, truth and justice to every context. They are dynamic and, indeed, have been interpreted in dynamic and evolutionary ways in other contexts. For example, the right to life has been interpreted to include the right to health in India. What a powerful precedent for a person living with HIV who wants to assert his right to accessible health care and treatment!

We therefore aim for a human rights model that is not divisive and where there are no categories, no special interests and no particular beneficiaries of human rights. By its very nature, the model upholds human rights for all. It is the basic sense of equity and equality that justifies human rights for persons living with HIV. Every individual is entitled to be treated with respect, with dignity and in accordance with the basic principles of equity.

Such an approach overcomes the hurdles faced by special interest groups, such as the groups most vulnerable to HIV, which have met with great societal resistance. Human rights that are all-encompassing and indivisible can accommodate such groupings.

No person is to be excluded from a broad vision of rights, regardless of which grouping or vulnerable community they happen to fall under. Indeed, this is an aspect of the pragmatic approach: recognizing that lobbying for specific rights may encounter controversial ideals and moralistic arguments and addressing this by a reorientation of the philosophical justification for rights.

A more enlightened ethos will recognize that all persons must be beneficiaries of human rights. We all deserve human rights, fairness and justice.

One could argue further that emphasizing vulnerable groups in relation to HIV somewhat distorts the reality, which is that *all* persons living with HIV are susceptible to discrimination and unfair treatment. For example, the child at school who is HIV positive and shunned by children, teachers and other parents is a victim of discrimination, as is the wife who is HIV positive because of her husband and is dismissed from work.

Broad-Based Nondiscrimination Legislative Agenda

From the previous discussion, it is apparent that, while rights conjure up the idea of constitutional protection, it may well be that some of the so-called rights about which we speak are located well outside of the boundaries of the constitution. Therefore, there needs to be a proactive legislative agenda, separate from the constitution, that will be in accord with fundamental human rights principles. Given that what we want to secure cannot be identified or located adequately in our constitutions, it is important to rely, more specifically, on ordinary legislation which targets issues important to the HIV phenomenon in a more pragmatic, direct way.

It is also desirable to promote broad-based strategies which do not isolate special interest groups not easily contemplated in existing law; these groups can be addressed in more general protections. The more plausible route is to promote protections and entitlements which are instrumental in promulgating a positive and helpful ethic not easily located either in our constitutions or in our orthodox conceptions of human rights. This leads to a broad antidiscrimination agenda which includes HIV in its remit.

The legal response must also take into account the medical aspects of HIV, since the fear and stigma engendered by HIV stems mainly from ignorance and myths which still surround the disease. Our laws and policies should not serve to fuel this misinformation.

If the premise that vulnerability to HIV and discrimination are consequences of deeper, wider inequities in the society is accepted, then the case for more all-inclusive grounds of discrimination and inequity, including grounds such as gender, race and even the more controversial ground of sexual orientation, is more persuasive. These are social constructs which make persons more vulnerable. We can therefore operate within a more embracing model of equality and nondiscrimination, interrogating any problems of discrimination (including those relating to HIV) and laying down a platform for a more egalitarian society.

General Nondiscrimination Legislative Agenda

Broad nondiscrimination and equality legislation, as distinct from constitutions, has tended to emerge only in the employment context in the Commonwealth Caribbean. Thus far, three of the independent countries have enacted such legislation (Guyana, St Lucia, and Trinidad and Tobago).[10] In addition, Grenada has nondiscrimination clauses in its employment legislation, while Dominica and St Vincent have more limited antidiscrimination provisions which prohibit dismissal for discriminatory reasons of race, sex, religion or political affiliation.[11]

In addition, the dependent territories of the region may have important provisions from UK legislation extended to them – in particular, the Human Rights Act 1988. Of special note is the specific inclusion of sexual orientation as a prohibited ground of discrimination in these territories. Further, in the Turks and Caicos Islands, a separate part of the Employment Ordinance is devoted to nondiscrimination, and this appears to be based on the St Lucia model.

Notwithstanding the existence of some useful antidiscrimination legislative provisions, only the Bahamas has enacted a specific provision prohibiting discrimination on the ground of HIV or AIDS, under section 6 of the Employment Act 2001. This is a bald statement of nondiscrimination, which provides no details or guiding principles on the scope of the clause, although it is suggested that, in interpreting the clause, one could draw on the emerging principles of nondiscrimination law.

In contrast to the sparse Bahamas formulation, where there is a general nondiscrimination statute, the legislation provides a road map for preventing discrimination. An important principle, for example, is that of indirect discrimination, which ensures that persons may be held liable for discrimination even if they do not intend to discriminate but their actions have a discriminatory impact. This is an important extension of the legal principle.

Just as important is the principle of accommodation, which requires the employer to facilitate the difference of the worker at the workplace, making special provision for that person to ensure that he or she can carry out his job. In the case of a person living with HIV, this might mean, for example, reasonable time off for medical treatment, home working or even redeployment to different tasks.

However, none of the general nondiscrimination statutes specifically mentions HIV as a ground of nondiscrimination. This would have to be inferred from the other grounds of discrimination. Significantly, where disability is a ground, jurisprudence from outside of the region, including the United States, establishes concretely that HIV may be treated as a disability, given that certain characteristics (such as psychological perception, prejudices and myths about a person's capabilities) are shared.[12]

Similarly, though with greater difficulty, sexual orientation may be inferred from the protection given on the ground of sex and provide relief to men who have sex with men.[13] This, indeed, was the result of the Belizean case of *Selgado*, argued on constitutional grounds.[14]

It is, of course, desirable for HIV to be included as a specific head of discrimination to ensure the broadest possible and most efficient coverage against discrimination on the grounds of HIV. Indeed, this is an emerging policy in the region. In St Lucia, for example, the new Labour Code has already made this adjustment. However, the law, while passed by parliament, has not yet been implemented. In the Turks and Caicos Islands, the Employment Ordinance was recently amended to include this ground and is awaiting passage through the legislative process.

HIV and the Rights of Immigrant Populations

The notion of rights or nondiscrimination for "all" in reference to HIV status is vividly tested in relation to immigrant populations. Given the movement of peoples, whether within the region or from countries outside of the region, our notion of human rights in relation to HIV must also be able to transcend questions of territorial jurisdiction.

In some cases, such as in relation to asylum seekers, this issue goes beyond discrimination and touches on issues of survival and the right to life. Generally, however, the immigrant issue concerns those who move for employment purposes. Such persons may have legal immigration status, or they may fall into the category of immigrants labelled *illegal* or *undocumented*.

The issue of immigrants in relation to HIV is of great importance in the region, given the high degree of migration in the Commonwealth Caribbean. It is a topic that is seldom addressed, which makes its predominance in this chapter even more significant. There may be several hurdles to immigrants securing rights in relation to HIV.

The objective must be to ensure that all persons living with HIV, including immigrants and mobile populations, have meaningful access to at least an adequate, minimum standard of medical treatment. The right to such access may be located under a number of internationally recognized human rights principles. It is also recognized that it is in the national interest of the state to grant such access – in particular, to be able to prevent the spread of the virus. The relevant guiding principles may be stated in the following way:

1. Every person has a right to health, an economic and cultural right as enshrined under the United Nations Convention on Economic, Social

and Cultural Rights. The right to health may also be derived from the broader right to life.

While it is recognized that states have leeway in determining how to translate this right in terms of dollars and cents, at a minimum, a state should do all in its power to ensure the health of those persons within its jurisdiction, especially in situations where its own citizens and the general population may be placed at risk because of health issues.

Public health grounds provide an additional basis for even irregular immigrants to be granted access to medical treatment, as opposed to immigration and justice grounds, since failure to do so poses additional health risks to the wider population, resulting in the state breaching its obligations. The right to access to treatment is to be balanced on economic, cost grounds. However, as a baseline, a person is entitled to a "minimum basket of health services" – in particular, antiretroviral treatment and primary health care.

Currently, the health cost-benefit analysis informing governments reveals that such a basic standard of care is not expensive and also has important long-term savings. This should encourage states that this is a reasonable expression of this principle and right. Given the substantial donor funding given to the region, it is difficult to justify excluding anyone, including the illegal immigrant population, from access to treatment.[15]

Enforcement issues are relevant here also, since a state violates the obligation to grant access if it does not put mechanisms in place to ensure that immigrants living with HIV have access to medical treatment. This may be due, for example, to structural obstacles, such as the refusal by employers to pay national insurance benefits where health care is dependent on social security or insurance. Some systems also require persons accessing treatment to identify their status, which poses another obstacle. This may act as a deterrent to illegal immigrants, even if treatment is not dependent on that status, because of the fear of being reported to the immigration authorities.

In the Commonwealth Caribbean, most countries provide access to medical treatment for their legal immigrant populations, though structural deficiencies may still exist. However, significant obstacles often relate to illegal immigrants. Suriname and St Maarten stand out as two examples which have more progressive policies in this regard, although there are difficulties in practice due to identifying nondocumented immigrants, making them aware of their entitlements and alleviating fears of deportation. In Barbados, however, there is a formal policy of denying health care benefits, including HIV treatment, to legal immigrants.

2.   Every person has a right to life and to the protection of his or her life
     and a right to human dignity.

     In recent times, international human rights law has recognized that
     these rights extend to a state protecting the life of nonresident "aliens"
     and other noncitizens where their lives are threatened because of lack
     of, or hindered access to, HIV treatment. We see this, for example, in
     recent asylum cases.[16] This principle is broad enough to encompass
     immigrants and mobile populations, including refugees and persons
     who travel across the Caribbean to access treatment because of stigma
     in their own countries. Indeed, the latter's standing before the law is
     greater than persons who come to a country to seek asylum.

     This also forms the basis for granting access to trafficked persons
     and can address the situation of children who need access to HIV
     treatment.

3.   The principles of equality and nondiscrimination are accepted as fun-
     damental principles of international and domestic human rights law.

     While constitutions may make exceptions in certain circumstances
     to the principle of nondiscrimination with regard to citizens – where
     a person resides in a state, pays taxes and contributes to a national
     health insurance scheme – it is suggested that there is no legitimate
     basis to apply this exception, and the principle of equality in its abso-
     lute sense must stand. As such, every immigrant person who contrib-
     utes to taxes and national insurance should have equal access to HIV
     treatment.

     The principle of nondiscrimination also encompasses the right to
     access and, of course, to life, regardless of gender or sexual orientation.

     In the region, constitutions typically permit the state to treat non-
     nationals differently. Consequently, such leeway given to the state
     will need to be made subservient to the more competitive rights of
     equality and equal access. Indeed, the lack of access to medical treat-
     ment can ground an action on the basis of cruel and inhumane treat-
     ment in the human rights context, as discussed in the sections that
     follow. This constitutes a powerful impetus for ensuring that rights
     are granted.

Emerging Jurisprudence on HIV, Asylum and Migration

There is an important, emerging jurisprudence which underscores the human
rights principles articulated previously. Many of these cases are from UK

courts and some involve Caribbean nationals. In these cases, the courts did not deem the fact that homosexuality or sodomy was illegal in the country of those seeking asylum from Africa and the Caribbean as relevant. It was sufficient to find that their lives and quality of life were under threat and needed to be protected. For example, it was enough to invoke human rights protection where a homosexual man claimed that his life was threatened because of his sexual orientation and the perception that he was HIV positive. It was also enough that another person living with HIV claimed that he was not able to access HIV treatment and that his life was consequently in danger. Those courts saw these applicants simply as persons in need of protection of the law, standing on equal footing with any other person, and they could be granted asylum in such exceptional cases. This is not to suggest that the relevant factual circumstances are unimportant, since the courts require a high threshold for the applicant to cross.

In *N v. Secretary of State for the Home Department*,[17] for example, it was found that article 3 of the EU Convention did not impose an obligation on a contracting state to provide aliens indefinitely with medical treatment which was unavailable in their home countries, even if the absence of such treatment would significantly shorten their lives. That article 3 could be extended to apply only in very exceptional circumstances where the present state of health of the person who was subject to expulsion was such that, on compelling humanitarian grounds, he ought not to be expelled, unless it could be shown that the medical facilities that he obviously needed were available to him in the receiving state. N's present state of health was not critical, and she could live for many decades with the right treatment. She was also fit to travel. Therefore, her case was distinguishable from that of a person whose illness had reached its terminal stage so that he was beyond the reach of medical treatment and was unfit to travel.[18]

Immigration and Regional Issues

There is to date no coherent regional policy on HIV as it relates to immigration issues, even within the context of the Caribbean community and the free movement regime. Here, official policy and practice often have little in common. There is a need to reform outdated, insensitive laws that are out of sync with medical data and human rights precepts. For example, dangerous loopholes exist in relation to "contagious diseases", which can include HIV, depending on how it is classified. Immigration statutes also claim discretion for the relevant authorities to deny entry to persons who are deemed "undesirable persons" without any clear definition of the term, with the danger that persons living with HIV can be categorized as such. The argument that such persons will represent a drain on the public purse is also one that can be utilized under such statutes, despite donor funding.[19]

Policymakers should therefore be requested to spell out that (1) people with HIV are not to be included among those "undesirable" categories and (2) HIV status does not constitute a "drain on the public purse", given the decreasing cost of treatment for HIV and the availability of donor funding.

Of utility, too, would be a rational, coherent, regionally integrated approach to the treatment and costs of treatment and social benefits for workers. This could include, for example, the portability of health insurance and benefits. This would mean that it would not matter where a person living with HIV resided, resulting in shared country burdens, especially from the point of view of countries with high inflows of immigrants.

Already, the cases reveal that Commonwealth Caribbean citizens are seeking asylum on the basis of HIV, claiming persecution, including that based on their sexual orientation, which is linked to the issue and lack of adequate medical treatment in their home countries. Human rights issues are being raised in relation to cruel and inhumane treatment.

Developing Human Rights Norms in the Traditional Employment Context

We have noted that *human rights* is a juristic concept applied traditionally to constitutions but that constitutions exist in the public law realm and not in the private law context in which most employment issues are confronted. The task is, therefore, to isolate principles of fairness and justice in the employment/ private law framework that may be applied to the issue of HIV.

Employment and Unfair Dismissal

One of the most useful principles to counter rights violations within the context of HIV is that of unfair dismissal. In the world of work, it is important to prevent employers from dismissing employees because of their HIV status. Unfair dismissal law has already cultivated suitable norms and principles for the treatment of HIV, but these have not yet been employed in the Commonwealth Caribbean. Indeed, these norms are little known, even by lawyers, and represent an untapped jurisprudence. What is required, therefore, is for such dicta to be highlighted to encourage similar results in our societies.

The basic rationale of the unfair dismissal concept is that a worker should not be deprived of his job and, by extension, his livelihood without a good, valid reason. To do otherwise results in unfairness – the locus of an unfair dismissal. In the case of *Chalk*,[20] for example, it was made clear that to *dismiss* persons because of their HIV status, when they were otherwise competent and capable of doing the job, would be unfair.

Certainly, the understanding of what is "unfair" in any employment context is a dynamic concept. Notwithstanding, the courts have taken an enlightened approach to HIV and have declared that, prima facie, dismissal on the ground of HIV is fundamentally unfair. For example, a person living with HIV could only be dismissed from their employment in the circumstance where he or she has been rendered incapacitated by the virus and is thereby unable to perform work tasks, such as when he or she has full-blown AIDS.

Another important principle derived from the unfair dismissal line and general nondiscrimination cases relating to HIV is the duty placed on the employer to accommodate the employee who is living with HIV. This could mean, for example, that the employee could be given extra time off from work to go for medical treatment or be reassigned to different tasks.

A further general principle is that the courts have been able to locate correctly the prejudice, misinformation and generally discriminatory attitudes which typically attach to HIV and have assessed such phenomena in the light of what is fair, reasonable and within an appropriate rights context. They have rightly concluded that perceptions, stigma and myth are irrelevant and not reasons to dismiss or deny employment. Such courts have reiterated that HIV must be judged by scientific data and that, today, medical science has demonstrated that there is very little risk of "catching" the virus by ordinary physical contact or interaction. The understanding of such harmful discriminatory attitudes was discussed in *South African Airways v. Hoffman*,[21] where the court underscored that they would not be tolerated. On what basis can an employee be dismissed when, in today's context, with the appropriate medical treatment, a person living with HIV can live a normal, functioning life? In fact, the latest scientific evidence reveals that persons being treated for HIV have a quite negligible rate of transmission of the disease, even during sexual intercourse.[22]

In addition, since dismissal law includes constructive dismissal, if the employer's conduct is discriminatory and causes the person living with HIV to leave employment, this would entitle the worker to remedies.

Right to Privacy and Confidentiality

The legal framework should be able to confront the dangers of a lack of confidentiality, particularly where constitutional adjudication cannot. In constitutional law in the region, the right of privacy is weakly protected and is restricted to search and seizure circumstances, particularly in the home. This is another pitfall of the constitutional framework.

It is understood that a lack of confidentiality discourages testing and treatment. This leads to practical questions, such as those involving the circumstances in which medical personnel can legitimately breach confidentiality and inform employers about the HIV status of employees or inform sexual partners – one of the questions considered in the CARICOM model law.[23]

Currently, the duty of confidentiality is not adequately protected in the Commonwealth Caribbean, and specific safeguards are needed in this regard. Nonetheless, given the principle of indirect discrimination, a claim could arise indirectly. For example, a breach of confidentiality which led to a person's sexual orientation being revealed would establish a claim of discrimination on the grounds of sexual orientation. However, this in no way undermines the argument for specific protection.

Insurance and Health Policy

Another area of concern in the employment context is the way in which insurance requirements have been allowed to impact the nondiscrimination agenda. While many national HIV policies are against compulsory testing for insurance purposes, the reality is that many employers can and do require such tests in order to be eligible for employment. Often, the HIV test is hidden, being one of several other medical tests carried out. The question is whether this is in any way unlawful or whether it should be outlawed. Does the harm to the individual outweigh the public interest?

In addition, insurance practices are out of sync with the medical realities of HIV, given that there is very little evidence of real risk in terms of incapacity or even early death today. In the United States, for example, an employer can compel testing at work, but the information gleaned can only be used for awareness and knowledge about what steps are needed to assist the workers (to accommodate them and other protections),[24] not to penalize them. The worker cannot be denied employment because of the result of the tests or discriminated against in any way.

The absence of appropriate insurance policies is due in part to the lack of information, which itself is fuelled by confidentiality. As noted previously, the courts have had scant respect for discriminatory actions due to misinformation and lack of information.

Modern Concepts of the Implied Terms of a Contract

Ordinary principles stated in the implied terms of contracts of employment may also be utilized to secure protections for those living with HIV. We may derive these from other cases relating to discrimination in employment, for example, on grounds of gender, including sexual harassment. The courts have been willing to extend the duties of mutual trust and confidence, an important implied term, to encompass situations where an employer or coworker sexually harasses another and, in so doing, violates the required relationship of trust.[25] In a similar fashion, discrimination against a person on account of their HIV status may violate this implied duty.

Litigation Strategies

One route for inculcating desirable values and encouraging a human rights agenda is to pursue litigation strategies using the existing tools at our disposal. Currently, the issue of HIV is underlitigated, mainly because of the very fear of discrimination which we seek to eliminate.

In many cases, what have been committed are simply legal wrongs for which the law already prescribes remedies. For example, there is no legal basis upon which a child can be denied her inheritance merely because she has been orphaned as a result of HIV. Such entitlements reside outside the traditional constitutional human rights framework. In such cases, the answer is more advocacy and not more laws.

Law has a norm-building, educative function and can inculcate positive values in society. It is not merely a passive response to social problems but must embrace a proactive and participatory approach. Litigation provides a platform for highlighting injustices in society and encouraging societies to think deeply about the need for new rights norms. Consequently, by underscoring more humane, egalitarian principles of equity and fairness in our law, we pave the way for these issues to become less contentious, and we make important strides towards becoming a more just society grounded in transformational notions of human rights.

Notes

1. These individuals are often described as "men having sex with men" (MSM).
2. See *Smith v. L.J. Williams* (1980) 32 WIR 395: the issue of discriminatory treatment required one to first prove that the denial of benefits (discrimination) extended to other applicants (workers) in similar positions.

3. See *Sanatan Dharma Maha Sabha of Trinidad and Tobago Inc. and Others v. Attorney General of Trinidad and Tobago* (2009) UKPC 17.

4. These are provisions inserted into the independence constitutions to expressly retain certain aspects of the law that were in existence preindependence. They have been infamous in their effect of restricting the ability of the various constitutions to be as dynamic as they arguably should be.

5. *Suratt and Others v. Attorney General of Trinidad and Tobago*, no. 2 (2008) UKPC 38

6. For example, the right to work, another economic and social right, is mentioned in the Constitution of Guyana but has not been made justiciable. Recently, however, in Belize, the court enforced a similar right found in the Constitution of Belize but only in a limited context. The UN Convention on Economic, Social and Cultural Rights contains such rights but give states considerable margins of appreciation in enforcing them.

7. See, for example, Rose-Marie Belle Antoine, "Policy and Law Reform: Emerging Perspectives on HIV/AIDS" (feature address, presented at the PANCAP Ninth Annual Meeting, 2009).

8. For example, the Commonwealth bills of rights are entrenched, and special majorities are required to change the provisions of the constitution.

9. See, for example, section 11 of the Constitution of Barbados, 1966.

10. Guyana also has a more general Equal Rights Act (1991), but this is largely superseded by the employment specific law.

11. See, for example, the Protection of Employment Act of Dominica.

12. See the US Disability Act and the case of *Quebec v. Boisbrand* (2000) 1 S.C.R. 665.

13. See *Pearce v. Governing Body of Mayfield School* (2001) IRLR CA.

14. *Selgado v. Attorney General of Belize*, Unreported, Supreme Court, Belize, July 14, 2004.

15. The Global Fund, for example, funds such treatment, making it possible for states in the region to offer the drugs free of charge. A person need not be a national of the country to access such treatment under the fund.

16. See Human Rights Watch, *Discrimination, Denial, and Deportation: Human Rights Abuses Affecting immigrants Living with HIV* (New York: Human Rights Watch, 2009).

17. Decision of the House of Lords (2005) UKHL 31 Court of Appeal Judgment (2003), EWCA.

18. *D v. United Kingdom* (1997) 24 EHRR 423, considered.

19. See Rose-Marie Belle Antoine, *The Report on Legal Issues in Relation to Freedom of Movement in CARICOM* (Georgetown, Guyana: CARICOM, 2010).

20. *Chalk v. USDC* (CA) 840 F. 2nd 701, 1988.

21. (2000) 20 ILLR 63; ZACC 17.

22. See S. Attia et al., "Sexual Transmission of HIV According to Viral Load and Antiretroviral Therapy: Systematic Review and Meta-Analysis", *AIDS* 23, no. 11 (2009). This article found that "there were no observed episodes of HIV transmission from people with undetectable viral load on highly active antiretroviral therapy" and estimated the overall rate of HIV transmission with undetectable viral load at 1.3 in 10,000 sexual encounters (0.013 per cent). In this study, viral load was considered undetectable if it was below 400 copies/ml. The findings of this study were further supported by the following research: J. Del Romero et al., "Combined Antiretroviral Treatment and Heterosexual Transmission of HIV-1: Cross Sectional and Prospective Cohort Study", *British Medical Journal* 340 (2010). In this study, involving 144 couples, the partner known to have HIV was taking combination antiretroviral treatment. These couples accounted for over seven thousand unprotected acts of intercourse, but no HIV seroconversion was observed among the HIV-negative partners. S. Reynolds et al., "ART Reduced the Rate of Sexual Transmission of HIV among HIV Discordant Couples in Rural Rakai, Uganda" (abstract 52a at the Sixteenth Conference on Retroviruses and Opportunistic Infection, 2009), http://retroconference.org/2009/Abstracts/35406.htm. In this study, 205 heterosexual HIV-positive couples were followed for a median of 1.5 years.

23. See "CARICOM Model Labour Law: Occupational Safety and Health", s. 69 (2), and "CARICOM Model Labour Law: Equality of Opportunity and Treatment in Employment and Occupation" (Georgetown, Guyana: CARICOM), http://www.caricom.org.

24. See, for example, the case of *Lorenzo Taylor Appellant v. Condoleezza Rice*, in Rice's official capacity as United States secretary of state, no. 05-5257.

25. See *Horkulak v. Cantor Fitzgerald International* (2003) EWHC 1918.

Chapter 7

HIV and Human Rights

The Role of International Organizations

Amalia Del Riego

Pan American Health Organization,
HIV Caribbean Office

HIV and AIDS have brought to the surface many unspoken (or very low spoken), hidden and denied realities in the region. I would like to focus my reflection on one aspect of the reality which in my opinion is critical to define the task at hand: sex. The Caribbean is well known as the region of the four Ss (sea, sand, sun and *sex*); there is a general sense of collective pride about that perception. The celebration of sex and sexuality is present in our culture, music and jokes. Paradoxically, societal structures continue to perpetuate a patriarchal fabric that results in intolerance, discrimination and violation of a fundamental human right: the right of any human being to enjoy his or her sexual life. HIV- and AIDS-related stigma and discrimination are therefore intrinsically linked to the taboos against sex/gender transgressors and prevent open discussion of sexuality in general. In the most perverse manifestation, stigma and discrimination permeates family, friends and community.

The consequences are indeed perverse and very present in the lives of many, even though most of the time they remain undocumented. My most recent contact with that reality was through a casual conversation with a participant in one of the Pan American Health Organization (PAHO) workshops. He confided, "I was sent to the street by my parents when I was sixteen and I admitted that I was gay . . . I didn't know where to go . . . I was just sixteen." Unfortunately, there are many more stories of very young boys that are rejected by their families and forced to become adults in an accelerated manner. The transition from adolescence to adulthood might take place within an alternative family structure; some become involved in a "gay fraternity", which may pose survival and developmental challenges for young homosexual boys.

There are also challenges for young girls. One female participant confided, "I went to the health centre to request an HIV and a pregnancy test. I was scared . . . the nurse sent me home to bring my mother . . . I was only fifteen." This is the nature of the beast, and that is what we need to stop, not sex.

A Caribbean with healthy and happy people, as it is envisioned by the Caribbean Community (CARICOM) in its Caribbean Cooperation in Health III,[1] is one that will promote and protect the rights of the young men and women like these and the rights of Caribbean people in general. From my perspective, the discussion about HIV and human rights is a discussion about health in general as a fundamental human right. The right to health is the cornerstone of the Constitution of the World Health Organization (WHO), signed in 1946 by sixty-one states. The constitution establishes, "The enjoyment of the highest attainable standard of health is one of the fundamental rights of every human being without distinction of race, religion, political belief, economic or social condition."[2] The HIV and AIDS epidemic has shaken the principles of the WHO constitution with the emergence of a deadly second epidemic – human rights abuses of those who are living with (or who are suspected of living with) the HIV virus. Discrimination and intolerance have caused thousands of people to lose their jobs, homes, and social standing and to be rejected by family and friends, denied vital medical care and support, unjustly imprisoned without due process and judicial guarantees, and even killed. Because of its association with behaviours that may be considered socially unacceptable and in some cases even illegal, HIV infection is widely stigmatized. This stigma stems from generalized fear and association of AIDS with sex, disease, and death and with behaviours deemed illegal, forbidden, or taboo, such as pre- and extramarital sex, sex work, homosexuality, and intravenous drug use.[3]

This takes me back to my initial reflection: the central role that sex plays in defining our approach to and outlook on HIV and AIDS. A simplistic approach will be to say that we need more, better, and safer sex for all, and the "all" is inclusive of those groups more vulnerable to human rights abuses – namely, men who have sex with men, transgender populations, male and female sex workers, young boys and girls, prison inmates, drug users, and immigrants (particularly illegal migrants).[4]

The Role of International Organizations and Partners

The Caribbean has embraced the human rights approach to HIV and the United Nation's Greater Involvement of People Living with HIV/AIDS (GIPA) declaration. International organizations have supported the region in this process and the states in meeting their human rights obligations. However, there is a need for scaled-up support of regional and national efforts to empower individuals and communities to claim their rights in the context of the HIV epidemic. A central part of this effort involves promoting and facilitating programmes, interventions and services that will enable the exercise of human rights such as personal liberty, privacy, work, and sexual and reproductive health rights, which are essential to human well-being and social and economic development.

The action platform has been established. This was before the signing of the WHO constitution in 1946. In the Americas, PAHO/WHO member states reaffirmed their commitment with the foundation of the WHO constitution during the Fiftieth Directing Council by approving resolution CD/50/12 on health and human rights.[5] In 1948, all the nations of the world endorsed the "Universal Declaration of Human Rights", which expresses the common recognition about what rights are and why they should exist for all people everywhere. All human rights elaborated in these and other treaties promote accountability in HIV- and AIDS-related issues. There is rich and diverse literature on human rights and HIV. The governments of the world made comprehensive commitments on human rights and HIV in the "Declaration of Commitment on HIV and AIDS" (2001) and the "Political Declaration on HIV and AIDS 2006".[6] UNAIDS and the Office of the UN High Commissioner for Human Rights have developed a set of guidelines for member states to assist them in designing and developing programmes, policies and legislation to promote and protect human rights in the context of HIV and AIDS.[7] Human rights are a cornerstone of the Caribbean Regional Strategic Framework (CRSF) against HIV and AIDS. The CRSF incorporates some of the targets of the "Declaration of Commitment" and recognizes the need for a human rights approach.[8] There have been major efforts aimed at sensitizing key stakeholders, political leaders and the community. The development of model legislation has been central in the work of the Pan Caribbean Partnership against HIV/AIDS (PANCAP) for a decade.[9] These regional efforts have been fully supported by international organizations and partners, and we have seen some changes, though the structural barriers persist.[10]

The challenge in the Caribbean – as in many other regions – continues to be the application of those principles and guidelines to policy, programmes and services at the country level to influence societal changes that will enable individuals to exercise their rights, in particular their sexual rights, without fear of rejection, stigma, discrimination and violence. A more country-focused approach to the interventions, while maintaining regional action, is therefore required. In this context, the role of international organizations and development partners in the Caribbean becomes even more relevant in supporting efforts to identify innovative solutions that will better respond to the evolving environment and emerging needs in the region.

I will not describe here what is already well defined in the various action frameworks for international organizations; rather, I will focus on some areas that in my opinion are of critical importance at this juncture in the Caribbean and, in some instances, unique to the realities of the region. Some of these propositions are in fact a product of collective thinking and consensus building of more than eighty stakeholders in the Caribbean, convened by PAHO/ WHO in collaboration with the Caribbean Vulnerable Communities Coalition (CVC) in 2009.[11] Their discussion involved improving access of key populations to comprehensive HIV health services, which is a tangible, practical solution for achieving the targets of zero new infections, zero deaths and zero discrimination.

Some of the action points for further consideration are as follows:

1. *A broader movement towards inclusion.* Collaboration and strategic alliances at the country and regional levels need to be strengthened and intensified. PANCAP needs support to carry out its mandates and move from developing model legislation (as they have done in the last decade) to the actual adoption/implementation in countries. This will require concerted efforts of UNAIDS and its co-sponsors and other key partners in the Caribbean, particularly the US President's Emergency Plan for AIDS Relief (PEPFAR), to promote strategic alliances with human rights advocates (beyond HIV), nongovernment organizations (NGOs) and the community at large. A complete legislative reform may not be possible in many countries, and even though there is consensus on the need for decriminalizing homosexuality, sex work and drug use, a phased approach can provide opportunities to move the agenda forward. There are two issues that need urgent resolution: the removal of restriction of travel on the basis of HIV status (endorsed by PANCAP in 2010) and the reform of public health legislation (or health legislation) to remove provisions that clearly represent barriers to access to care (i.e., laws that prohibit people under eighteen from accessing sexual and reproductive health services without parental consent, effectively denying access to many sexually active young people).[12]

2. *A bold regional advocacy campaign to support inclusion efforts.* The Caribbean has been successful in regional communication efforts for the prevention of HIV. The Caribbean Broadcast Media Partnership

on HIV/AIDS (CBMP) LIVE-UP campaign is well recognized as a best practice. I wish to challenge international organizations, in particular UNAIDS and its co-sponsors and the PEPFAR, to support the CBMP to undertake a regional advocacy campaign to support inclusion efforts, highlighting the links between HIV and AIDS and human rights and directly supporting PANCAP efforts to move with the adoption and implementation of the model legislation. We need to break the silence!

3. *Concerted efforts to support the networks of people living with HIV or AIDS and vulnerable communities in reorienting and expanding their work to improve laws and policies.* A critical role of the international organizations and partners in the Caribbean involves providing support for the efforts for the reorientation and strengthening of the Caribbean Regional People Living with HIV/AIDS (CRN+) and local networks of people living with HIV or AIDS to respond to the emerging realities in the region. CRN+ and its constituency ought to play a key role in the implementation of campaigns and social mobilization programmes to ensure that HIV advocates, activists and affected populations know their rights and laws relevant to HIV, as well as existing mechanisms for redress. However, first and foremost is to address the sustainability of CRN+ and the networks and to establish strategic alliances with other networks, in particular CVC and other nontraditional networks. A coordinated approach between UNAIDS, PANCAP and partners is a "must" in this very critical juncture for the organizations that have been present for decades in the Caribbean, articulating the rights of individuals and the community of people living with HIV or AIDS into concrete demands. CRN+ is a prime example and is now challenged to sustain its efforts.

4. *Direct technical support and capacity building.* This is one of the key areas of intervention for international organizations. Overall, more awareness has been raised and there are various degrees of understanding of the fundamental linkages between HIV and human rights in the region. However, the use of human rights norms and standards to guide policies, programmes and services is still limited, and policymakers, programme managers and service providers are still not comfortable using human rights norms and standards to guide the actions taken by or on the behalf of governments in all matters affecting the response to HIV and AIDS. Moving from concepts to action requires genuine attention to building their capacity to recognize and promote the

synergy between health and human rights and to appreciate more fully the potential gains when health and other interventions are guided by human rights principles. Those involved in programme development and service delivery must become more familiar with the practicalities of genuinely using international human rights law in their practice.

An area of special consideration in the Caribbean is the sensitization and capacity building of providers, in particular health providers, on sexuality and sexual health issues. Knowledge of human rights will not be sufficient to promote changes in attitudes, behaviours and practices. Many health providers feel uncomfortable in dealing with issues related to sexuality and sexual health and do not have the skills for the provision of care that will take into consideration the special needs of sexually diverse populations. The training package on men's health and sexual diversity, developed by PAHO/WHO in collaboration with Caribbean experts and international partners, is a good example of concrete and innovative actions for capacity building. The dissemination and use of this training package is a concrete, practical intervention to be supported by international organizations.

In addition, international organizations can support sensitization and capacity building of judges, ombudspersons, the police and officers of other relevant agencies in the criminal justice system to enable a better understanding of the international treaty obligations that they may be called upon to enforce. The UNAIDS initiative in this area is under way and should be strengthened.

5. *Dissemination of international human rights norms, standards and mechanisms that protect people living with HIV or AIDS and vulnerable communities.* The dissemination of international human rights norms and standards, including the "International Guidelines for Human Rights and HIV/AIDS", is a clear mandate of UNAIDS and its co-sponsors and one that continues to be relevant in the region. Perhaps innovation is needed to reach the community at large and transcend policymakers, programme managers and service providers – hence the required alliance and support to the established networks of people living with HIV or AIDS and vulnerable communities. International organizations actively working in the Caribbean can also facilitate collaboration with regional and international human rights bodies charged with promoting and protecting the human rights of those living with HIV or AIDS, including participation in hearings and the provision of technical opinions.

6. *A bold approach to the issue of migration, HIV and human rights.*
Anecdotal and documented violation of the human rights of immigrants, in particular illegal immigrants, continues to be a challenge in the Caribbean. Existing policies and practices in many countries result in barriers to care for immigrants, with severe implications for public health. In a few Caribbean countries, the public sector provides full and free health services to all in need, no questions asked. However, in most of Caribbean countries, immigrants (in particular undocumented immigrants) have limited access to health services. Limitations can be in the form of types of services offered or higher copays. The health system's evaluations in several countries supported by PAHO have documented reluctance among undocumented immigrants to use health services as a result of the occurrence of raids from immigration services and fear of deportation. In addition, language and cultural barriers limit migrant clients from gaining the full benefits of health services.[13]

In general, undocumented immigrants concentrate on the fringes of big cities in areas with high crime rates, poverty, overcrowding, social disintegration, and a lack of social and health services. Their uncertain legal status creates insecurity in everyday life and drives their political and economic marginalization.[14] Instances of sexual exploitation and trafficking have also been documented in the region. During the past ten years, several Caribbean countries, including Belize, Guyana, the Dominican Republic and Suriname, have been identified as transit and destination countries for women and children trafficked for the purpose of sexual exploitation. Trafficked persons have little ability to negotiate safer sex, and trafficked sex workers may be subjected to additional exploitation by police, customs officers and other authorities, including demands for sex and demands for pay for entry or protection.[15]

The impact of migration on the HIV epidemic is widely recognized and one that will require a regional approach and consensus building. UNAIDS and its co-sponsors, in collaboration with the PANCAP, are in the best position to generate a policy dialogue on this issue – one that will bring together governments to debate some hard topics and identify feasible solutions. This might be as difficult as the decriminalization of the behaviours themselves (and perhaps is intrinsically linked). That, however, if not addressed by a sound public health approach, will continue to fuel the HIV and AIDS epidemic in the region. As well captured by one of the most moving of Bob Marley's songs, the Caribbean is the "one love" region: mobility from island to island is part of our nature and will not stop, whether it is regulated or unregulated. That is the heritage from our ancestors and a result of complex socioeconomic determinants that will not be resolved soon. Therefore, we cannot ignore this very important determinant of the HIV and AIDS epidemic in the region. International organizations, in particular UNAIDS and its co-sponsors, are best positioned and, I will say, have the obligation to support CARICOM and PANCAP in facilitating a policy dialogue which is most needed.

7. *Direct technical support for the scale-up of comprehensive services to key populations through a primary health care approach.* Availability of a full range of health services utilizing a primary health care approach is a critical condition to ensure access for all. Integration of HIV and sexual/reproductive health services in primary care service delivery is particularly important to overcome stigma and discrimination. If STI patients are seen only in STI clinics and persons living with HIV are seen only in HIV units, then visiting these facilities marks and stigmatizes users, which compromises confidentiality. Integration of HIV with other health services will also improve the cost-effectiveness and sustainability of HIV services and will create the opportunity for leveraging of HIV resources to strengthen health systems. From the perspective of the key populations, the integrated package of health services and the delivery of those services must include availability of a continuum of medical and psychosocial services, convenient opening hours, and efficient and client-centred staff.[16]

   Collaboration between the public sector, private sector and civil society is critical, since many key populations seek health services outside of the public sector. International organizations and partners, in particular UNAIDS, PAHO/WHO and PEPFAR, can play important roles in advocacy, direct technical support and harmonization.

8. *Sharing experiences across countries and institutions and promoting horizontal collaboration.* There are many ongoing interventions and efforts in most of the Caribbean countries. A critical role for international organizations is to facilitate a platform for sharing of experiences across countries, which will allow a discussion on successes and challenges and will also promote horizontal collaboration. Horizontal collaboration (or in the PAHO language, "technical cooperation among countries", or TCC) is a powerful intervention to deal with the complexity and sensitivity of HIV and human rights and one that should be more utilized. By facilitating

debate between countries, exchanges and open discussion of both good and not-so-good practices, countries can embrace even further the principle of solidarity which is highly appreciated in the Caribbean.

9. *Mobilization of resources (human and financial) to support national and regional efforts.* International organizations ought to support efforts for the mobilization of resources needed to scale up interventions to reduce stigma and discrimination and to remove legal barriers. This does not necessarily mean more funding but better use of our human capital. There is expertise in the region that can and should be better utilized under a key principle: this is our problem, this is our region, and we have the obligation to resolve it.

Notes

1. CARICOM, "Caribbean Cooperation in Health Phase III: Investing in Health for Sustainable Development", http://www.caricom.org/jsp/community _organs/health/cch_iii_summary.pdf.
2. PAHO/WHO, "Human Rights and Health: Persons Living with HIV/AIDS" (Washington, DC, 2008).
3. Ibid.
4. UNAIDS, "Keeping Score III: The Voice of the Caribbean People" (Trinidad and Tobago, 2011).
5. PAHO/WHO, "Health and Human Rights: Resolution CD50/12" (Fiftieth Directing Council, Washington, DC, 2010).
6. UNAIDS, Office of the United Nations High Commissioner for Human Rights, "International Guidelines on HIV/AIDS and Human Rights, 2006 Consolidated Version" (Geneva, Switzerland, 2006).
7. Ibid.
8. CARICOM and PANCAP, "Caribbean Regional Strategic Framework on HIV and AIDS 2008–2012" (September 2008).
9. PANCAP, "Regional Policy and Model Legislation to Address HIV and AIDS-Related Discrimination: Summary of the Desk Review" (Georgetown, Guyana, 2010).
10. Ibid.
11. PAHO/WHO, "Improving Access of Key Populations to Comprehensive HIV Health Services: Towards a Caribbean Consensus" (draft report, 2010).
12. UNFPA, "Young People and Times of Change: Talking about Life, Love and Sexuality" (fact sheet, 2009), http://safaids.net/files/Adolescence%20and%20 Preg%20Position%20Paper.pdf.

Amalia Del Riego

13. PAHO/WHO, "Improving Access".
14. P. Brodwin, "Marginality and Cultural Intimacy in a Transnational Haitian Community", occasional paper 91 (Department of Anthropology, University of Wisconsin-Milwaukee, 2001).
15. Ibid.
16. Ibid.

Chapter 8

Current Legal and Institutional Responses to HIV Stigma and Discrimination

F. Ayana Hypolite

CARICOM Secretariat / Pan Caribbean
Partnership against HIV and AIDS

In the Caribbean, people living with HIV or AIDS and vulnerable communities face discrimination in many spheres of life, including employment, education, access to health care, and physical violence and harassment in their homes and communities. Many are without access to justice or other mechanisms for redress and fear the repercussions of seeking such remedies. Previous regional efforts to record and address incidents of HIV-related discrimination through antidiscrimination reporting and recourse mechanisms such as human rights desks have achieved limited success due to inadequate or weak legislative and human rights frameworks.

The Regional Response

The "Caribbean Partnership Commitment", which birthed the Pan Caribbean Partnership against HIV/AIDS (PANCAP), made reference to the "devastating social and economic impact" of the epidemic and recognized that "intolerance, homophobia and discrimination against people living with HIV or AIDS and of those vulnerable to infection drive the epidemic underground and contribute to further spread of the virus". This document was a call to action for the CARICOM Heads of Government and all partners to commit to efforts to reduce "stigma, discrimination and exclusion of people living with HIV or AIDS and protections of their human rights and dignity".

In 2002, regional partners came together to develop an action plan around law, ethics and human rights, with funding from partners such as the Canadian International Development Agency (CIDA); the Global Fund to Fight AIDS,

Tuberculosis and Malaria (GFATM); and the World Bank, and they have
pursued various elements of this plan with varying success. The action plan
formed the basis of a regional work plan which was then funded by CIDA (the
PANCAP Law, Ethics and Human Rights – LEHR project). Under this project,
legislative assessments were conducted in six countries (Guyana, Dominica,
St Vincent and the Grenadines, St Lucia, and St Kitts and Nevis); these findings
were collated and discussed at a regional consultation to find common policy
areas for action. Codes of practice were also developed for and by psychosocial
and medical practitioners in order to ensure that principles and standards of
good practice were observed in the provision of HIV care and support and
that discriminatory practice was reduced or eliminated.

Other PANCAP partners, including the University of the West Indies
Caribbean HIV and AIDS Regional Training Network (UWICHART) and the
University of the West Indies HIV AIDS Response Programme (UWI- HARP),
have tackled capacity building for health care workers so that people living with
HIV or AIDS receive adequate standards of care. The LEHR project, in collaboration with the Caribbean Regional Network of People Living with HIV/
AIDS (CRN+), also supported the sensitization of two subregional groups of
legal practitioners and people living with HIV or AIDS around HIV legal issues and advocacy. A meeting of HIV and human rights activists was also held
under this project to develop a common platform for human rights–based
action on HIV.

CRN+, through the Health Economics Unit at the University of the West
Indies, has also collaborated with PANCAP to host an HIV law, ethics and
human rights meeting and has developed guidelines for rights-based approaches in the HIV response. CRN+ has also pioneered the establishment
of human rights recourse mechanisms and the development of guidelines for
their operation so that violations of the human rights of people living with
HIV or AIDS might be reported and appropriately addressed.

The legislative assessments (under the LEHR project as well as other national assessments) informed the development of the PANCAP antidiscrimination model policy and legislation.

The draft antidiscrimination model policy and accompanying legislation
funded by the World Bank address discrimination in access to HIV prevention, treatment, and care services and also in other spheres, including the
workplace, education, insurance and prisons, among others. These models,
which have already been sent out to country programmes, will pass through a
regional approval processes via CARICOM and then be adopted and adapted
at the national level. Funding for these initiatives has been budgeted under the
PANCAP Global Fund Round project.

A number of Caribbean policies and declarations (e.g., those developed for the workplace [national and enterprise level], education sector and faith-based organizations) encourage nondiscrimination, respect for the rights of people living with HIV or AIDS and advocacy against stigma and discrimination.

Behaviour change communication and advocacy strategies, frameworks, and multimedia campaigns have also been launched throughout the region by Caribbean Epidemiology Centre (CAREC), CARICOM, UNICEF and UNDP, among others. The PANCAP Champions for Change initiative, funded by the United Kingdom Department for International Development, also involved persons of influence in various spheres (sports icons, political leaders, religious leaders, media, etc.) in advocating for the rights of people living with HIV or AIDS.

The evaluation of this initiative and its three regional consultations and the recommendations therein has led to the establishment of the PANCAP Regional Stigma and Discrimination Unit in Barbados. This unit, which has now entered the implementation phase of its project life, will provide technical assistance to countries in research, programming, advocacy (including human rights messaging, empowerment and advocacy) and best practice dissemination around HIV stigma and discrimination.

Conclusion

In the absence of a supportive policy and legislative environment, newly sensitized practitioners and their clients do not have an effective system for redress. Legislative reform must also be accompanied by efforts to sensitize the political directorate, mobilize the legal fraternity (including law students) and address the restrictive costs of litigation. It is critical that the connectivity between HIV stigma and discrimination and human rights and the impact on access to prevention, treatment, care and support services and national development are understood and emphasized.

The following items are recommended:

1. The legal fraternity should be supported to articulate a strategy that will outline the creation and facilitation of an enabling environment in which people living with HIV or AIDS and attorneys will be empowered to come together to go to court to test the strength of existing legislation. This strategy may include background research into best practices; publication of cases from both local and other jurisdictions; support for research for test cases; the creation of literature that will be easy to read by both laypersons and professionals; and the mobilization

of law schools, legal aid clinics, law societies and regional nongovernment organizations. It will also aim to support and expand the informal network of legal practitioners.

2. Legal practitioners, academics and political leaders, as well as professionals that are already sensitized and engaged in the regional response to HIV, should continue to support the sensitization of their constituents and the regional model policy and legislation and resulting national level legislation.

3. People living with HIV or AIDS and at risk populations should be empowered to advocate on their own behalf. This is central.

4. Medical, legal, psychosocial and other professionals should be exposed to HIV legal-ethical and human rights issues during training.

Bibliography

Caribbean Conference of Churches. "Guidelines for Caribbean Faith-Based Organisations on Developing Policies and Action Plans to Deal with HIV/AIDS". Barbados: CCC, 2004.

Caribbean Health Research Council (CHRC) and Caribbean Regional Network of People Living with HIV (CRN+). "Quality of Life of People Living with HIV/AIDS in the Caribbean". Barbados: CHRC, 2007.

Francis, C. "Regional Model Code of Practice for Psychosocial Practitioners in HIV and AIDS Care". Guyana: CARICOM and PANCAP, 2008.

Gaitry Pargass, G. "Regional Guidelines for a Human Rights Referral and Response System to Violations against Persons Living with HIV/AIDS (PLWHA)". Guyana: PANCAP, 2007.

Hypolite, A. "Report of an Initial Assessment of HIV and AIDS Stigma and Discrimination Recourse Mechanisms in Six Countries of the Caribbean Region". Guyana: CARICOM, 2008.

International Labour Organization. "ILO Code of Practice on HIV/AIDS and the World of Work". Geneva: ILO, 2001.

Royes, H. "PANCAP Survey of Stigma and Discrimination in Six Caribbean Countries". Guyana: PANCAP, 2007.

Chapter 9

HIV, AIDS and Human Rights in the Caribbean

An International Perspective

Clare K. Roberts

Former President and Commissioner of the
Inter-American Commission on Human Rights

I considered it a signal honour to have been invited to present a lecture to the plenary session of the important and timely symposium on HIV and AIDS and human rights. The timeliness of this symposium must be emphasized because it comes sharply on the heels of the international conference on AIDS held in Vienna, Austria, in July this year. The theme of that conference was "rights here, right now". Thus we are here looking at the same subject but focusing on the Caribbean region. Nevertheless, the urgency is the same. Indeed the urgency is greater than for most places considering the statistics.

Statistical Background

By way of background, let me recite some statistics that are not sufficiently grasped in this region. Our people are not aware of just how serious the situation is. In the global AIDS pandemic, the Caribbean is the second most affected region in the world. Among adults aged fifteen to forty-four, AIDS has become the leading cause of death.[1] The region's adult prevalence rate is 1.6 per cent, with national rates ranging from 0.2 per cent to 3.1 in the Bahamas.[2] HIV transmission occurs largely through heterosexual intercourse, with two-thirds of AIDS cases in this region attributed to this route. Sex between men is also a significant route of transmission, even though it is heavily stigmatized and illegal in many areas.[3] HIV transmission through intravenous drug use remains rare, except in Bermuda and Puerto Rico.

In 2007, the population in the Caribbean was 32,024,000.[4] The total adult prevalence rate was 1.0 per cent and 17,000 people (adults and children) contracted the HIV virus.[5] An estimated total of 11,000 people died that year. Another estimated 230,000 persons live with the virus in the region. The rate of HIV in the Caribbean is four times that of North America, South Asia, Southeast Asia and Latin America. The rate is thirty-five times that of East Asia and ten times the rate in western Europe.

The Human Rights Reality

Those are the statistics; now let us look at the human rights reality regarding persons living with HIV or AIDS. HIV-related stigma and discrimination are extremely common in the Caribbean. In some cases, prejudice towards people living with HIV is linked with homophobia; sex between men carries a high risk of HIV transmission and, as elsewhere, people in the Caribbean often associate HIV with homosexuality, despite the fact that the majority of infections occur through heterosexual sex.[6]

I quote from an editorial in a newspaper in the Caribbean: "Despite the fact that they have rights, including the right to work and the right to privacy, the stigma continues against people living with HIV or AIDS. As a result these individuals become intimidated and do not seek the necessary medical attention out of fear of being rejected by their communities and families or losing their social status. But this is dangerous, as delayed medical attention speeds up deterioration of health."[7]

The disclosure of a person's HIV status may solicit "a broad spectrum of discriminatory acts" against the victims. The editorial continues, "Persons have been disowned by family members, evicted from their homes, lost their jobs either through dismissal or quit due to unbearable acts of stigma and discrimination."

Despite general knowledge that the virus is only spread through bodily fluids, blood, semen, vaginal fluid or saliva, society continues to scorn the infected by not wanting to share the same space as them or even touch them. In fact, many feel threatened breathing the same air in close proximity to a person living with HIV or AIDS. Children are being discriminated against at school, and some have suffered at the hands of health care professions.

Another Caribbean reality is the attitude of intolerance that is shown to men who have sex with men. A Caribbean gay rights activist states, "Gays and lesbians in Jamaica exist with the possibility that you might be chased, you might be run down, you might be killed because of your sexual orientation, and when a day ends when that does not happen, we give thanks."[8]

This problem is not helped by the fact that in most countries of the Caribbean the law criminalizes sex between men and also sex work. UNAIDS reports that, of the Caribbean countries that submitted data for its 2006 global report, over three-fourths had laws that hinder prevention and treatment services to vulnerable and high-risk populations. This includes outlawing sex between men and not providing condoms to certain groups, such as prisoners.

The prison population consists of, to a large extent, young men in crowded areas. Indeed, in most prisons in the Caribbean, young men are "stacked". There is no rehabilitation programme, so these young men are merely "doing time".

Stigma and Discrimination in the Caribbean

It is generally acknowledged that stigma and discrimination are helping to fuel the HIV epidemics of Caribbean countries. One HIV-positive man in Jamaica stated, "With HIV, because it's seen as a gay thing, there's a lot of shame. If someone finds out they are positive, they're afraid that everyone will assume they are gay, so it's best to keep it to yourself."[9]

Some progress is being made in overcoming this problem, particularly through the work of organizations of people living with HIV and nongovernmental organizations that work with vulnerable populations.[10] Many HIV prevention campaigns include messages against stigma.

However, there is still an urgent need for stronger and more coordinated efforts to fight this problem. Since HIV-related stigma is often linked with negative attitudes towards marginalized groups, there is a particular need for a review of the legislation of Caribbean countries that may be fuelling discrimination against such groups.

The Role of the Inter-American Commission on Human Rights

The Inter-American system for the protection and promotion of human rights has played its part by using the tools at its disposal to attempt to alleviate this dire situation. I therefore believe it is essential that advocates and activists for the protection of persons with HIV or AIDS are intimately aware of the Inter-American system of human rights and how the use of the system can protect the fundamental human rights of these persons. The Inter-American Commission on Human Rights ("commission", or IACHR) and the Inter-American Court of Human Rights ("court") are the two bodies within the Organization of the American States (OAS), created to promote the observance and defence of human rights in the hemisphere. While the Inter-American system recognizes and respects state sovereignty, the member states of the OAS believed it was necessary to establish a regional system to ensure compliance with the human rights treaties they established. The commission was created as a central component of this system.

The commission has been called "the conscience" of the region. It has also been called "the engine" of the Inter-American human rights system. The main function of the commission is to promote respect for and defence of human rights. In the exercise of its mandate, it has the following functions and powers:[11]

1. Develop an awareness of human rights among the peoples of America.

2. Make recommendations to the governments of the member states, when it considers such action advisable, for the adoption of progressive measures in favour of human rights within the framework of their domestic law and constitutional provisions as well as appropriate measures to further the observance of those rights.

3. Prepare studies or reports that it considers advisable in the performance of its duties.

4. Request the governments of the member states to supply it with information on the measures adopted by them in matters of human rights.

5. Respond, through the General Secretariat of the OAS, to inquiries made by the member states on matters related to human rights and, within the limits of its possibilities, provide those states with the advisory services they request.

6. Take action on petitions and other communications pursuant to its authority under the provisions of articles 44 through 51 of this convention.

7. Submit an annual report to the General Assembly of the OAS.

Since the establishment of the commission in 1959, there have been cases on a wide variety of issues for the improvement of enjoyment of fundamental rights of persons in the Americas. The Inter-American system has resolved matters involving discrimination based on race and sex, freedom of expression, rights of women and children, rights of persons with mental and physical challenges, violence against women, property rights, and right to health, among others.

In recent years, the commission has taken on HIV and AIDS human-rights-related issues. The commission is able to use the tools at its disposal to ensure that the rights of persons living with HIV or AIDS are protected. These tools include the processing of complaints of human rights abuses that are brought to its attention – the case system.

Numerous human rights treaties have been prepared and adopted by the OAS since its creation in 1948. However, the principal instruments interpreted and applied by the commission are the American Declaration on the Rights and Duties of Man and the American Convention on Human Rights. All thirty-five member states of the OAS are considered to be legally bound by the American declaration. Currently twenty-four member states have ratified the American convention, six of which are Caribbean member states.[12] Three of these Caribbean states have also accepted the contentious jurisdiction of the Inter-American Court of Human Rights: Barbados, Haiti and Suriname, meaning that matters from these jurisdictions can be presented and heard by the Court.

In the OAS system, the commission has primary responsibility for responding to and processing petitions of alleged human rights violations. Under article 44 of the American Convention on Human Rights, the commission accepts petitions from any individual or legally recognized nongovernmental organization (NGO) about human rights violations. This right of petition is available once domestic remedies have been exhausted. The commission also has the authority to issue precautionary measures in urgent cases where there is risk of irreparable harm to a victim of human rights abuse. The commission is the first responder and, in many cases, the final arbiter of the thousands of human rights petitions brought to the system each year.

It is the only regional mechanism in the Americas that monitors state compliance with an established set of human rights standards. The system functions as a facilitator between government and civil society to ensure that human rights and freedoms remain integrated in government policy and planning and that these rights and freedoms are not left behind in the pursuit of economic development. The recommendations of the commission and decisions of the court have been instrumental in assisting member states to re-examine legislation and policies in the area of human rights.

Human rights activists and lawyers in Latin America are generally more familiar with the Inter-American system. This may be a result of the political history of Latin America. Today, Latin American lawyers and NGOs are the dominant users of the Inter-American human rights system. There is a need to change that picture. The commission has pushed for universal ratification of the American Convention on Human Rights, but ratification of Inter-American treaties has not been a priority for some Caribbean member states. This may be partially due to the limited knowledge of the system in the region. NGOs should be advising, influencing and agitating policymakers to ratify all human rights treaties in the Inter-American system so that Caribbean victims of human rights abuse can have the full use of the system. If human rights activists are unfamiliar with the system or do not see the benefits for victims of human rights abuse, their participation will remain limited. The people of the Caribbean need the system in the constant struggle to protect the human rights of Caribbean people and to bring about societies in the Caribbean where human rights are recognized and respected at every level of society.

IACHR Mechanisms to Address HIV

It is pertinent to give a brief overview of how the Inter-American system of human rights works. Some of the mechanisms that can be utilized by the system to address HIV include the following:

- Prepare reports and special studies on the rights of persons infected with HIV and, more broadly, studies on issues pertaining to elimination of discrimination against such persons.
- Hold hearings during regular sessions having to do with alleged violations.
- Undertake consultations and prepare recommendations to member states regarding the modification of existing laws and articles related to the rights of persons infected with HIV or AIDS.
- Make on-site visits to the countries of the region. During the visits, the commission gathers information and investigates the most relevant problems related to persons living with HIV or AIDS.
- Draft admissibility and merits reports on case petitions as well as thematic, country and annual reports.[13]

The IACHR Response to HIV Cases

The commission has so far not had many opportunities to decide cases dealing with HIV or AIDS. Nevertheless, I bring to your attention some precedents which will give you an insight of the approach taken by the commission to the right to health.

Regarding HIV, the following decisions of the Inter-American Commission on Human Rights can be found:

The first example is Jorge Odir Miranda Cortez et al., a case from El Salvador. In that case, the commission received a petition alleging liability on the part of El Salvador with respect to Jorge Odir Miranda Cortez and twenty-six other persons who were HIV positive.

The petition alleged that the state had violated the right to life, health and well-being of the alleged victims in this case, inasmuch as it had not provided them with the triple therapy medication needed to prevent them from dying and to improve their quality of life. The commission declared the petition admissible with regards to the alleged violation of articles 2 (obligation of the state to legislate), 24 (equal protection under the law), 25 (judicial protection) and 26 (progressive development of economic, social and cultural rights) of the American convention.

The Inter-American commission concluded that the Salvadoran state did violate article 26 (economic, social and cultural rights). The commission decided not to render a decision with respect to the arguments on article 4 (right to life) or article 5 (right to humane treatment) of the American convention "because of the subsidiary nature of the corresponding arguments in this case".

The second example is a case from Mexico: J.S.C.H and M.G.S.[14] This admissibility report refers to two petitions. The first one was presented on behalf of J.S.C.H., a former driver with the rank of second lieutenant in the Secretariat of National Defence. The other was presented on behalf of M.G.S., a former infantry corporal in the Secretariat of National Defence. The petitions alleged discrimination against the alleged victims in that they were discharged from the Mexican Army because they were HIV positive, as well as for alleged violation of their rights to a fair trial and judicial protection. The commission declared the petitions admissible with regard to alleged violations of articles 2 (domestic legal effect), 5(1) (humane treatment), 8(1) (fair trial), 11 (right to privacy), and 24 (equal protection) of the American convention, in conjunction with the general obligation to observe and ensure rights provided in article 1(1) of that international instrument.

The other case I bring to your attention is the case, *TGG*,[15] from Ecuador. This admissibility report refers to a petition presented against Ecuador for its alleged responsibility for injury done to the female child TGGL, due to alleged infection with HIV and AIDS through a transfusion of blood supplied by the provincial Red Cross in the city of Cuenca, Province of Azuay, on 22 June 1998 and administered at the Pablo Jaramillo Crespo Foundation Humanitarian Clinic. The petition also alleged a failure to prosecute and punish those responsible.

After analysing the positions of the parties, the commission decided to declare the case admissible for purposes of examining the claim regarding the alleged violation of articles 4(1) (right to life), 5(1) (humane treatment), 8(1) (fair trial), 19 (rights of the child) and 25(1) (judicial protection) as they relate to article 1(1) of the American convention.

In addition, the commission has granted several precautionary measures relating to victims with HIV or AIDS. Tara J. Melish, in a chapter on social jurisprudence,[16] points out that between 2000 and 2003, the commission granted precautionary measures on behalf of four hundred persons carrying HIV or AIDS in ten member states of the OAS. In almost all these cases, the commission requested the state to provide the beneficiaries with the "medical examination and treatment indispensable for their survival". In some cases, it specified that this should include "comprehensive treatment and antiretroviral medications necessary to prevent death, as well as the necessary hospital, pharmacological and nutritional care needed to strengthen their immune system and prevent infections".

There is a clear trend with regard to access to treatment and its impact on human rights.

Case Studies from the IACHR on HIV

The commission also granted precautionary measures on behalf of Jorge Odir Miranda Cortez and twenty-six other members of the Asociación Atlacatl on 29 February 2000, thereby accepting that their rights to life were in grave danger since they required care from state institutions to access the medicine they needed for treatment and considering that HIV is a life-threatening disease. The commission requested that the Salvadoran state provide treatment and antiretroviral drugs, as well as the pertinent hospital, pharmacological and nutritional care. The IACHR received information from both parties on the actions taken to care for the aforementioned persons.

On 26 June 2000, the board of directors of the Salvadoran Social Security Institute authorized the procurement of the triple antiretroviral therapy for persons who are HIV positive or have AIDS in that country. Starting on that date, the state began to provide the requested treatment. The precautionary measures expired on 29 August 2000, at the end of the six-month period initially requested by the commission.

Further, the Inter-American commission granted precautionary measures on behalf of Juan Pablo Améstica Cáceres, Manuel Orlando Farías and Náyade Orieta Rojas Vera of Chile. These three individuals were HIV positive and contacted the IACHR because they believed their rights to life and health were in serious danger as a result of a lack of drugs and medical attention to treat their HIV. In its communication of 20 November 2001, the IACHR informed the Chilean state that these individuals urgently needed basic assistance from state institutions in order to secure the drugs needed for their treatment; it therefore requested the adoption of urgent measures to ensure them access to the medicines needed for their survival and to medical examinations for the regular monitoring of their health conditions.

On 5 December 2001, the state described the preliminary steps taken at the Ministry of Health and reported that Juan Pablo Améstica, Manuel Orlando Farías and Náyade Orieta Rojas Vera were receiving medication and undergoing examinations in order for their health conditions to be monitored by the state's services. It also requested additional time in which to submit further information on the case.

Again, on 3 October 2002, the commission granted precautionary measures on behalf of fifty-two persons, including two minors, who were carriers of the human immunodeficiency virus and alleged that in many cases they had turned to the state public health systems but not undergone the tests necessary to determine how the disease was progressing or received the antiretroviral treatment needed for them to survive. On 22 January 2003, the state presented a photocopy of the report of the National Program on STDs, HIV and AIDS.

On 2 October 2002, the commission granted precautionary measures on behalf of one person living with HIV or AIDS. According to the request, on 15 August 2002, the beneficiary, who lived alone and did not have any income, became unemployed and hence was cut off from social insurance. Because the Colombian state offered access to treatment for this disease only through that vehicle, the beneficiary was automatically removed from the HIV and AIDS programme that he had been involved with since November 1994. That programme provided him with antiretroviral treatment (AZT 3TCIDV). According to Pan American Health Organization standards, suspension of this treatment for a person infected with HIV or AIDS is fatal. The commission asked the state to resume the beneficiary's treatment. In response, the state took steps to include the beneficiary in an ad hoc programme providing access to antiretroviral treatment.

On 14 August 2002, the commission granted precautionary measures on behalf of ten carriers of HIV or AIDS. The petitioners alleged that the beneficiaries went to health centres or hospitals but were not given the drug treatment needed to fight the disease. As a result, the immune systems of these ten persons were in a critical state, and they did not have access to clinical tests to monitor how the disease was progressing. On 3 September 2002, the state indicated that it would provide comprehensive care to the beneficiaries within four months and would supply drugs to selected patients who met the criteria set by the National Commission on Antiretroviral Drugs, in accordance with the availability of the resources allocated for 2002. On 16 and 26 September 2002, the commission broadened the precautionary measures on behalf of several other persons, at the petitioners' request, covering 119 persons with HIV or AIDS.

The IACHR has also examined matters in relation to testing for HIV. On 9 July 2002, the commission granted precautionary measures on behalf of six Ecuadorian citizens who claimed to be HIV or AIDS carriers. The petitioners argued, inter alia, that state health agencies had failed to provide the beneficiaries with basic testing to determine the course of the disease as well as adequate treatment. The commission requested that the state provide the beneficiaries with the medical examination and treatment indispensable for their survival. The petitioners filed a second, third and fourth request, bringing the total number of affected persons, by 12 August 2002, to fifty-four. With each request, the commission extended the precautionary measures granted previously. On 26 August 2002, the state indicated that the original six HIV or AIDS carriers were receiving medical attention and that the Ministry of Health had acquired medication to prevent mother-child transmission for 100 women and to assist approximately 120 persons with HIV. Subsequently, the petitioners filed additional fifth and sixth requests, bringing the total number of affected persons by 23 September 2002 to 153 persons. Precautionary measures were requested in these cases as well. On 15 October 2002, the commission held a hearing on this matter, at the request of the state.

It is also noteworthy that on 19 August 2005 the commission granted precautionary measures in favour of Andrea Mortlock in the context of a petition, which alleged violations of Mortlock's rights under the American Declaration of the Rights and Duties of Man. The petitioners claimed that Mortlock was a forty-one-year-old Jamaican national detained at the Passaic County Jail in Patterson, New Jersey, who had lived in the United States since 1979, had lived with HIV or AIDS since 1989 and suffered from a number of related serious and life-threatening illnesses, including neuropathy and extreme wasting. They also claimed that Mortlock was at imminent risk of deportation to Jamaica and that her life and physical integrity were threatened as a result because many of the drugs that she was receiving were not available in Jamaica at all. She alleged that people with HIV or AIDS in Jamaica with visible signs of their illness were unable to receive medical care, were denied access to public and even private transportation, and could be the victims of physical violence. Murdock had no family, doctor, friends or acquaintances in Jamaica, as her entire family resided in the United States. In view of these circumstances, the commission asked the United States to refrain from deporting Mortlock to Jamaica, pending the commission's examination of her petition on the basis that Mortlock's deportation would render any eventual decision by the commission ineffective and would cause irreparable harm. On 23 August 2005, the state informed the commission that the commission's request had been forwarded to the US Department of Homeland Security and to the Passaic County Jail in New Jersey.

Rights to Life and Humane Treatment in the Context of HIV

The following provisions of the American convention guarantee the rights to life and to humane treatment:

Article 4. Right to Life

1. Every person has the right to have his life respected. This right shall be protected by law and, in general, from the moment of conception. No one shall be arbitrarily deprived of his life.

Article 5. Right to Humane Treatment

1. Every person has the right to have his physical, mental and moral integrity respected.

2. No one shall be subjected to torture or to cruel, inhuman or degrading punishment or treatment. All persons deprived of their liberty shall be treated with respect for the inherent dignity of the human person.

In the commission, the right to life is regarded as a right that is not exhausted or violated only when agents of the state act deliberately to deprive a person of life (such as in extrajudicial executions, summary executions); it is understood that the right to life is also a positive right and not simply a right of freedom. Consequently, it may also be violated by state omissions. In sum, therefore, there are also state omissions that lead to the death of a person.

The failure by the state to deliver free antiretroviral drugs to persons living with HIV or AIDS, whose need for them is based on objective and scientific considerations but who are unable to buy them owing to financial or other constraints, may represent a violation of the right to life, without prejudice to the violation that such an omission might represent with respect to the right to health, in view of the necessary interdependence and indivisibility of human rights.

The same reasoning applies regarding the right to humane treatment, which leads to the conclusion that the failure to deliver the drugs entails a state omission that causes physical and emotional suffering, which constitutes inhumane treatment that violates and infringes the right to physical integrity.

The Principle of Nondiscrimination

The principle of nondiscrimination is an aspect of the very essence of the Inter-American system of human rights. In this regard, the Inter-American court has ruled the following in its Proposed Amendments to the Naturalization Provisions of the Constitution of Costa Rica:

> The notion of equality springs directly from the oneness of the human family and is linked to the essential dignity of the individual. That principle cannot be reconciled with the notion that a given group has the right to privileged treatment because of its perceived superiority. It is equally irreconcilable with that notion to characterize a group as inferior and treat it with hostility or otherwise subject it to discrimination in the enjoyment of rights which are accorded to others not so classified. Precisely because equality and nondiscrimination are inherent in the idea of the oneness in dignity and worth of all human beings, it follows that not all differences in legal treatment are discriminatory as such, for not all differences in treatment are in themselves offensive to human dignity.[17]

The European Court of Human Rights has held that a difference in treatment is only discriminatory when it "has no objective and reasonable justification". There may well exist certain factual inequalities that might legitimately give rise to inequalities in legal treatment that do not violate principles of justice. They may in fact be instrumental in achieving justice or in protecting those who find themselves in a weak legal position. For example, the law's imposition of limits on the legal capacity of minors or mentally incompetent persons, who lack the capacity to protect their interests, cannot be deemed discrimination on the grounds of age or social status.

Accordingly, no discrimination exists if the difference in treatment has a legitimate purpose and if it does not lead to situations which are contrary to justice, to reason or to the nature of things. It follows that there would be no discrimination in differences in treatment of individuals by a state when the classifications selected are based on substantial factual differences and there exists a reasonable relationship of proportionality between these differences and the aims of the legal rule under review. These aims may not be unjust or unreasonable – that is, they may not be arbitrary, capricious, despotic or in conflict with the essential oneness and dignity of humankind.[18]

Generally speaking, it should be mentioned that persons living with HIV or AIDS very often suffer discrimination in a variety of forms. This circumstance magnifies the negative impact of the disease on their lives and leads to other problems, such as restrictions on access to employment, housing, health care and social support systems. There can be no doubt that the principle of nondiscrimination must be very strictly observed to ensure the human rights of persons affected by HIV or AIDS. Public health considerations must also be taken into account since the stigmatization of, or discrimination against, a person who carries the virus can lead to reluctance to go for medical treatment, which creates difficulties for preventing infection.

Life with Dignity

I further submit that persons living with HIV or AIDS have a right to live their lives with dignity. The dicta of the Inter-American Court of Human Rights support this position. For instance, one case determined, "One of the obligations that the State must inescapably undertake as guarantor, to protect and ensure the right to life, is that of generating minimum living conditions that are compatible with the dignity of the human person and of not creating conditions that hinder or impede it. In this regard, the State has the duty to take positive, concrete measures geared toward fulfilment of the right to a decent life, especially in the case of persons who are vulnerable and at risk, whose care becomes a high priority."[19]

Proposals for Moving Forward

I strongly advocate that each Caribbean country develop a human-rights-driven national plan for the prevention and treatment of HIV or AIDS and ensure that a section in the national human rights plan develops a strategy for persons living with HIV or AIDS. The process of creating the national plan will also serve the purpose of bringing the question of human rights of persons living with HIV or AIDS off the back burner.

It is also vital that there is a programme to raise the awareness level of all in the society – including the victims, activists, NGOs, persons involved in the treatment of persons living with HIV or AIDS, parliamentarians, ministers of religion, and lawyers – to end stigmatization, discrimination and exclusion of persons living with HIV or AIDS.

I further suggest that those living with HIV or AIDS, including advocates must be made aware that in addition to domestic remedies, there is international responsibility placed on the states of the Caribbean as well as the rest of the Americas for the protection of their rights and for sanction where their rights are violated. These avenues must be pursued for persons living with HIV or AIDS. Such persons are not defenceless, but they need to be aware.

My final message to persons living with HIV or AIDS I give with the help of Dylan Thomas, the Welsh poet, "Do not go gentle into that good night, rage, rage against the dying of the light", and (I would add) fight for your rights!

Notes

1. UNAIDS, "Epidemic Update 2004: Caribbean Fact Sheet" (2004).
2. UNAIDS/WHO, "AIDS Epidemic Update" (2005).
3. Byron Buckley, "Buggery and Health – What the Gay-Rights Lobby Doesn't Tell You", *Gleaner*, 13 November 2011.
4. Population Reference Bureau, "World Population Data Sheet" (2007).
5. UNAIDS/WHO, "AIDS Epidemic Update" (December 2007), 7.
6. This is a recent development. Initially the incidents of HIV were higher in men who have sex with men (MSM). Currently, women account for 53 per cent of HIV cases reported in the Caribbean. The highest percentage occurs in persons who are sex workers. See UNAIDS/WHO, "Report on Global AIDS Epidemic" (2008).
7. "Stigma and Discrimination Will Not Get Rid of HIV", *Daily Observer*, 23 June 2010, 2.
8. Gareth Williams, "The Jamaica Forum for Lesbians, All-Sexuals and Gays (J-FLAG)".
9. S. Cole, "Closet of the Caribbean", *Positive Nation*, April 2006.
10. For example, the work of the Caribbean Regional Network of People Living with HIV/AIDS (CRN+).
11. "The American Convention on Human Rights", article 41.
12. Barbados, Dominica, Grenada, Jamaica, Haití and Suriname ratified the American Convention. Trinidad and Tobago denounced the American Convention in 1998, which became effective in 1999.
13. Report 29/01/case 12.249 of the IACHR.
14. Report 02/09, Petitions 302-04 and 386-04 of the IACHR.
15. Report 89/09, Petition 663-06 of the IACHR.
16. Malcolm Langford, ed., *Social Jurisprudence – Emerging Trends in International and Comparative Law* (Cambridge: Cambridge University Press, 2008), 368.
17. Advisory opinion OC-4/84 of 19 January 1984, series A, no. 4: 104.

18. For further information, see United Nations, *Human Rights in the Administration of Justice: A Manual on Human Rights for Judges, Prosecutors and Lawyers* (New York: United Nations, 2005), 653.
19. See *Yakye Axa Indigenous Community v. Paraguay*, judgment of 17 June 2005, series C, no. 125, par. 162–63.

Chapter 10

A Snapshot of Legal and Institutional Responses to HIV and Human Rights in the Caribbean

Veronica S.P. Cenac

Board Member, Caribbean Vulnerable
Communities Coalition, St Lucia

HIV and AIDS continue to be one of the greatest threats to life, dignity and respect for human rights. Some among us have reacted with caution, care and compassion, in the acceptance and acknowledgement that we are all humans endowed equally with dignity and freedom. Others have reacted with hatred, scorn and fear and have rejected the duty of care that we owe to our fellow man.

Twenty-nine years[1] since the first reported case in the Caribbean, stigma and discrimination is alive and well. It continues to plague our highly religious, highly moralistic societies, which cast people living with HIV or AIDS (PLWHA) as "sinners", "outcasts" or "deviants". The various stereotypes associated with HIV have also contributed to the perception of HIV as a disease that affects only certain people, especially those who are already stigmatized because of their sexual behaviour, gender, race or socioeconomic status.

The response being coordinated to address the human rights imperatives raised by HIV and AIDS is improving.[2] An analysis of existing responses is therefore important at this stage in order to assess their efficacy.

This chapter is divided into three parts. First, a snapshot of the existing legal frameworks will be provided, drawing from national assessments on the laws and policies related to HIV conducted in various Caribbean Community (CARICOM) countries between 2003 and 2008, briefly illustrating the legislative responses. Second, the findings of an assessment commissioned by UNAIDS, Barbados and the Eastern Caribbean on the effectiveness of one of the recourse mechanisms set up to respond to instances of discrimination and other rights violations perpetrated against PLWHA – human rights desks established under the Caribbean Regional Network of People with HIV/AIDS (CRN+) Global Fund Project.[3] The desks were reviewed as an example of institutional response and are the focus of this chapter. Third, in conclusion, the author recommends that there is a need for a complaints mechanism addressing abuses against all vulnerable populations (not only PLWHA), given that these populations face similar levels of discrimination. Isolating HIV human rights responses is inherently stigmatizing, and the denial of rights and lack of focus on these populations have exacerbated increasingly high levels of infection. Documenting human rights violations is an essential step in encouraging policy change and helps monitor laws and policies even where protective provisions exist.

Legislative Responses

Priority area 1 of the Caribbean Regional Strategic Framework 2002 to 2006, "Law, Ethics and Human Rights",[4] called for the conduct of national legal assessments to review the legislative response to HIV and to recommend policy and legislative amendments to address stigma and discrimination.

Accordingly, through funding from the Canadian International Development Agency (CIDA), assessments were conducted by the Pan Caribbean Partnership against HIV/AIDS in Dominica, Grenada, Guyana, St Kitts and Nevis, St Lucia, St Vincent and the Grenadines, and Belize. Assessments were also conducted in Barbados, Jamaica, Suriname, and Trinidad and Tobago under other bilateral arrangements. An analysis of the national reports which were available for review, including the reports for Dominica, Grenada, Guyana, St Kitts and Nevis, St Lucia, St Vincent and the Grenadines, Belize, Barbados, and Suriname, reveal that governments in the region have adopted stigmatizing and discriminatory legal and policy measures, including compulsory screening and testing of the military, police and prisoners; compulsory notification of HIV cases; and compulsory screening of pregnant women. Other measures include screening of persons applying for visas and citizenship, mandatory testing of persons seeking work permits, pre-employment screening and the introduction of criminal laws to punish the wilful transmission of HIV. Existing laws, which generally exacerbate stigma and discrimination and limit access to treatment among some vulnerable groups, include buggery or sodomy laws, laws criminalizing prostitution, laws criminalizing drug use, laws deeming HIV an infectious disease and age of consent in relation to the treatment of minors. Progressive measures include antidiscrimination legislation in employment, broad antidiscrimination legislation and constitutional protections for right to health, right to work.

The following section on the existing legislative framework draws on the assessments of laws and policies related to HIV and AIDS reports that were available for Dominica, Grenada, Guyana, St Kitts and Nevis, St Lucia, St Vincent and the Grenadines, Belize, Barbados, and Suriname. The reports were conducted between 2004 and 2008 and refer to the state of the law at the date of the conduct of the assessment.[5]

Antidiscrimination Legislation in the Caribbean Region

Guyana stands out as having broad antidiscrimination legislation, while in Grenada and St Lucia the antidiscrimination legislation is restricted to the area of employment law. Dominica, St Kitts and Nevis, St Vincent and the Grenadines, Belize, Barbados, and Suriname do not appear to have any specific or general antidiscrimination legislation.

There is a substantial body of antidiscrimination legislation in Guyana, contained in both the constitution and in specific statutes that seek to promote equality between the sexes and prevent discrimination. The constitution prohibits discrimination on the grounds of *race, place of origin, political opinion, colour, creed, age, disability, marital status, sex, gender, language, birth, social class, pregnancy, religion, conscience, belief or culture* (s. 149[2]).[6] The constitution also protects free choice of employment, equality before the law, equality of birth status and equality of women (s. 249-F).

The Equality Rights Act (1990) further decrees equal rights for women. Section 4 of the Prevention of Discrimination Act (1977) prohibits discrimination on grounds *including race, sex, religion, colour, ethnic origin, indigenous population, national extraction, social origin, economic status, disability, family responsibilities, pregnancy, marital status and age*. Prohibited areas of discrimination include recruitment, employment, training and membership of professional bodies.

In Grenada the Employment Act (1999) was passed to set out the legal rights and responsibilities of employees and employers. Section 74 outlines the prohibited grounds for dismissal, which are a person's race, colour, national, extraction, social origin, religion, political opinion, sex, marital status and family responsibility or disability. Section 26 of the act seeks to prohibit discrimination with respect to recruitment, training, promotion, terms and conditions of employment, termination of employment or other matters arising out of the employment relationship. Health status is not a ground, but it is arguable that HIV can come within the definition of "disability."

The Equality of Opportunity and Treatment in Employment and Occupation Act, chapter 16.14 of the Revised Laws of Saint Lucia (2001), constitutes the sole antidiscrimination legislation in St Lucia. It is very progressive in that it aims to promote equal opportunity by eliminating unfair discrimination, directly or indirectly, against an employee, in any employment policy or practice, including discrimination on the grounds of race, sex, religion, colour, ethnic origin, family responsibilities, pregnancy, marital status and disability. Note again that health status is not a ground of discrimination.[7]

While the Bahamas and Bermuda were not reviewed under the PANCAP law ethics and human rights project the Employment Act (2001) in Bahamas and the Human Rights Act (1981) of Bermuda are worthy of special note here.

The Bahamas Employment Act (2001)[8] prohibits discrimination in public or private employment, except in the disciplined forces (armed force, police and prison services). Section 6 of the act prohibits discrimination on the grounds of race, creed, sex, marital status, political opinion, age, HIV or AIDS status, or disability (subject to reasonable accommodation). Note that HIV or AIDS status is a ground separate from disability in the act. The act defines the prohibited discrimination as refusal to offer employment, not affording access to opportunities for promotion or training or other benefits, dismissal of the employee, and subjecting the employee to other detriment. The act also expressly prohibits the prescreening of an employee for HIV or AIDS.

In Bermuda, the Human Rights Act (1981)[9] was amended in 2000 to revise the definition of *disabled person* to include a person who has "any degree of physical disability, infirmity, malformation, or disfigurement that is caused by bodily injury, birth defect or illness, including . . . acquired immune deficiency syndrome, human immunodeficiency virus."

The act prohibits discrimination on the grounds of disability in the area of housing; goods, facilities and services; employment; membership in organizations; advertising; and contracts. An exception exists if the discrimination was reasonable or excusable in all the circumstances. Employers are required to take reasonable steps to accommodate employees with disabilities.

Constitutional Protections Nondiscrimination

Constitutional protection against discrimination is restricted on grounds of sex, race, place of origin, political opinions, colour or creed in St Lucia, St Vincent and the Grenadines, St Kitts and Nevis, Barbados, Grenada, and Belize. No provision is made for "other status" that may arguably envisage categories including health status, disability or sexual orientation. In contrast, the Constitution of Suriname, article 8 (2), states that "no one shall be discriminated against on the basis of birth, sex, race, language, religion, education, political opinion, economic position or any other status."

Right to Health

The arguments for guaranteeing legislative protection of the right to access treatment stems from an acceptance of a right to health as a fundamental human right. The right to health is recognized in developing country constitutions including Costa Rica (articles 21 and 70 of the 1949 constitution), Ghana (article 24), Guatemala (articles 93–95 of the 1985 constitution) and Kenya (articles 70–85). In Venezuela, the right to health is clearly defined in the 2000 Bolivarian constitution. It recognizes access to treatment as a component of the right to health, and HIV treatment has been included in the Essential Drugs List since 1999. National and Provincial legal provisions to ensure access to HIV or AIDS treatment have been repeatedly upheld through decisions in the courts.

The following countries in the Caribbean recognize the right to health: Cuba at article 50 of the revised Cuban constitution,[10] the Dominican Republic at article 8 of the constitution,[11] and in the Preamble to the Haitian constitution.[12] For the countries considered in this review, only Guyana and Suriname have constitutional protection of the right to health.

In Guyana article 25 of the constitution states, "Every citizen has the right to free medical attention and also to social care in case of old age and disability . . . Every person in Guyana is entitled to the basic right to a happy, creative and productive life, free from hunger, disease, ignorance and want."

In Suriname, article 36 of the Surinamese constitution guarantees right to health to everyone residing in Suriname. It explicitly mentions the following: "Everyone has the right to health" (article 36 [1]) and "the state shall promote general health care by systematic improvement of living and working conditions and shall give information on the protection of health" (article 36 [2]).

Right to Work

For the countries considered in this review, only Suriname, Belize and Guyana have constitutional protection of the right to work.

In Suriname article 24 of the constitution gives the state the general obligation to create an environment in which optimal fulfilment of the basic need to work can be achieved. Two other articles provide individual citizens in general and specifically employees infected with or affected by HIV or AIDS with some protection of their right to work.[13]

In Belize article 15 of the constitution protects an individual from being denied the right to gain a living by work that he freely chooses or accepts. However, the Labour Act does not specifically prohibit discrimination on the grounds of HIV and AIDS.

Article 22 of the Guyana constitution states that "every citizen has the right to work and its free selection in accordance with social requirements and personal qualifications. He has the right to be rewarded according to the nature, quality and quantity of his work. Women and men have the right to equal pay for equal work."

Right to Privacy

Privacy is a human right, according to article 12 of the Universal Declaration of Human Rights:[14] "No one shall be subjected to arbitrary interference with his privacy, family, home or correspondence nor to attacks upon his honour and reputation. Everyone has the right to protection against such interference or attacks."

Except for a perambulatory call for "respect for [his] family life, personal privacy, the privacy of his home and other property", no substantive "right to privacy" exists for the individual in the constitutions of St Lucia, St Vincent and the Grenadines, St Kitts and Nevis, Barbados, Grenada, and Belize.

Redress for infringement of rights is available only with respect to those rights contained in the enforcement provisions. The absence of a clear provision protecting the right to privacy is a major gap in tackling stigma and discrimination related to HIV and AIDS. The right to privacy is constitutionally protected in Suriname.[15]

Public Health Law

One of the most important public health issues facing the world currently is the *HIV Disease*. In relation to HIV and AIDS, specific areas of importance are prevention and treatment services, HIV testing, epidemiological surveillance, infection controls and blood safety. The principal piece of legislation relating to public health is generally Public Health Acts.

In many countries, HIV or AIDS is not a notifiable or communicable, contagious or infectious disease (Suriname,[16] Dominica,[17] and St Kitts and Nevis[18]). This means that (1) there is no power to authorize the restriction of liberty or the detention of PLWHA; (2) there is no power to quarantine, particularly within a prison environment; and (3) there is no restriction on persons entering the state under the immigration acts, which generally restrict the entry of a person suffering from a communicable or infectious disease.

In Belize, statutory instrument (SI) 32/1987, passed under the Public Health Act, renders HIV an infectious disease and makes the persons infected susceptible to legislation requiring quarantine of persons with infectious diseases. There were no reported cases cited in the assessment report where the law was imposed against persons living with HIV. Under the law of Belize as currently enacted, there is no general legal requirement for HIV or AIDS to be a notifiable, public health disease.

In St Lucia, statutory instrument no. 21 of 1991 deemed HIV and AIDS *notifiable diseases*. This requires the notification of all cases to the chief medical officer. The potential for harm by this mandatory disclosure has been severely diminished by the institution of coding at the outset of the epidemic and by its universal use. This system has now been officially sanctioned by the National AIDS Programme and is promulgated in the National HIV/AIDS/STI Protocols (March 2006).

Testing

TESTING OF PREGNANT WOMEN

There was much debate among nurses and other health professionals on the testing of pregnant women and strong views were expressed by some nurses of the need to know the patient's status at the point of delivery. There is, however, strong authority from the Supreme Court of Canada and provincial appellate courts suggesting that forced HIV testing by the state or pursuant to the state authority is prima facie illegal.[19]

In Suriname, mandatory testing of pregnant women was reported notwithstanding laws that require voluntary and informed consent before one can receive medical treatment. The legal challenge against mandatory testing in Suriname is based on article 9(1) of the Surinamese constitution, which provides for the right to physical, mental and moral integrity.

In Dominica, infection-control nurses at the Princess Margaret Hospital reported that in cases of tuberculosis, HIV testing is mandatory, and in cases of pelvic inflammatory disease, HIV testing is recommended. The assessment report noted that in interviews with medical personnel, it appeared that testing without obtaining specific informed consent is widely practised.

It was reported that in Grenada as well, tests are conducted on pregnant women without their informed consent.

In Barbados, notwithstanding government policies to the contrary, the police force and the defence force conduct pre-employment HIV screening of their recruits.

In St Kitts and Nevis under the Defence Force Act No. 10 of 1997, recruits for the defence force are required to undergo a medical examination in order to ascertain their physical fitness in accordance with section 9 of the act. In practice, an HIV test is one of the required tests, and a potential recruit will not be retained if the test is positive. Progressively, police service recruits in the federation are not required to take an HIV test.

In St Lucia, recruitment within the police service and fire service requires a medical examination to determine fitness. One of the key tests includes a test for HIV. There were reports from the focus groups discussions with these two groups, indicating that where a test is positive, the prospective officer will not be hired. Of concern as well was the issue of privacy and confidentiality, as the test results go directly from the test site (laboratory, private doctor) to the police or fire service.

TESTING FOR WORK PERMITS AND CITIZENSHIP

In St Kitts and Nevis under the Saint Christopher and Nevis Citizenship Act no. 1 of 1984, all applicants for citizenship other than children by descent who are under twelve years of age are required to take an HIV test as part of the application. The rationale for the test, which is not encapsulated in any amendment or regulation to the Citizenship Act, is that "the country needs to know so that it can protect its citizens. And it needs to know the impact on the health system."[20] Where a potential applicant tests positive, the application is denied and the person is asked or is required to leave the state.

The Immigration and Passport (Amendment) Regulations, statutory instrument (SI) no. 33 of 1991, require "proof for having passed an HIV test". Therefore, all applicants for work permits entering St Kitts and Nevis are required to be tested for HIV. Where a potential applicant tests positive, the application is denied and the person is asked or required to leave the state. It appears that with respect to work permits, the government has reversed its policy; however, amendments to the law have not been made.

In Suriname, applications for work permits are made under section 27E of the Immigration and Passport (Amendment) Act 19 of 2003, which provides as follows:

(1) An application for a work permit shall be addressed to the minister who may grant the work permit either with or without conditions or may refuse to grant it.

(2) All applications for work permit shall be in such form as may be prescribed.

The same medical form for residence is also used for work permit applicants, and it makes mention of an HIV test. Though not explicitly mentioned in any policy document, it is reasonable to infer that HIV-positive persons will not be granted work or residence permits.

In Barbados, the immigration department recommended that an HIV-infected person could become an excessive charge on the health services. Therefore, as the Immigration Act deals with prohibited persons, HIV should be included as one of the communicable diseases designated within the Health Services Communicable Diseases Regulations and should be a ground upon which one may be refused entry.[21] This recommendation has, thankfully, not been implemented.

TESTING OF PRISONERS

In St Kitts and Nevis all inmates entering prison, whether as a remand or a convicted prisoner, are required to take an HIV test upon entry into the institution. Prisoners are not informed of their results. The results are received by the medical officer responsible for the prison and not by other prison authorities.

In St Lucia, prisoners in the Bordelais Correctional Facility, particularly new inmates, are tested for HIV. Although the prison authority indicated that the test was voluntary, there was evidence from the inmates that they were not aware of being tested for HIV. In breach of confidentiality rules, the medical reports are received by prison authorities and not by the inmate directly.

TESTING FOR INSURANCE

There was much evidence that testing for HIV is required for life insurance and medical insurance for all countries under review. While it may be argued that insurance coverage is a voluntary activity, this is negated by the fact that many financial institutions require life insurance for securing a mortgage or loan for residential or business purposes. An HIV test is now a standard test requested by insurance companies for health or life policies. On the other hand, persons living with HIV have been routinely denied coverage and suffer disclosure of test results leading to exposure of the PLWHA. This unsatisfactory situation continues to be a major complaint against the industry.

Confidentiality

With the exception of Suriname, Belize, and St Kitts and Nevis, it appears that none of the countries under consideration has specific legislation providing protection against breaches of confidentiality. All the countries reported that this was one of the major problems in addressing stigma and discrimination.

In Suriname confidentiality is statutorily enjoined upon anyone who acquires information on account of his or her job. The concept of statutory confidentiality is found in article 332 of the Criminal Code and article 38 of the Civil Service Code (Bulletin of Acts and Decrees 1962, no. 195). This law very explicitly states the obligation to confidentiality of civil servants, which includes government-employed physicians and other health workers. According to article 1613 of the Surinamese Civil Code, the relation between health workers and patients can be qualified as an agreement for rendering services. Under article 332 of the Criminal Code, which governs general obligation to confidentiality, the health workers are bound to confidentiality. Should a physician use the services of other supportive professionals, then these professionals have an obligation to confidentiality, which is derived from the physician. This was ruled by the High Court of the Netherlands on 30 November 1927 (NJ. 1928, page 265, W. 11772).

In Belize there are no laws specifically imposing sanctions for breach of confidentiality. The only two avenues of redress for breach of confidentiality are the Medical Council or the Nurses and Midwives Council for disciplinary action to be taken.[22] Since there is a right to privacy protected under the constitution, there is also the option of bringing an administrative action in the Supreme Court to recover damages.[23] However, the cost of securing legal counsel for such proceedings places this option outside the reach of most individuals.

The common law principle of doctor-patient confidentiality applies in the other countries reviewed. In English common law systems (in this case St Lucia is included), physicians have a duty of confidentiality to their patients. Physicians owe a duty of care to their patients to maintain all information generated in the course of a medial relationship, and the patient has a right to such confidentiality.

In Grenada, confidentiality is viewed as a major problem. There are no laws to require confidentiality or to protect persons against breaches.

In Dominica, there are no laws requiring the protection of information other than the common law duty of care. In an effort to address unlawful breaches of confidentiality, coding is used in the laboratory in Dominica.

Where the result is positive, only the national epidemiologist has access to information on the patient's sex, age, status and address. However, the same is not practised in the hospital, where a patient's status is recorded in the medical file.

In Barbados during the initial response to the epidemic, confidentiality was compromised in a number of different ways, from the provision of specially known clinics, to isolation in wards, to whisperings or euphemisms used, to the special marking of records. While there is no legislation, these practices have largely been abandoned due to education and training in the health sector and workplaces.

In St Kitts and Nevis there is a perception of a systemic lack of confidentiality, particularly in the public health care system, at the hospital, pharmacy, laboratory and other health facilities. Health care providers admit that there are instances where confidentiality is unintentionally breached and that there is a lack of privacy on the hospital wards.

There are clear legislative requirements for the protection of confidentiality of patient information by nurses.[24] Notwithstanding, there was much evidence to the contrary. Reasons for this may be that the provisions of the legislation are not enforced, or that, in the absence of a sufficient penalty, there is no incentive to adhere to the Nurses and Midwives (Registration) Act no. 18 of 2005.

At present, a code is utilized when testing for HIV. However, when an individual presents at a laboratory for testing, there is some likelihood that a connection will be made to the identity of the patient, notwithstanding the code, due to the small size of the country. Further, the form for an HIV test has a distinct yellow backing, unlike other laboratory forms.

In St Lucia the assessment found that breaches of confidentiality in the health service are systematic and deeply rooted. There was significant evidence from the focus groups of high levels of breaches of confidentiality. Unlawful disclosure in St Lucia has led to consequential widespread discrimination; this was considered one of the most significant challenges to tackling stigma and discrimination. Persons reported being run out of their communities and fired from jobs, houses have been burnt, and it was reported that one person committed suicide when a talk show host disclosed their status on radio.[25]

Disclosure-Partner Notification

Most reports recorded that health care workers are conflicted over the issue of partner notification, as they are often in a quandary as to whose rights they are to protect: their patient's or the partner's. Doctors agree that they cannot disclose to the patient's partner without the patient's consent. The general view is that the patient should always be responsible for disclosure to a partner.

Contact-tracing programmes are in place in St Lucia and Suriname. In Suriname, the contact-tracing policy is based on the Law on Contagious Diseases. It is also used as a method for effectively preventing the spread of sexually transmitted infections by breaking the chain of STIs.

In St Kitts and Nevis, however, there is no contact-tracing programme and none was recommended on the basis that the small size of the population would hinder the ability of the contact tracer to operate in a confidential manner.

In Dominica, there is no legal authorization, practice guidelines or written policy on partner notification in cases of HIV and AIDS in Dominica.

In Barbados, contact tracing is referred to in its communicable diseases regulations. Barbados recommends a code system for determining the conditions under which confidentiality can be broken in disease tracing.

These are as follows: (1) The infected person has been tested and counselled and knows the result of the test and how the disease is transmitted or can cause harm; (2) the counsellor has made all efforts to have the person inform those who are at risk or have been at risk for transmission of the disease and has offered assistance in doing so, through confidential means; (3) the counsellor is convinced that a specific third party or parties are being put at risk for transmission of the disease and has so informed the designated public health medical officers and has been instructed by that officer to break confidentiality to the specific third party or parties; (4) where public health officials determine that a person is deliberately endangering others, they may, with the permission of the designated public health medical officer (rather than the police), bring the matter before the court. The court may impose sanctions which may vary from community service to restrictions in a manner and place designated by the court.

Access to Treatment

The international community, both government and nongovernmental organizations,[26] have promoted legislative protections guaranteeing access to antiretroviral drugs.[27]

Revised Guideline 6 (2002) International Guidelines provides that

> states should enact legislation to provide for the regulation of HIV-related goods, services and information, so as to ensure widespread availability of quality prevention measures and services, adequate HIV

prevention and care information, and safe and effective medication at an affordable price.

States should also take measures necessary to ensure for all persons, on a sustained and equal basis, the availability and accessibility of quality goods, services and information for HIV prevention, treatment, care and support, including antiretroviral and other safe and effective medicines, diagnostics and related technologies for preventive, curative and palliative care of HIV and related opportunistic infections and conditions.

States should take such measures at both the domestic and international levels, with particular attention to vulnerable individuals and populations.[28]

Other than countries which guarantee a right to health, there are no legislative provisions securing the right to access treatment in the countries reviewed.

Notwithstanding, all countries subject to this review currently provide free antiretroviral drugs (ARV) and, in the case of Barbados, highly active antiretroviral therapy (HAART) to PLHIV. With respect to the OECS countries mentioned (St Lucia, St Kitts and Nevis, Grenada, and Dominica) there is some concern that with the closure of the Round 3 OECS Global Fund to fight AIDS, Tuberculosis and Malaria (GFATM) Grant in August 2010, free treatment to newly infected persons will not be possible.

With respect to Barbados, the policy is to provide free treatment to nationals. Testing is provided free of cost in most government assigned institutions in all countries.

Criminal Law

Wilful Transmission[29]

In Belize, sections 46.01 and 73.02 of the Criminal Code chapter 101 of the revised edition of Laws 2000 list reckless or wilful transmission of HIV or AIDS as a criminal offence.

In St Lucia section 140 of the Criminal Code 2004 provides as follows:

Transmission of HIV:

140. (1) Any person who, knowing that he or she suffers from Acquired Immune Deficiency Syndrome commonly known as AIDS, intentionally or recklessly infects another person with the human-immuno deficiency virus known as HIV, whether through sexual intercourse or any other

means by which the disease may be transmitted to another person, commits an offence of aggravated assault and is liable on conviction on indictment to prison for ten years.

(2) It is no defence for a person charged with an offence under subsection (1), to prove that the act was committed with the consent of the other person.

St Vincent and the Grenadines, Barbados, and Suriname do not list such offences; however, in St Vincent and the Grenadines, under section 291 of the Criminal Code, cap. 124, any person who unlawfully or negligently does any act which he knows, or has reason to believe, to be likely to cause the spread of any infectious or contagious disease is guilty of an offence and liable to imprisonment for one year.

It appears that a person who deliberately infects another person with HIV knowing that he is living with that disease may be prosecuted under that provision.

In Barbados, sections 19 and 26 of the Barbados Offences against the Person act could be used to prosecute persons who in section 19 "endanger life and safety" and in section 26 "assault another occasioning harm".

In Suriname, under the Surinamese Criminal Law 11, it is virtually impossible to prosecute persons who intentionally infect others. One would have to produce lawful evidence to show the intention of the defendant; that the defendant was HIV positive at the moment of transmission; and the victim could not have been infected with the HIV virus other than through the defendant.

In Grenada, St Kitts and Nevis, and Dominica, there is no specific legislation against wilful transmission, and its introduction is not recommended.

Laws Relating to Buggery or Sodomy[30]

While homosexuality is not considered illegal, eleven of the independent CARICOM states have laws that in practice criminalize consensual sex between adult males. The UK overseas territories have introduced laws to effectively decriminalize homosexuality, and Dutch laws relevant to Aruba and the Netherlands Antilles prohibit discrimination against individuals on the basis of their sexual orientation. The Dominican Republic, Cuba, Suriname and the Bahamas have no criminal sanction against consensual same sex.

In Belize, section 53 of the Criminal Code criminalizes unnatural crimes. The section does not specifically state that sodomy is a crime, but it is used to criminalize acts of sodomy. In practice, however, the section has only been invoked to bring charges against male adults who sexually assault boys or other men. The police indicate that they treat sexual intercourse between consenting adults, whether male or female, as a matter of privacy of such adults, preferring not to get involved.

In Grenada, section 431 of the Criminal Code, cap. 1 (1994 continuous revised edition) states the following: "If any two persons are guilty of unnatural connection . . . each person shall be liable to imprisonment for ten years."

In Dominica, buggery is an offence under section 16 of the Sexual Offences Act no. 1 of 1998:

16. (1)   A person who commits buggery is guilty of an offence and liable on conviction to imprisonment for –
   (a) twenty-five years, if committed by an adult on a minor;
   (b) ten years, if committed by an adult on another adult; or
   (c) five years, if committed by a minor.

In St Lucia, section 133 of the Criminal Code (2004) criminalizes buggery:

(1) A person who commits buggery commits an offence and is liable on conviction on indictment to imprisonment for:
   (a) life if committed with force and without the consent of the other person;
   (b) ten years, in any other case.
(2) any person who attempts to commit buggery, or commits an assault with intent to commit buggery, commits an offence and is liable to imprisonment for five years.

In St Kitts and Nevis, the Offences against the Person Ordinance, chapter 56 of the Revised Laws 1961, section 56, provides, "Whoever is convicted of the abominable crime of buggery, committed either with mankind or any animal, shall be liable to be imprisoned for any term not exceeding ten years, with or without hard labour."

In St Vincent and the Grenadines, the Criminal Code (1990) Edition 101, sections 146 and 148 provide the following:

146. Any person who
   (a) commits buggery with any other person;
   (b) commits buggery with an animal; or
   (c) permits any person to commit buggery with him or her; is
guilty of an offence and liable to imprisonment for ten years.

148. –Any person, who in public or private, commits an act of gross indecency with another person of the same sex, or procures or attempts to procure another person of the same sex to commit an act of gross indecency with him or her, is guilty of an offence and liable to imprisonment for five years.

In Barbados, the Sexual Offences Act 1992, chapter 154, section 9 provides the following: "Any person who commits buggery is guilty of an offence and is liable on conviction on indictment to imprisonment for life."

In Guyana, it is an offence for a man to commit an act of "gross indecency" with another male person in public or private, including procuring or attempting to procure such an act. In accordance with section 351 of the Criminal Law Offences Act cap. 8.01, the offence is punishable on indictment by imprisonment for up to two years. Section 353 of the Criminal Law Offences Act criminalizes buggery which is punishable on indictment by life imprisonment. Attempted buggery is punishable by imprisonment for a period of up to ten years.

All reports recommended the decriminalization of consensual adult sexual relations.

Sex Work

There are no prohibitions against sex work in Suriname. However, prostitution is an offence in all other countries under review. The laws relating to sex work cover a range of activities including prostitution. All countries under review contain prohibitions including

- soliciting, living off earnings, loitering and wandering in public places;[31]
- procuring for the purposes of prostitution;[32]
- use of premises as a brothel;[33]
- laws sanctioning idle and disorderly persons, rogues, vagabonds and vagrants;[34]
- immigration laws;[35]
- procuring of minors.[36]

In law the term "sex work" is a misnomer or legal fiction. Instead, legislative provisions define sex workers as "prostitutes" and "night walkers" and regulate aspects of "prostitution" and "brothels". Less directly, those engaged in sex work might be deemed "vagrants", "disorderly", "rogues" and "vagabonds".[37]

Sex workers face grave physical and sexual violence, threats to themselves and families, harassment, sexual violation and even murder at the hands of their clients and pimps. They report being raped and robbed by clients, police officers and strangers who see them working on the streets. Many report narrow escapes from even more severe injury and murder.

They are also unlikely to seek sexual and reproductive health services for fear of the discrimination that may occur. In many countries sex workers are viewed as drivers of the epidemic and the provision of certain services to sex workers, including the provision of condoms seen as encouraging and facilitating this immoral and illegal activity.

Education

In Grenada, the Education Act 2002, section 22(3), requires parents of children who are under the age of eighteen to make their children's medical or other conditions known to the principal of the school. Section 23 imposes on every principal the obligation to establish and maintain a student record for each student. This section also gives the right to examine the record to the student, parent and sponsor of the student.

In St Kitts and Nevis and St Lucia,[38] the education acts, which are CARICOM model legislations, establish a right to education. Section 28 progressively establishes prohibited grounds of discrimination: "Subject to the provisions of this Act, a person who is eligible for admission to a public educational institution or an assisted school as a student shall not be refused admission on any discriminatory grounds including race, place of origin, political opinion, colour, creed, sex, or subject to the provisions of this Act, mental or physical handicap." HIV is not covered as a ground of discrimination.

Prison

Although prisoners are regarded as a high-risk population, legislation in Belize governing the prison department makes no provision for prevention, treatment and care of inmates or staff and does not prohibit mandatory testing.

In Grenada, St Lucia, and St Kitts and Nevis, distribution of condoms to prisoners was felt to be very problematic and considered illegal, based on buggery or sodomy laws. The prison authorities believe that the distribution of condoms in the prison would be an admission that homosexuality exists in the prison and that this might also be condoning homosexuality.

In Dominica under the Prisons Act, chapter 12:70, there is no medical examination on reception of prisoners, as provided for in section 18. At present, some volunteers and Ross University students carry out medical examination of inmates. There is also no mandatory testing of prisoners for HIV. Condoms are not issued to prisoners.

In St Vincent and the Grenadines, section 21 of the Prisons Act (chapter 281), mandates that the "prison medical officer, who shall record the state of health of the prisoner, must examine every prisoner entering Her Majesty's Prisons".

This provision subjects the prisoner to compulsory medical treatment. There is no requirement that his medical status will be kept confidential. It is possible that the ordinary prison officer may have access to the prisoner's health records.

In Guyana, apart from general provisions dealing with entitlement to medical treatment, the Prisons Act cap. 11.01 does not specifically address HIV prevention. There is no requirement to educate prisoners regarding safe practices or to provide them with a means of prevention such as condoms. There is no provision regarding voluntary testing or prohibiting mandatory testing or the provision of counselling. These findings were also made in the reports of all the countries under review with the exception of Suriname. The most contentious issue remains the availability of condoms within the prison, which was largely regarded as impossible to consider in the face of buggery laws.

Drug Use

The criminalization of drug use and its impact on HIV was considered in three of the national assessment reports—that is, Barbados, St Lucia, and St Kitts and Nevis. However, drug use is highly criminalized in the Caribbean, and the "war on drugs" has led to large numbers of offenders being incarcerated for drug-related offences.

All countries under review criminalize the use of "controlled drugs", including marijuana, cocaine and heroin, among others.[39] See by way of example the Drugs Act (Prevention of Misuse), chapter 3.02 of the Revised Laws of Saint Lucia (2001). Section 8 of the Drugs Act criminalizes the possession of and trafficking of controlled drugs, including heroin, cocaine, opium, morphine and cannabis (also known as marijuana).

Human rights abuses against people who use drugs are widespread and impede HIV prevention, treatment and care efforts. These abuses include denial of harm reduction services, discrimination in accessing antiretroviral therapy (ART), abusive law enforcement practices, and disproportionate criminal penalties.[40] The threat of arrest or police abuse creates a climate of fear for drug users, driving them away from lifesaving HIV prevention and other health services and fostering risky practices.

Recommendations were made for alternative sentencing to treatment programmes, including needle or syringe exchanges where appropriate. The intersection between drug use and sex work and drug use and prisoners continues to be a major gap in prevention efforts. There is considerable merit in shifting the focus from criminalization of drug users to reducing harm and addressing rehabilitation.[41]

Assessment of Human Rights Desks

This section presents the findings of an assessment commissioned by UNAIDS, Barbados and the Eastern Caribbean. The assessment reviewed the functioning of the desks in five countries of the Organization of Eastern Caribbean States (OECS) – Antigua and Barbuda, Grenada, St Kitts and Nevis, St Lucia, and St Vincent and the Grenadines – and considered the operation of the desks under two components:

1. Institutional and administrative arrangements
   • Selection of the advocates, adequacy of training, ability to define the issues and provide guidance
   • Infrastructure, including location, facilities, access and support
   • Reporting mechanisms

2. Substantive issues
   • Broad areas of human rights violations
   • Level of redress achieved
   • Reasons for anywhere redress was unsuccessful

The report also built on an initial assessment of the HIV and AIDS stigma and recourse mechanisms in six countries of the Caribbean – Antigua and Barbuda, Grenada, Guyana, Jamaica, St Vincent and the Grenadines, and Trinidad and Tobago – compiled by Ayana Hypolite for the Pan Caribbean Partnership against HIV/AIDS (PANCAP) in December 2008 which reviewed the functioning of the desks in these countries.

The human rights desks were a key component of the CRN+ global fund project "Strengthening the Community of PLWHA and Those Affected by HIV/AIDS in the Caribbean: A Community-Based Initiative", which was approved by the Global Fund in July 2004 and implemented following signing of the grant agreement after June 2005. See programme 3.4: "Establish a specialized system in each National Network or Programme to receive and respond to complaints pertaining to human rights violations to PLWHA through the appropriate and relevant authorities in each country."

Eleven human rights desks were set up in Antigua and Barbuda, the Dominican Republic, Guyana, Grenada, Haiti, Jamaica, St Kitts and Nevis, St Lucia, St Vincent and the Grenadines, Suriname, and Trinidad and Tobago as part of the CRN+ Global Fund Project.

This assessment is concerned with the desks set up in Antigua and Barbuda, Grenada, St Kitts and Nevis, St Lucia, and St Vincent and the Grenadines. The original project did not include activities in Dominica or Barbados.

Methodology

The individuals selected for interviews included human rights advocates and former advocates (where the desks are no longer operational), national AIDS programme coordinators (NAPCs), supervisors of advocates, lawyers assigned to human rights desks or who volunteer pro bono services, staff of legal aid clinics, staff of sexually transmitted infections (STI) clinics, networks of PLWHA, members of organizations working with or representing other vulnerable groups, staff of social services ministries, psychosocial support providers, HIV and AIDS NGOs, human rights organizations, other NGOs, CRN+, Caribbean Coalition of National AIDS Programme Coordinators (CCNAPC), stigma and discrimination units, and the OECS HIV/AIDS Project Unit (HAPU).

Compilation and Desk Review of Documents

The project attempted to compile copies of all complaints filed with the desks from the inception of the project in 2006 to 2010 from various sources, including CRN+, human rights advocates, NAPCs and the OECS HAPU, which collected data from the desks under the OECS Global Fund to fight AIDS, Tuberculosis and Malaria (GFATM) Grant.

A literature review of studies on stigma and discrimination in the Caribbean was also undertaken. Requests were sent to the agencies and individuals for copies of the documented reports. Information was also obtained in print and from the Internet.

Limitations

The main constraints in the study were as follows:

1. *Severe limitations on interviews.* It was difficult to secure the attendance of participants for the telephone interviews.

2. *Availability of reports.* In most countries, no one entity, organization or person had all the information. Locating the reports was time consuming and difficult.

3. *No resources for travel.* The fact that the consultant could not travel to the countries further exacerbated the collection of complaints and extended the reporting time of the consultancy.

General Project Design

Purpose

The purpose of the human rights desks was to receive, document and respond to complaints filed by PLWHA in target countries and to educate PLWHA on their rights and avenues for redress.

Structure

The human rights advocate was selected from members of the in-country network after an open application and interview process. The desk was set up either at a national AIDS programme or in country network or other NGO which would take responsibility for supervising the advocate. The Terms of Reference of the Advocate which was established as a part-time position was quite extensive and included undertaking continuous monitoring of actions to address complaints towards resolution and redress.

Training

The project designed regional guidelines for a human rights referral and response system, and the advocates received a three-day training programme on the guidelines. Local attorneys were engaged to provide follow-up training on human rights and national laws of relevance to the work of the desks.

Monitoring

Advocates were required to complete a monthly attendance register and monthly report forms detailing the complaints received and work of the desk in the reporting period.

Access and Uptake

Access to the desk was designed to be either by calling or by personal interview with the advocate. Other agencies, including treatment clinics, were encouraged to refer patients to the desk.

The CRN+ Global Fund Project was not approved for a second round funding, and the project closed in 2009. However, some of the human rights desks set up under the project ceased operating as early as November 2008 due to financial constraints. Table 10.1 indicates the state of the desks in the countries under consideration.

Observations on Institutional and Administrative Arrangements

The following findings on the institutional and administrative arrangements were made:

1. The training received by human rights advocates was woefully inadequate.

   At the inception of the desks in 2006 and 2007, the advocates from Grenada, St Kitts and Nevis, St Vincent and the Grenadines, and other regional counterparts participated in a three-day workshop conducted by CCNAPC on Regional Guidelines for a Human Rights Referral and Response System to Violations against Persons Living with HIV. In the cases of Antigua and Barbuda and St Lucia, new advocates are in place and both have received no special training in human rights, law or ethics.

Table 10.1. Present state of human rights desks in countries under consideration

COUNTRY	STATUS	LOCATION/ PREVIOUS LOCATION	FUNDING PROVIDER
Antigua and Barbuda	Functioning	The Health Hope and HIV (HHH) Foundation	HHH Foundation with support from the Ministry of Health
Grenada	Closed	National AIDS Directorate	–
St Kitts and Nevis	Functioning	Ministry of Health – Health Promotion Unit	Ministry of Health
St Lucia	Functioning	AIDS Action Foundation	AIDS Action Foundation
St Vincent and the Grenadines	Closed	Ministry of Health – National AIDS Programme	–

In the PANCAP Report, it was revealed that advocates in the countries considered had a functional understanding of Human Rights. In this Study a similar observation could not be made. Only two of the advocates demonstrated an understanding of legal and human rights issues. However, this may be due to the inadequacy of the training referred to previously.

To function more efficiently, the desk requires, *inter alia*, an advocate who should at a minimum be able to dissect the issues, determine whether a legal response is necessary or whether the complaint can be addressed through some intervention by the advocate (mediation) or where psychosocial support is required.

2. There was a lack of access to national laws and other materials.

    The advocate's ability to function effectively was further hampered by a lack of access to national laws and other materials.

3. There was a lack of basic equipment, including computers and dedicated telephone lines and a lack of privacy.

    In some countries, office space, telephone and fax lines were shared with other offices, diminishing the privacy required when accessing the desks and complaints follow-up. In some cases advocates do not have independent access to the desk, which limits the time frame within which persons can come to the desk or call in to report complaints.

4. The referral systems were mainly informal.

    Many of the cases coming within the purview of the desk could not be adequately addressed without the ability of the advocate to refer the matter to other appropriate entities. At the inception of the project, no emphasis or resources were focused on developing a structured referral system in country. A referral system is absolutely necessary for the efficient functioning of this kind of mechanism regardless of where it is located.

5. There was an inherent conflict created by placing the desks within government HIV departments and other stigmatized locations.

    In Grenada, the desk is located in the National AIDS Directorate (NAD) and set up as the Project Coordinating Unit for the World Bank Programme on HIV. Since the NAD is identified as an HIV Unit, persons felt stigmatized if they went there, as only persons who have an "HIV" issue would go there. Placing the desk within a government entity also raised a conflict of interest, as human rights protections are generally against the state.

The desks in St Vincent and the Grenadines and St Kitts and Nevis have similar challenges. Both are placed within the National AIDS Programme. Advocates reported that "tucked within the Ministry" as they were, persons would not come to the desk and would not call as there is mistrust in a government department.

The expectation that the mere presence of the desk – in the absence of sufficiently trained and qualified personnel and confidential settings – translates to persons reporting instances of abuse or violations was perhaps too ambitious, and unfortunately this sentiment is supported by the evidence.

Observations on Cases Reported

There were weak monitoring and evaluation systems. Out of a total of eighty-seven cases reported, information on the nature of the complaints and the steps taken to secure a resolution were only available for eighteen of the cases. Sixty-nine of the cases reported could not be located, as there was no documentation system in place at the state level. Advocates were charged with the responsibility of establishing a database of complaints received and outcomes to allow for further research and to influence legislative reform. However, the monthly reporting requirements did not include this essential task, and with some exceptions (Antigua and Barbuda and St Lucia), there is little information to determine whether any redress was obtained other than the referral.

The only requirement was that the cases be recorded and referred, where necessary, to the appropriate authority. There was no requirement to follow up on these matters, determine the outcome or provide redress.

One of the reasons for this gap resides in the fact that global fund grants are performance-based grants. There is certainly much to be commended with this approach. However, one of the drawbacks has been an overriding concern about numbers as a measure of achievement; indicators are therefore designed around quantitative targets.

The emphasis of the project on collecting the number of cases, as opposed to the nature of the violations necessary to inform legislative and policy changes, has resulted in the loss of an extremely valuable advocacy tool. This does a severe disservice to those who were brave enough to report abuses.

Low Reporting

The epidemic of stigma and discrimination is so embedded in the psyche of service providers, activists, programme managers, NGOs and every person involved in reducing the impact of HIV and AIDS that it is taken for granted. No evidence of violations is required; we know that it is happening. Anecdotal reports of abuses abound in annual UN Reports, the PANCAP-sponsored National Legislative Assessments and other commissioned studies which have provided evidence of a range of abuses which occur daily. However, there is very little documented evidence of these abuses. The desks were meant to address this gap.

Advocates in the countries under consideration reported receiving complaints regarding (1) discrimination by health care providers (HCP); (2) discrimination in securing insurance; (3) breaches of confidentiality, mainly by HCP and family members; (4) harassment and victimization from the community and family; (5) denial of health services or discrimination in accessing health services (particularly with prisoners); (6) discrimination in employment and dismissals; (7) lack of accommodation; and (8) discrimination in schools.

However, over a period of approximately two years, only eighty-seven cases were reported across five countries in the OECS region. It is clear that either there is severe underreporting or the extent of the problem has been exaggerated. However, the informant interviews and focus group discussions revealed that many cases were not reported to the desk for a number of reasons, including location, lack of visibility of the desk, fear of HIV-related stigma, fear of disclosure and lack of trust.

The Case for a Reporting Mechanism

Documenting human rights violations is an essential step in encouraging policy change and monitoring laws and policies, even where protective provisions exist.

Facts need to be collected and documented to support a specific allegation with evidence. It allows advocates, human rights organizations and governments to (1) provide assistance when needed, (2) seek redress and remedies, (3) change policies, (4) change behaviour and attitudes of authorities and (5) raise public awareness.

All respondents supported the continuation of the desk; however, there was a consensus of opinion that the desk should be expanded and thereby positioned appropriately to record complaints on all human rights abuses related to HIV – not solely on abuses experienced by PLWHA. Therefore, the desk should report on violations faced by women, vulnerable children, prisoners, substance users, homosexuals and other sexual minorities, sex workers, and the general public.

The Case for Integrating the Human Rights Response

Vulnerable groups typically experience stigma from multiple sources (e.g., drug use, sexuality, gender, sex work, HIV). Thus interventions that address only HIV stigma may not improve prospects for these groups or facilitate the response to AIDS.

As mentioned previously, all respondents in the five countries recommended the expansion of the desk to consider general human rights abuses, removing the focus on HIV. Respondents indicated that the focus on HIV attached stigma to the desk, and persons did not access the services for fear of being labelled HIV positive or associated with HIV. This focus also limited the ability to advertise the desk widely: the greater the association with HIV, the greater the likelihood of a perception that only PLWHA would approach the desk.

Resources will continue to be wasted if the focus is solely on PLWHA. This study is evidence of that. There was severe underreporting, weak monitoring and nonacceptance by the public because of the programme's association with HIV. In order to collect and deal with instances of violations, the stigmatized HIV human rights desk needs to be remodelled and emerge as a true human rights desk.

Conclusion

The original project design has revealed a number of weaknesses, including (1) inadequate training of human rights advocates, (2) lack of access to national laws and other materials, (3) lack of basic equipment, (4) lack of privacy, (5) lack of referral systems, (6) inherent conflict created by placing the desks within government departments and (7) weak monitoring and evaluation systems.

Documenting human rights violations is an essential step in encouraging policy change and monitoring of laws and policies. For the desks to be sustainable, the human rights advocate must operate within a framework where there is access to additional legal and psychosocial support and where clients are not fearful of breaches of confidentiality and further stigma and discrimination by attempting to protect their rights.

Two revised project designs have been presented for consideration; they are not exhaustive and must take account of local realities. They do, however, address the weaknesses of the existing system while expanding coverage of violations beyond HIV and AIDS.

Option 1: Fully integrate desk within existing legal services provider.
Redesign the desk to move from stand-alone, single-person manned entity operating within an NGO or a government department to an integrated desk within an established human rights organization or legal aid clinic where they exist reporting on all human rights violations.

Option 2: Create various points of access for reporting abuses.
Train entities which already receive and document human rights abuses to record complaints and to act or refer. Within this recommended framework all reports or copies of reports would be forwarded to the Human Rights Advocate for compilation, tracking and maintenance of a complaints register. Clients would therefore be able to report abuses where they are most comfortable and where there is trust. This framework requires training among a wider pool of persons to enable proper consideration of the complaints.

At a minimum, the human rights reporting mechanism should (1) target all human rights violations perpetrated against vulnerable populations (not only PLWHA), (2) be located outside a government entity or a location which is stigmatized while being accessible to target clients, (3) be supported by a formal referral system expanding access to additional legal and psychosocial services, and (4) be manned by a properly trained advocate who engenders a sense of confidence through professional competence.

Notes

1. The first documented reported case was Haiti in 1981. See United Nations Joint Programme on HIV/AIDS (UNAIDS)–Caribbean Regional Support Team, "Keeping Score II: A Progress Report towards Universal Access to HIV Prevention Treatment, Care and Support in the Caribbean", UNAIDS 2 (2008): 22.
2. Indeed, in the first working meeting of the Caribbean Vulnerable Communities Coalition (CVC) on human rights held in the Dominican Republic in September 2009, a symposium of this nature was envisaged. Now under the guidance of Sir George Alleyne, UNAIDS, PANCAP, the University of the West Indies and other regional partners including CVC, the extent to

which the human rights of persons vulnerable to HIV and PLWHA are respected, protected and fulfilled will be addressed in order to propose possible avenues and responses for strengthening the human rights and HIV agenda.

3. The desks were established in approximately eleven countries in the region to receive and respond to complaints of human rights abuses against PLWHA.

4. PANCAP, "Caribbean Regional Strategic Framework on HIV/AIDS 2002–2006", http://www.caricom.org/jsp/projects/hiv-aidsstrategicframework.pdf.

5. Suriname 2003, Barbados 2004, Guyana 2004, Dominica 2005, St Vincent and the Grenadines 2005, St Lucia 2006, St Kitts and Nevis 2007, Grenada 2008, Belize 2008.

6. Guyana's 1980 constitution. In the National Assessment Report on HIV/AIDS, Law Ethics and Human Rights in Guyana by the National AIDS Committee, July 2004, he noted at page 76 that "in 2000 a bill to amend the Constitution, which would have added sexual orientation as a prohibited ground of discrimination, was passed by the Parliament but lapsed after the President failed to sign it into law".

7. See section 3 of the act.

8. Employment Act (2001) no. 73 of 2000, s. 6. http://www.lexbahamas.com/Employment%20Act%202001.pdf.

9. See Laws of Bermuda, Human Rights Act no. 41 of 1981. http://www.bermudalaws.bm/Laws/Consolidated%20Laws/Human%20Rights%20Act%201981.pdf.

10. Article 50 of the revised Cuban constitution states, "Everyone has the right to health protection and care. The state guarantees this right by providing free medical and hospital care by means of the installations of the rural medical service network, polyclinics, hospitals and preventive and specialist treatment centres; by providing free dental care; by promoting the health publicity campaigns, health education, regular medical examinations, general vaccinations and other measures to prevent the outbreak of disease."

11. Article 8 states, "With the aim of strengthening its stability and well-being, its moral, religious and cultural life, the family shall receive the broadest possible protection from the State. (a) maternity, regardless of the condition or status of the woman, shall enjoy the protection of the public powers and shall be entitled to public assistance in case of desertion. The State shall adopt measures of hygiene and other steps designed to prevent infant mortality insofar as possible and to attain the healthy development of children."

12. The 1987 Haitian constitution states, "Strengthen national unity by eliminating all discrimination between the urban and rural populations, by accepting the community of languages and culture and by recognizing the right

to progress, information, education, health, employment and leisure for all citizens."

13. See article 6, which states that anyone has the right to work within his capacities. Article 8, sub. 2, states that no one shall be discriminated against on the basis of birth, sex, race, language, education, political opinion, economic position or *any other status*. The "'other' status" quality implies that no one, including those with a disability, should be discriminated against, which arguably may include someone who is HIV positive.

14. United Nations, Universal Declaration of Human Rights, http://www.un.org/en/documents/udhr/index.shtml.

15. Although the right to privacy is protected in Suriname, it appears that human rights promulgated by the constitution or in international instruments, for example, the Universal Declaration of Human Rights, which have the force of law in Suriname as a monist state, may be restricted by national law. In Suriname, the law of 7 December 1953, concerning the regulations to prevent and combat contagious diseases (Bulletin of Act and Decrees 1953, no. 137), is an example of such a legal restriction. This law regulates that a matter of overriding importance will have preference before the oath of confidentiality and thus the right to privacy.

16. See the Law on Contagious Disease (Bulletin of Acts and Decrees 1953, no. 137) and the Law on Venereal Diseases (Bulletin of Acts and Decrees 1944, no. 31).

17. Environmental Health Services Act 8 of 1997.

18. Public Health Act no. 22 of 1969.

19. *R v. Dyment* 2SCR 417 (1998) at 431–32.

20. PANCAP (2007), "Saint Kitts and Nevis Final Report on Law Ethics and Human Rights", 35.

21. The report recommendation is similar to the position in the Cayman Islands, which provides that only citizens and permanent residents of five years duration or more are entitled to access government financed services without the payment of fees.

22. See Medical Practitioner's Registration Act, chapter 318 of the Laws of Belize, 2000 and Nurses and Midwives Act, chapter 321 of the Laws of Belize, 2000.

23. Supreme Court of Judicature Rules, chapter 91 of the Laws of Belize 2000.

24. Nurses and Midwives (Registration) Act no. 18 of 2005.

25. PANCAP, Saint Lucia Assessment on HIV/AIDS Law, Ethics and Human Rights, 2007, 55.

26. ICASO, *The International Guidelines on HIV and Human Rights: An Assessment of National Responses* (Toronto: ICASO, 2002), http://data.unaids.org/pub/report/2002/20020701_icaso_human_rights_en.pdf.

27. In April 2002, UNCHR adopted two resolutions relating to access to medication. Resolution 2002/32 recognizes that access to medication is a "fundamental element" for progressively realizing article 12 of the International Covenant on Economic, Social and Cultural Rights (ICESCR).
28. Revised Guideline 6 of the International Guidelines on HIV/AIDS and Human Rights, http://data.unaids.org/Publications/IRC-pub07/jc1252-internguidelines _en.pdf.
29. Other than St Lucia and Belize, the Bahamas and Bermuda also criminalize the transmission or exposure of HIV. The Bahamas Sexual Offences and Domestic Violence Act, chapter 99, s. 8(2) makes wilful transmission an offence. In Bermuda, s. 324 (1) of the Criminal Code (Sexual Offences) Amendment Act, 1993, states that a sexual assault has been committed if the person has a sexual disease and engages in a sexual act with another without informing the other party about the disease.
30. Countries that criminalize include Antigua and Barbuda, Jamaica, Belize, St Lucia, Trinidad and Tobago, Grenada, St Vincent and the Grenadines, Barbados, and St Kitts and Nevis, Dominica, and Guyana. Countries that do not criminalize include the Dutch territories, the UK Overseas Territories, the Bahamas, Cuba, the Dominican Republic and Suriname.
31. Dominica Sexual Offences Act 1998 s. 25 (living off the earnings); Grenada Criminal Code Art. 137 (loitering for the purpose of prostitution); Saint Kitts and Nevis Small Charges Ordinance chapter 75, s. 39; Saint Lucia Criminal Code 2004 s. 150 (loitering) and s. 151 (living off the earnings); Barbados Minor Offences Act s. 2 (loitering); Belize Summary Jurisdiction Offences Act s. 4 (loitering).
32. Dominica Sexual Offences Act 1998 ss. 18, 22 and 23; Barbados Sexual Offences Act 1992 ss. 13 and 14; Belize Criminal Code cap. 101 ss. 49, 50.
33. Dominica Sexual Offences Act 1998 ss. 23 and 24; Saint Lucia Criminal Code 2004 s. 143; Barbados Sexual Offences Act 1992 ss. 17 and 18; Belize Criminal Code cap. 101, s. 50.
34. Dominica Small Charges Act 1891 cap. 10:39, s. 30; Saint Lucia Criminal Code 2004 ss. 525, 560 and 563.
35. Dominica Immigration and Passport Act cap. s. 3 (a); Grenada Immigration Act 1990 cap. 145 s. 3; Saint Kitts and Nevis Immigration Act 2002, Schedule 1 s. 3; Saint Lucia Immigration Act 2001 s. 4; Saint Vincent and the Grenadines Immigration (Restriction) Act cap. 78 s. 4; Barbados Immigration Act cap. 190 Schedule 1 s. 3.
36. Dominica Sexual Offences Act 1998 ss. 18 and 21; Grenada Criminal Code 1994 Cap. 1 s. 188; St Kitts and Nevis Small Charges Ordinance chapter 75, s. 39; Saint Lucia Criminal Code 2004 s. 141; Barbados Sexual Offences Act 1992 ss. 13 and 17.

37. T. Robinson, "A Legal Analysis of Sex Work in the Anglophone Caribbean", UNIFEM, UNAIDS, April 2007.

38. Saint Lucia Education Act, chapter 18.01 of the Revised Laws of Saint Lucia 2001 s. 14; Saint Christopher and Nevis Education Act no. 9 of 2005 s. 14.

39. Barbados Drug Abuse (Prevention and Control) Act cap. 131.

40. International Harm Reduction Association (IHRA). *Harm Reduction and Human Rights the Global Response to Injection-Driven HIV Epidemics: Submission to the Office of the High Commissioner for Human Rights for the biennial report on HIV/AIDS requested by Commission on Human Rights Resolution E/CN.4/RES/2005/84* (London: IHRA, 2008), http://www.ttag.info/pdf/HR2SubmissiontoOHCHR.pdf.

41. Axel Klein, Marcus Day and Anthony Harriot, eds., *Caribbean Drugs* (New York: Zed Books, 2004).

Chapter 11

Discrimination and Access to Treatment of HIV and AIDS

Douglas Slater

Minister of Foreign Affairs, Foreign Trade and
Consumer Affairs, St Vincent and the Grenadines

HIV and AIDS began to be seen in the region in the early 1980s.[1] Uncertainty, fear and the association of the disease with men who have sex with men (MSM) in a predominantly homophobic society, combined with religious and other cultural taboos regarding sexually transmitted infections (STIs), provide a platform for discrimination and stigma against people living with HIV or AIDS (PLWHA).

Discrimination may have various definitions and concepts, but essentially it involves the practice of rejection and exclusion by a person or persons towards others in a set category or group, including the refusal of services, as may be the case regarding PLWHA.[2]

The onset of HIV has evoked responses of various natures and dimensions. I believe the fact that it is primarily a sexually transmitted disease, coupled with the early perception that it was a disease spread mainly by MSM, has caused many persons, especially in most religious cultures and also in some sociopolitical environments, to respond in discriminatory ways.[3] Some of these responses are considered blatantly discriminatory and even challenge concepts of basic human rights. Persons in authority, either professional or political, who have moral, ethical and even legal obligations to be antidiscriminatory, have been found wanting! But aren't politicians and other professionals, including our health care workers, the product of our general society?

This discrimination has seriously hampered the Herculean efforts of many persons who have over the years worked on controlling the scourge of the HIV epidemic. Wherever this is found, it needs to be urgently and dispassionately addressed. Is there the political will? Are our citizens willing or ready to accept the need for change through tolerance? Can we afford not to find a solution?

Health Care Industry Discrimination and the Response to the Prevention and Treatment of HIV and AIDS

While recognizing the serious health and developmental challenges that an uncontrolled epidemic may cause, the health and political authorities were virtually set in a "prevention" mode up to the early 2000s.[4] The development of several antiretroviral drugs (ARVs) in the late 1990s and early 2000s, coupled with the establishment of the UN Global Fund and other funding mechanisms such as the World Bank, the Clinton Foundation, UNAIDS, the UK Department for International Development, USAID and so on, provided new opportunities to provide treatment to persons infected with HIV.[5]

Provision of and access to treatment are not as simple as they may seem. This requires an organized structure of human and material resources. The human factor is the crux of the issue regarding discrimination and access. In order to establish the necessary structure, what is required is a coming together of political will, technical recognition and commitment to the desired response. For example, a previously proposed approach recommended that each country establish a specific unit with various professionals such as counsellors, public health nurses and psychologists. This invariably requires increases in the number of staff in the public service establishments or reallocation of new duties to the existing staff. There was notable resistance in many jurisdictions in the Caribbean Community (CARICOM) to this, from the political as well as the professional bodies. Some thought that HIV was a condition brought on by careless persons and did not merit the financial and human resources required. A review of the time taken among the various CARICOM countries to establish an AIDS unit may be a reflection of this type of inherent discrimination.[6]

A similar case can be made regarding the process of acquiring and offering ARVs to citizens of various countries.[7] In short, those countries with stronger political will and a health staff with the stronger willingness to respond favourably to the idea of treatment of HIV responded accordingly, which is demonstrated by the date of availability of ARVs.[8]

Despite generalized policy decisions to offer treatment to persons with HIV, there have been varying levels of discrimination, leading to less accessible ARVs and medications. I would emphasize more discrimination meted out by health care professionals and ancillary workers, but at a political level we must also be aware of sentiments that may have affected access to treatment.

There have been incidences of expressed homophobia by politicians in various countries and controversial, if not undesirable, statements by some.[9] In some instances, ministers have been publicly criticized for suggesting measures that would facilitate access to treatment.

Formal studies and anecdotal reports indicate that there remain challenges among our health staff that negatively impact access to treatment. Examples include nurses being judgemental regarding sexual contact, seemingly wanting information to be used as gossip rather than for benefit of patient care, and counsellors demonstrating "scorn" when clients try to use bathroom facilities used by staff.

There are many stories of breach of confidentiality by several staff members who are knowledgeable of clients' HIV status.[10] Studies indicate that "generally" the survival rate for HIV and AIDS patients is higher among practitioners with more experience in HIV and AIDS management.[11] Service providers need to be more aware of how their prejudices affect clients' health-seeking behaviour and develop sensitivity to enable them to effectively work with PLWHA.

According to the 2010 Country Progress Report for St Vincent, during the reporting period, approximately a hundred health care workers were trained in Provider-Initiated Training and Counselling (PITC). Even though St Vincent has not yet created national guidelines on the implementation of PITC at health centres, the WHO guidelines, which address confidentiality, informed consent and access to quality counselling, are guiding the national implementation process. Also, the health care workers were trained in Voluntary Counselling and Testing (VCT), and twenty-three workers were trained in HIV rapid testing.[12]

In St Vincent and the Grenadines, a study done in 2005 of seventy-seven public health care providers indicated that just about half or 49 per cent showed a positive attitude towards PLWHA.[13]

Table 11.1. Of the public facilities sampled, the percentage of providers with an accepting attitude towards PLWHA (St Vincent Health Report, 2005)

Total number of public providers	*Percentage of public providers with a positive attitude towards PLWHA*
77	49
77	49

* Totals based on six questions related to HIV and AIDS stigma

Recommendations and Strategies

The following are some recommended strategies for decreasing stigma and discrimination towards PLWHA:

1. Continuous sensitization of all health care workers during either their formal training or other organized sessions (e.g., a conference or meeting discussing desirable behaviour with respect to PLWHA). Example target groups include medical students, nursing students, pharmacists and lab technicians.

2. Education of policymakers and other relevant authorities on human rights issues related to PLWHA. Example target groups include parliamentarians, the legal fraternity (from law school to the judiciary), teachers and the media.

3. Formulation, promotion and establishment of legislation to decrease discrimination against PLWHA. This may require legislation related to issues of human rights and HIV control.

The establishment of a sociopolitical environment with a desirable anti-discriminatory stance in CARICOM requires a progressive and proactive cadre of legislators. This will involve the political will to (1) understand the implications of discrimination on the control of HIV, (2) be cognizant of the various factors leading to or conducive to discriminatory practices, (3) be bold enough to formulate the necessary legislation, and (4) ensure that the relevant authorities of law enforcement are facilitated and encouraged to enforce the antidiscriminatory laws.

Notes

1. See Human Development Sector Management Unit, "HIV/AIDS in the Caribbean: Issues and Options – A Background Report" (Latin America and the Caribbean Region: The World Bank, 2010), 8, http://www.un.org/works/goingon/HIVAIDSCaribbean.pdf.
2. Under s. 13(3) of the Constitution of Saint Vincent, the term *discriminatory* means "affording different treatment to different persons attributable wholly or mainly to their respective descriptions by sex, race, place of origin, political opinions, color or creed whereby persons of one such description are subjected to disabilities or restrictions to which persons of another such

descriptions are not made subject or are recorded privileges of advantages which are not accorded to persons of another such description".

3. R. Parker and P. Aggleton, "HIV/AIDS-Related Stigma and Discrimination: A Conceptual Framework and an Agenda for Action" (USAID, May 2002).

4. Former president of the United States George Bush implemented the faith-based abstinence-only method in the fight against HIV and AIDS, advocating for abstinence over condom use.

5. In 2004, the World Bank provided St Vincent and the Grenadines with US$7 million financing to reduce HIV infections, provide treatment for PLWHA, and strengthen institutional capacity to scale up HIV and AIDS prevention and control activities in St Vincent and the Grenadines. The project helped to provide ARV drugs to those in need. See Lee Morrison and Alejandra Viveros, "World Bank Approves US$7 Million for HIV/AIDS Prevention and Treatment in St. Vincent and the Grenadines" (2004), http://web.worldbank .org/external/default/main?pagePK=34370&piPK=34424&theSitePK =4607&menuPK=34463&contentMDK=20223479.

6. It must be noted there have been strong efforts by Caribbean countries to combat the epidemic. For example, Barbados is known for its comprehensive HIV and AIDS education in secondary schools. However, despite these individual country's successes, what is really needed most is "a multi-sectoral national response that engages government, civil society and international donors, as well as scaled-up efforts to serve entire national populations". See Human Development Sector Management Unit, "HIV/ AIDS in the Caribbean", 21.

7. In the Caribbean, countries such as Cuba, Barbados, Trinidad and Tobago, and Guyana offer ARV treatment either 100 per cent free of cost or at highly subsidized prices. See CARICOM Secretariat, "PANCAP at 10: Glimpsing Its Scorecard" (2010), http://www.caricom.org/jsp/pressreleases/press_releases _2010/pres430_10.jsp.

8. In 2002, the Pan Caribbean Partnership against HIV/AIDS signed an agreement with six pharmaceutical companies to provide access to cheaper ARVs. Progress since then has been uneven, partly due to wide differences in drug prices. In the Dominican Republic, Jamaica and Haiti, HIV treatment coverage reaches less than half those in need, at 47 per cent, 46 per cent and 43 per cent, respectively. Overall in the Caribbean, the ARV coverage is 29 per cent. WHO/UNAIDS/UNICEF, "Towards Universal Access: Scaling Up Priority HIV/AIDS Interventions in the Health Sector" (2010), http://www.who.int/ HIV/pub/2010progressreport/en/index.html.

9. In an interview with BBC in 2008, the former prime minister of Jamaica, Bruce Golding, stated there was no room for gays in his cabinet.

10. Breaches in confidentiality propagate stigma and discrimination; voluntary disclosure is ideal. For more information on the importance of not breaching confidentiality, see Caribbean HIV/AIDS Alliance, "The Right to Privacy and Protection of Confidentiality for People Living with HIV" (briefing paper, 2010), http://www.caribbeanHIVaidsalliance.org/uploaded/Consent%20 and%20Confidentiality%2010.08.10_1.pdf.

11. USAID, "St. Vincent and the Grenadines, HIV and AIDS Service Provision Assessment Survey Report" (2005), 27–28, http://www.cpc.unc.edu/measure/ publications/tr-07-46/at.../document.

12. See UNAIDS, "Saint Vincent and the Grenadines: 2010 Country Progress Report" (2010), http://www.unaids.org/en/dataanalysis/monitoringcountryprogress/ 2010progressreportssubmittedbycountries/saintvincentandthegrenadines _2010_country_progress_report_en.pdf.

13. Ibid., 28.

Chapter 12

HIV Infection and the AIDS Epidemic in the Caribbean

HIV Transmission, Treatment and Prevention

Michel de Groulard

Senior Regional Programme Adviser, UNAIDS, Trinidad and Tobago

The Caribbean HIV Epidemic

In 2008, 240,000 people were estimated to be living with HIV (up from 210,000 in 2001). The adult HIV prevalence was about 1.1 per cent, making the Caribbean the second most HIV-affected region in the world, after sub-Saharan Africa.[1]

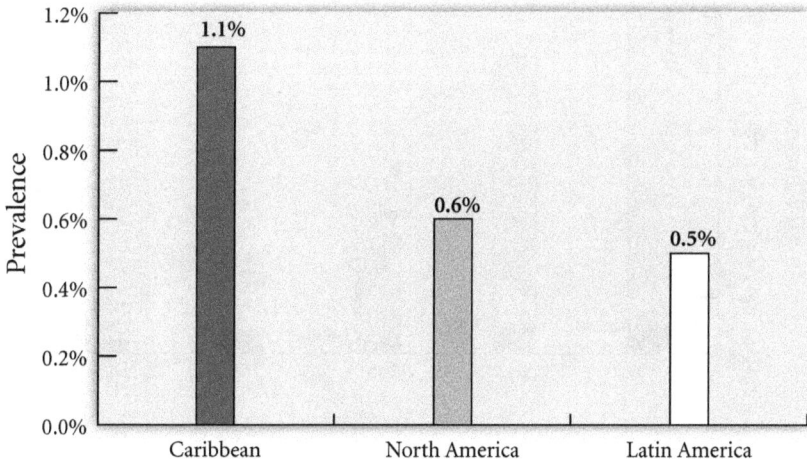

Figure 12.1. Estimated Adult HIV Prevalence in the Three Regions of the Americas (UNAIDS/WHO 2007)

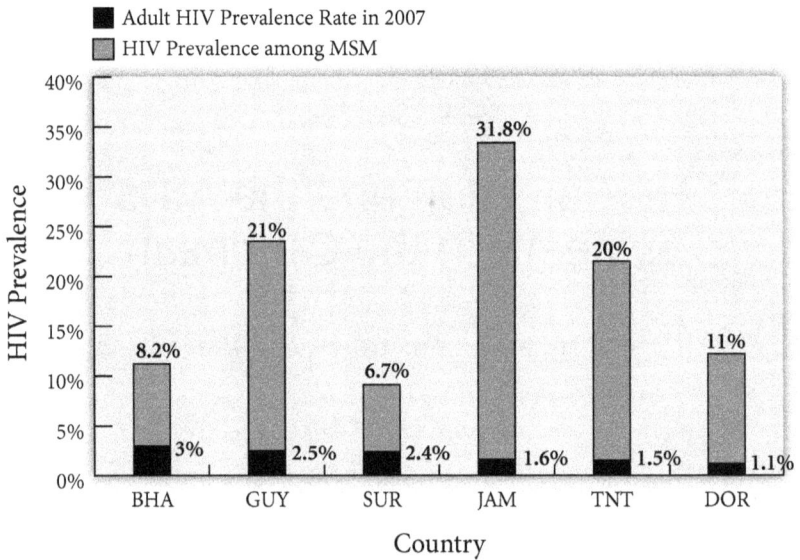

Figure 12.2. Comparing Adult HIV Prevalence and HIV: Prevalence among Caribbean MSM, 2005–7

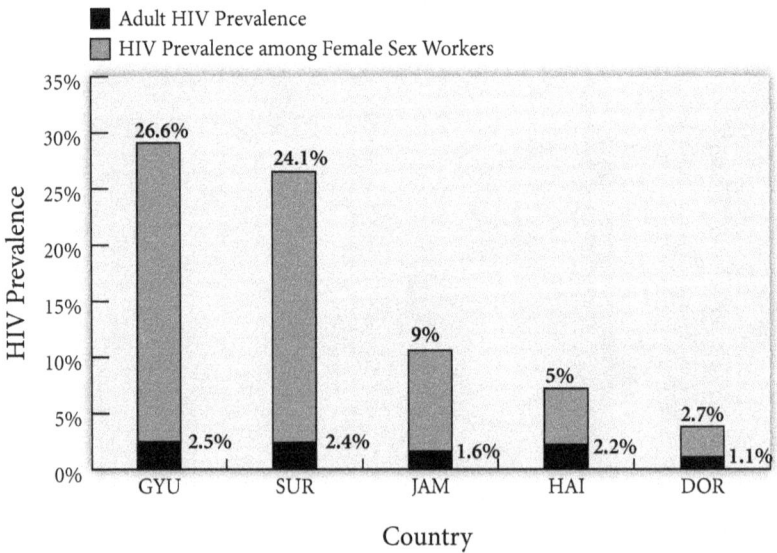

Figure 12.3. Comparing Adult HIV Prevalence with HIV Prevalence among Female Sex Workers in the Caribbean, 2005–7

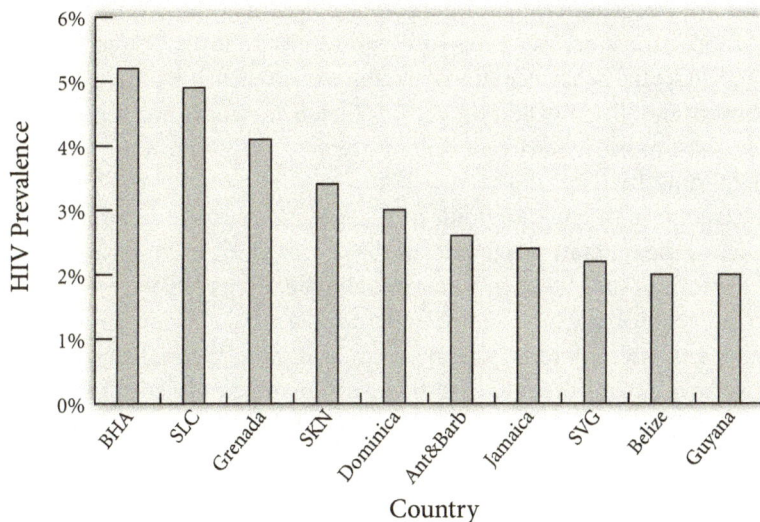

Figure 12.4. HIV Prevalence among Prisoners in Ten Caribbean Countries, 2004–6

In 2008, it was estimated that 12,000 persons died of AIDS-related infections or diseases (38 per day). AIDS is the leading cause of death among people ages twenty-five to forty-four. There were 20,000 new HIV infections (55 per day) in 2008. HIV prevalence remains high among men who have sex with men (MSM), sex workers, prisoners, crack-cocaine users and young people.[2]

There are fundamental differences between concentrated and generalized epidemics, especially in terms of their dynamics and the responses they generate. *Concentrated epidemic* means that there are higher levels of the virus in certain targeted areas (e.g., AIDS rates in urban versus rural areas). *Generalized epidemic* refers to consistently high levels throughout a region (e.g., AIDS prevalence rates in Barbados).[3] The Caribbean HIV epidemic, however, is complex and more heterogeneous, being classified as a generalized epidemic having large pockets of concentrated epidemics among specific groups of the population.

Challenges for the Response

Although the HIV epidemic appears to have stabilized in many countries, it has done so at a high level of new infection reported every year (approximately 20,000).

MSM and sex workers (male and female) are disproportionately infected with and affected by HIV. However, this epidemiological evidence has not significantly influenced expenditure patterns. The majority of persons in these population groups are not reached by prevention efforts. Colonial laws still criminalize sexual behaviours and orientations and help perpetuate notions of immorality and illegality that hinder Caribbean citizens from exercising some of their most basic rights: freedom of movement without fear of violence and the right to health care.[4]

The change in the gender profile of the epidemic over the last thirty years is evidence of the generational impact of the norms of masculinity and femininity in Caribbean societies. The economic climate, deep pockets of poverty and a new information age have altered patterns of sexual behaviour and increased women's vulnerability to HIV. Transactional sex and the exchange of sex for security have caught the region's leaders off guard, as adolescent and female sexual behaviours are different from what was assumed to prevail at the start of the epidemic.[5]

A *prevention revolution* is needed. If the number of new cases of HIV is not reduced, the number of people needing treatment will increase. Effective prevention is necessary to reduce treatment costs. The voice of Caribbean leaders must be heard to shape the discourse around sex, sexuality, sexual orientation, morality and young people's sexuality if the silence, shame and fear of open, informed discussion are to be broken. We need to use combined prevention approaches: evidence-informed options that can reach the populations most affected with clear, unambiguous information, support and services. As resources become scarcer, prevention funding must be allocated to the most effective interventions and to the most affected target populations.

Overall access to treatment is estimated to be just over 48 per cent in the Caribbean.[6] Treatment is part of prevention. The stigma attached to HIV prevents people from seeking treatment. This must be removed. The systems for delivering treatment must be made more efficient. Caribbean governments must place increased emphasis on lowering the cost of treatment and engage more actively in price negotiations with pharmaceutical companies. Civil society must be supported to help expand the reach of treatment, care and support as part of a new approach to prevention.

The epidemic is far from over; more evidence-based interventions are needed within a context of human rights and a sustained long-term commitment. Human rights violations fuel the epidemic by increasing people's vulnerability to infection. In addition, human rights violations also often follow infection, and people living with HIV are subjected to various forms of discrimination and ill treatment, including harassment, arbitrary arrest and, in some cases, torture. Laws that perpetuate stigma and discrimination,

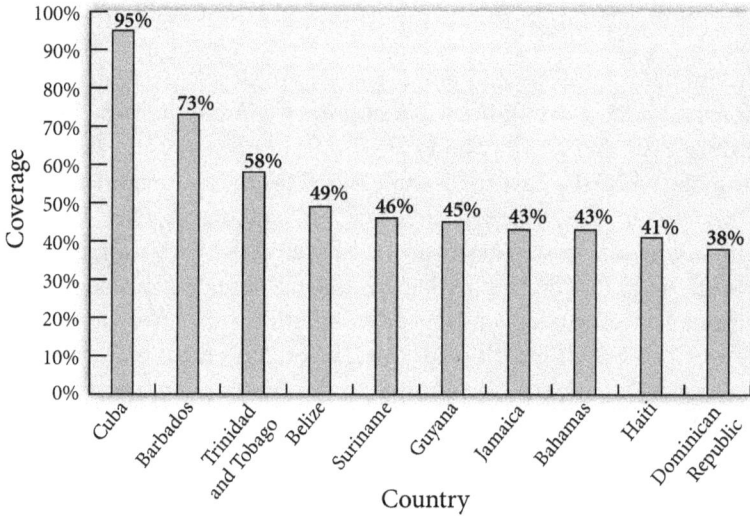

Figure 12.5. Antiretroviral Treatment Coverage in the Ten Larger Caribbean Countries (UNAIDS 2008)

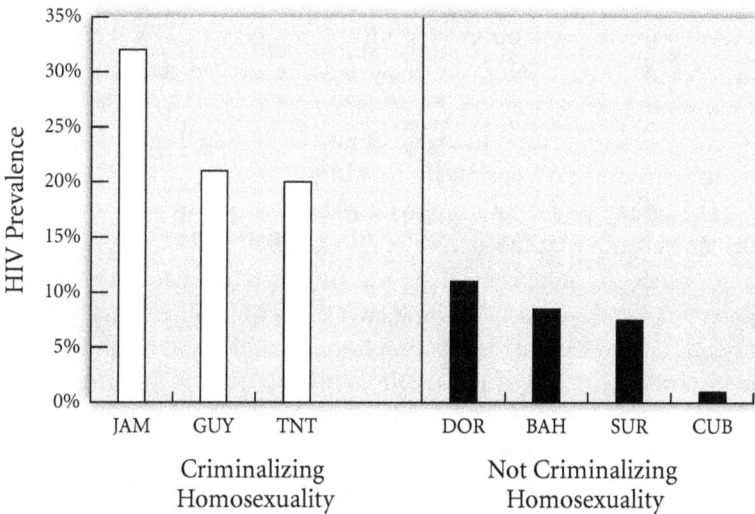

Figure 12.6. HIV Prevalence among MSM in Caribbean Countries That Both Criminalize and Do Not Criminalize Homosexuality (UNAIDS 2008)

limit access to health care and fuel the spread of HIV are not in the national interest.

Discriminatory policies and practices result in people being denied access to information, support and services necessary to make informed decisions and reduce their vulnerability and risk of infection. As a result, about half of people living with HIV have inadequate access to care and treatment.

In many countries, colonial laws and policies that legalize stigma and discrimination still exist. These have been characterized by some as "state-sponsored stigma and discrimination". Indeed, in eleven Caribbean states, laws prohibiting homosexual acts and sex work are still in place. Very few countries have explicit antidiscrimination laws and, where they exist, they are not fully used because of the risk of disclosure of one's sexual orientation, sexual practices or HIV status during the search for redress in the legal system.

In some instances, mandatory HIV testing without consent occurs during recruitment for the protective services; during entry into prison; during applications for citizenship, health or life insurance; in clinical settings for particular conditions; and during pregnancy. The extent of pre-employment screening is not known, despite the fact that it has been reported to be widespread.

Moving Forward

The vulnerability of women to HIV infection appears to be increasing, yet few resources and programmes are dedicated to address their particular needs. Programmes to change harmful gender norms that condone violence against women and coercive sex should be instituted, including those that help build parenting skills and police capacity to address domestic violence and rape. Gender norms among men must also be addressed.

State laws are often a reflection of religious beliefs and sociocultural norms in communities. A multipronged approach is therefore necessary to address human rights issues – from changing laws that criminalize sexual behaviour and orientations to creating less homophobic societies and communities and an environment which is empowering and supportive of all groups of the population.

Criminalization can be addressed by law reform aimed at the removal of punitive laws. More needs to be done to create and support effective outreach to all populations. This means investing major resources in peer-led outreach programmes. It also means investing sufficient resources to change the social and legal environment to support such outreach.

The training of health care workers to reduce stigma and discrimination against people living with HIV or AIDS in key populations is also needed.

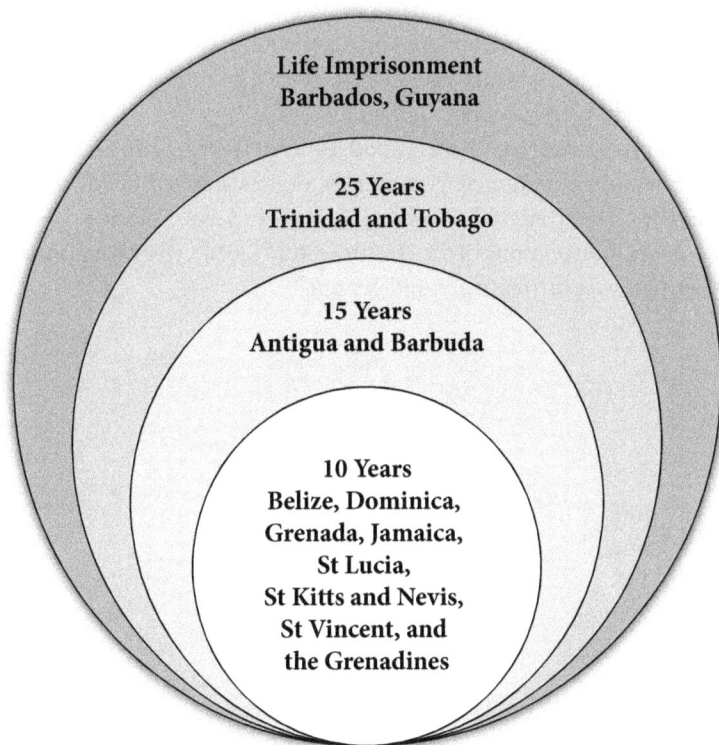

Figure 12.7. Penalties for Practising Homosexual Acts in Selected Caribbean Countries

Health care workers would also benefit from training in confidentiality, informed consent and universal precautions as well as the ability to detect and address domestic violence. Where outreach services are hampered by police action, it would be useful to sensitize police to HIV in terms of their own vulnerability and to highlight the important role they can play in providing a protected space for outreach programmes for MSM, sex workers and people who use drugs.

Notes

1. WHO/UNAIDS, "AIDS Epidemic Update" (December 2007), 7, http://data .unaids.org/pub/epislides/2007/2007_epiupdate_en.pdf.
2. J.P. Figueroa, "The HIV Epidemic in the Caribbean: Meeting the Challenges of Achieving Universal Access to Prevention, Treatment and Care", *West Indian Medical Journal* 57, no. 3 (2008).

3. UNAIDS, "Frequently Asked Questions", http://www.unaids.org.vn/sitee/index .php?Itemid=28&id=14&option=com_content&task=blogcategory#i15.
4. Sir Ronald Sanders, "Gays Have Rights Too: The Caribbean Dilemma", *Jamaica Observer*, 13 November 2011.
5. CARICOM Secretariat, "Background Paper: HIV/AIDS in the Caribbean", http://www.caricom.org/jsp/community_organs/aids.jsp?menu=cob.
6. WHO/UNAIDS/UNICEF, "Towards Universal Access: Scaling Up Priority HIV/AIDS Interventions in the Health Sector" (2010), www.who.int/hiv/pub/ 2010progressreport/report/en/index.html.

Chapter 13

HIV and AIDS in the Workplace

Business Coalitions

Colin T. Brewer

Immediate Past President, Barbados AIDS Foundation

As a representative of the business community, my first task is to outline the principles under which private business functions.

Managers of business corporations are charged with the responsibility to maximize the long-term financial return on the capital employed in the enterprise while operating within the framework of the law – nothing more, nothing less. Accordingly, if managers utilize corporate resources to fund charitable or social programmes, they must be able to demonstrate to their investors and employees that, directly or indirectly, these expenditures will enhance profitability in the short, medium or long term. If they failed to do so, they would be quite properly subject to censure.

It is not the place of business enterprise to determine or to act on its perception of human rights; instead, governments must legislate where they believe there is conflict between the business sector and the human rights of individual members of society. We must also remember that a treatment of human rights is included in the Barbados constitution and in those of most of the Commonwealth Caribbean countries.[1] Representatives of labour may, appropriately, also hold management accountable for potential human rights violations.

HIV and AIDS awareness programmes in the workplace are one of the most important national initiatives required to meet the challenge of HIV and AIDS in Barbados, as more than 80 per cent of those infected are of working age.[2] Prevention is the battleground issue in a country that has achieved a great deal in the areas of care and support but where the incidence of the virus continues to increase. Workplaces are the trenches where the war will eventually need to be won.[3]

If there is potential conflict between the rights of employees in regard to the HIV pandemic and the goals of private business, then we must seek ground where there is mutuality of interest so to circumvent the conflict. We must sympathetically study and seek to understand the paradigms under which each function and synthesize positions that both may support.

Enlightened self-interest often causes business managers to anticipate the concerns of the legislature and the labour unions, but this is usually only possible in large corporations that can afford to designate personnel to consider such social policy responses. Barbados is largely an economy of small and microenterprises that cannot commit resources to contemplate such issues.[4]

We can avoid conflict between business and human rights, as there is a strong business case for private enterprise to invest in the development of workplace policies and programmes to remove stigma and to educate and inform on questions relating to HIV and AIDS.[5] However, if we are to have a meaningful response in a country of small and microenterprises, then there must be a pooling of resources into a single-issue business coalition to inform and advise business of the appropriate responses to the crisis.[6] This particular solution is highly appropriate for small island developing states.[7]

Business Coalitions in Barbados

The AIDS Foundation of Barbados (AFBI; of which I am a member) is such a business coalition and is charged with the responsibility of persuading individual business enterprises to introduce HIV and AIDS policy statements as well as programmes to inform and advise employees of the dangers of the HIV virus and how to avoid infection. The AFBI further informs members that the extent of the HIV problem is not known but the incidence of infection continues to rise. The possibility of reaching epidemic proportions is a realistic concern, and this is the reason the government considers HIV the single largest health challenge in our society. The AFBI also acts as a government lobbyist on behalf of the working people and companies of Barbados.

The AFBI draws from several studies undertaken by businesses in sub-Saharan Africa and Brazil.[8] These societies have wrestled with the challenge of the virus for a long time. Many studies were introduced over a decade ago; consequently, there has been time to evaluate the costs and the quantifiable benefits of support for these workplace health education initiatives in HIV and AIDS. The reduction of staff replacement and training costs and the enhancement of productivity as a result of increased morale in the workforce have been shown to exceed the cost of such programmes to these corporations.

After evaluating these financial results, companies have generally ramped up the expenditure on such programmes.[9]

The AFBI uses the International Labour Office's Code of Conduct as a template for the development of policies to deal with matters such as non-discrimination, confidentiality and privacy. There is a ten-point plan for the development of continuous workplace education.[10] These documents are consonant with the UN Declaration of Human Rights.

We at the AFBI concur with the intervention programme and the eight major themes which are posited by UNAIDS, as these themes encapsulate the core activities which, when implemented, meet the challenges of human rights in the workplace. The main themes which we urge our members to incorporate in their HIV and AIDS policy statements are as follows: the right to work (the right not to be fired on the basis of HIV status), the right to health (access to all health care prevention services such as condoms and the ability to attend doctor appointments during work hours), the right not to be discriminated or stigmatized (no discrimination on the basis of real or perceived HIV status), the right to privacy (protection against mandatory testing for both current employees and job applicants, with HIV status kept confidential), and the right to education/information (access to HIV education on prevention, including information on sexual and reproductive health as well as relevant counselling and appropriate referral).

Since inception, the primary focus of the AFBI has been on education to reduce stigma and discrimination, as this is the key to changing sexual behaviour patterns in a positive way to reduce the incidence of the virus. The human rights of the individual who may be infected or affected by the virus need to be upheld.

Accordingly, if the business community continues to grow in support of the AFBI's efforts and responds to the matters encapsulated in the UN Declaration of Human Rights, there will be no need for legislative intervention to protect workers infected or affected by HIV and AIDS.[11] A volunteer force is always better than a conscripted army.

However, the AFBI does not have the resources to provide the level of support needed to optimize this initiative. We wish to have far greater resources to take this message to all Barbadians working in the private business sector. We have limited financial support from the government and are grateful for this support, but the resources provided to the private sector are small compared to the resources provided to workers in the public sector, where each ministry has had the opportunity to develop significant programmes for all their staff. The AFBI currently serves approximately 10 per cent of the local private sector workforce only. We wish to be staffed up to provide adequate support to all Barbadian workers and their employers that request the introduction of sustained education programmes on HIV and AIDS.[12]

The AFBI supports regional initiatives that are being undertaken currently to build a Caribbean-wide business coalition network.[13] This endeavour requires coordinated development and financial support. The funding for such a venture to succeed and make a genuine contribution needs to be expanded considerably.

Conclusion

We view a national charter as a "best practices" mechanism. Accordingly, we formally launched the AFBI on 1 December 2010 and invited businesses to sign it as evidence of their commitment to the principles enshrined in the document.[14]

The publication of this charter is an opportunity to once again demonstrate the urgency of the challenge. The government, the business community and other interested parties need to show a shared commitment to win the war against HIV and AIDS. This initiative might be subsequently spread out throughout the Caribbean.

Notes

1. Each Commonwealth Caribbean constitution has a bill of rights that addresses human rights. However, in accordance with the state action doctrine, it governs human rights violations between the state and citizens rather than between private individuals.
2. See "Human Rights Key to Prevention and Control of AIDS", *Barbados Advocate*, 12 December 2010, http://www.barbadosadvocate.com/newsitem .asp?more=politics&NewsID=14380. See also National HIV/AIDS Commission, "United Nations General Assembly Special Session (UNGASS) Country Report 2010: Barbados" (reporting period January 2008–December 2009), http://www.unaids.org/en/dataanalysis/monitoringcountryprogress/ 2010progressreportssubmittedbycountries/barbados_2010_country _progress_report_en.pdf.
3. The workplace is one area where HIV-infected persons are affected. The ILO Code of Practice, principle 4.1 ("Recognition of HIV/AIDS as a Workplace Issue"), reads, "HIV/AIDS is a workplace issue and should be treated like any other serious illness/condition in the workplace." Principle 4.2 ("Non-Discrimination") reads, "In the spirit of decent work and respect for human rights and dignity of persons infected or affected by HIV/AIDS, there should

be no discrimination against workers based upon real or perceived HIV status." International Labour Office (ILO), "HIV/AIDS and the World of Work" (ILO Code of Practice, ILO Global Programme on HIV/AIDS and the World of Work, Geneva, Switzerland, 2001), http://www.ilo.org/wcmsp5/groups/public/.../@ilo ... /wcms_113783.pdf.

4. Micro and small enterprises have been more affected by the HIV epidemic than any other sector of economic activity. See International Labour Office (ILO), "Helping Micro and Small Enterprises Cope with HIV/AIDS" (Geneva, Switzerland, 2006).

5. Environmental and Social Development Department (CES), "HIV/AIDS in the Workplace" (Good practice notice [number 2], International Financial Corporation [IFC], World Bank Group, 2002), http://www.ifc.org/ifcext/enviro.nsf/.../p_HIVeng/$FILE/HIVAIDSEng.pdf.

6. National business coalitions enable companies to leverage their resources more effectively to combat the diseases. Coalitions assist companies by facilitating information sharing; permitting economies of scale in the development of workplace HIV and AIDS products and services; and creating a strong, unified front for public policy debate and advocacy. Elizabeth J. Ashbourne, ed., "HIV/AIDS Business Coalitions: Guidelines for Building Business Coalitions against HIV/AIDS" (International Bank for Reconstruction and Development and the World Bank, Washington, DC, 2004), http://data.unaids.org/pub/Manual/2004/business_coalitions_guidelines_en.pdf.

7. The United Nations Department of Economic and Social Affairs identifies fifty-one SIDS located in three regions: Africa, Asia and the Pacific, and Latin America and the Caribbean. Of these fifty-one, twenty are located within the Caribbean region. SIDS face certain issues, such as fragility of an open economy, reliance on one industry (usually tourism) and unsustainable high external debt. In Barbados, the challenge to find necessary resources to fund effective prevention, treatment and care programmes is all the more exacerbated by its World Bank classification as a high-income country and its concurrent classification as a SIDS by the United Nations Commission on Sustainable Development (CSD). See National HIV/AIDS Commission, "UNGASS Country Report 2010: Barbados".

8. Francesca Boldrini and Chris Timble, "The State of Business Coalitions in Sub-Saharan Africa" (Global Health Initiative, World Economic Forum, 2006), https://members.weforum.org/pdf/GHI/The_State_of_Business_Coalitions_in_Sub_Saharan_Africa.pdf. See also Peter DeYoung, "Private Sector Intervention Case Example: Nestle, Brazil" (Global Health Initiative, World Economic Forum, 2003), http://www.aidsfoundationbarbados.org/cms/index.php/resources/international-response/private-sector-intervention-case-study-nestle.

9. The small and micro enterprises will feel the impact of HIV and AIDS through increased expenditures on medical and health costs, funeral costs and death benefits, as well as recruitment and training needs due to lost personnel as well as decrease in revenue due to higher absenteeism, low worker morale and high staff turnover. See Environmental and Social Development Department (CES), "HIV/AIDS in the Workplace".
10. International Labour Office (ILO), "HIV/AIDS and the World of Work".
11. The international treaties that address human rights, such as the United Declaration of Human Rights, do not expressly mention HIV and AIDS; however, specific human rights that are protected in these documents are relevant to HIV and AIDS and therefore are means by which the human rights of people living with HIV or AIDS are protected. These include, inter alia, the right to nondiscrimination, the right to health and the right to work. See Program on International Health and Human Rights, François-Xavier Bagnoud Center for Health and Human Rights, Harvard School of Public Health and the International Council of AIDS Service Organizations (ICASO), "HIV/AIDS and Human Rights in a Nutshell: A Quick and Useful Guide for Action, as Well as a Framework to Carry HIV/AIDS and Human Rights Actions Forward" (2004), http://globalhealth.usc.edu/Home/Resources/Pages/~/media/3B27BC433DB44B68B161AF3B5E769032.ashx.
12. See "Report of President to the AGM of AIDS Foundation" (23 June 2010), http://www.aidsfoundationbarbados.org/cms/index.php/about-afbi/reports/presidents-report-2010.
13. One such regional initiative is the Pan-Caribbean Business Coalition on HIV/AIDS (PCBC), which was formed in 2005 under the chairmanship of Sir George Alleyne in order to fill gaps in national AIDS programmes across the region. The PCBC supports five national business coalition members in its network at the regional level: Barbados, Belize, Guyana, Jamaica and Suriname. See Pan Caribbean Business Coalition (PCBC), "PCBC Profile" (World Economic Forum, 2008), https://members.weforum.org/pdf/GHI/Caribbean.pdf.
14. AIDS Foundation of Barbados, "The Business Pulse: Raising Awareness within the Workplace" 3, no. 1 (2011): 1–2, http://www.pancap.org/docs/AFBI%20Newsletter%20Vol3%20Issue1.pdf.

Part 2

Experiences and Life Challenges

Chapter 14

Discrimination and Access to Treatment

Yolanda Simon

Executive Director, Caribbean Regional Network of People
Living with HIV/AIDS, Trinidad and Tobago

In this chapter, I attempt to address key issues surrounding access to treatment from the perspective of the community of persons living with HIV or AIDS (PLWHA) – a community of which I have been a member for more than two decades. I invite you to take a journey with me as I survey the history of access to treatment and explore the relationship of PLWHA to treatment – the challenges and gaps, the effects of discrimination and its implications on treatment adherence. I will also reflect on the "partnership" framework in the context of representations of PLWHA and will conclude by stressing the need to chart a new course that is inclusive of all.

In a perfect world, increased access to treatment should result in more PLWHA seeking treatment. Unfortunately, we do not live in a perfect world, and discrimination against PLWHA continues to be one of the many barriers to mitigating the impact of HIV and AIDS.[1] While many reasons and opinions have been put forward on this, the most significant voices have been – and continue to be – left out of the conversation: the voices of PLWHA. It is time to look at discrimination with regard to access to treatment from the inside out.

Almost three decades into the pandemic, why is discrimination – real or imagined – such an important factor when it comes to access to treatment? Despite all the advancements that have been made at every level, why does discrimination still persist as a seemingly insurmountable hurdle? Let me remind you of what the early days of the epidemic were like in Trinidad and Tobago and the rest of the Caribbean.

Following my diagnosis with HIV/AIDS at a time when little distinction was made between the two (i.e., if you tested HIV positive, you were said to have AIDS), I went through a period of much pain and hopelessness, thinking that my death was imminent. A fortuitous meeting with a clinical psychologist helped me realize that I was not going to keel over and die anytime soon and rekindled in me a determination to take my life into my own hands. I made a conscious decision to actively seek care, treatment and support. I soon discovered that while there were many pockets of support, care and treatment were nonexistent.

In the late 1980s and early 1990, there was absolutely no access to treatment. The disease did not even have a name until 1986, and it was only one year later that AZT, the drug used to treat HIV, was released in developed countries. People became fearful due to the general ignorance surrounding this newly discovered disease. This fear, heightened by the fact that its predominant mode of transmission was through unprotected sexual intercourse, fuelled the stigma and subsequent discrimination about the disease that has mushroomed into a major stumbling block over the years.

In those early years, treatment consisted of medications for opportunistic infections, bolstered by prayer and hope. The community of PLWHA as we know it today did not exist. We speculated about who might have HIV in whispered tones and only spoke about the "victims" when they finally sought care and treatment, which almost always was too late. Hence the community was isolated, invisible and lived underground.[2]

In this early environment, I made a conscious decision *not* to question the hand that fate had dealt me but rather to go with the flow. Then I got involved with the National AIDS Programme, which brought me into contact with many infected persons over the years. I heard many horror stories about PLWHA losing their jobs, being put out of their homes and, in extreme cases, being murdered.[3] This, coupled with the realization that the collective body politic at that time was not prepared to be engaged, cemented the fact that I was in the battle of my life, and if things were to change, I *had* to be a part of that process.

The government's response was the establishment of the National AIDS Programme, as well as one site for infectious diseases (including HIV and AIDS). This, of course, would come to be known as "the AIDS place", so that when people took that journey of a thousand steps to get to the front door, they were sure to be branded as AIDS victims by onlookers. Still, through it all, I kept my appointments and went to the clinic.

For the first seven years following my diagnosis, I received practically no treatment. The only drug available at that time was AZT and, while it gave some measure of hope, there was little or no access to it locally and the cost was prohibitive. When, in 1995, I was diagnosed with my first and only major illness to date – cryptococcal meningitis – I decided to take a serious look at treatment options. I officially started treatment in January 1996 and switched to highly active antiretroviral therapy (HAART) one year later. This meant that I had to take several combinations of drugs to treat retroviruses.[4] At that time, antiretrovirals (ARVs) were not accessible in the Caribbean: all my meds came from the United States. People living with the disease continued to be invisible and continued to die.

Discrimination preceded access to treatment. When the first cases of HIV appeared in the Caribbean in the early 1980s, with Haiti having the first reported case, the group most affected was homosexual males, fuelling an already heightened sense of moral outrage and resulting in the group being labelled and ostracized. According to Gareth Williams, leader of the Jamaica Forum for Lesbians, All-Sexuals and Gays (J-FLAG), "Gays and lesbians in Jamaica exist with the possibility that you might be chased, you might be run down, you might be killed because of your sexual orientation, and when a day ends when that does not happen, we give thanks."[5]

Add to the mix an absence of political will and the following picture emerges: a diagnosis of HIV meant death for those who did not have the resources to fly to North America or Europe for treatment. It also meant a loss of employment, eviction and ostracism by family, friends and the community. Arguably, more people with AIDS died from shame, isolation and loneliness in those days than from the disease itself. Even now, the suicide rate for persons with the virus is three times greater than average figures.[6] Fear and ignorance fanned the flames of discrimination, the mortality rate soared and the future looked uncertain.

In 1996, two events took place that were to have a lasting and profound impact on HIV and AIDS, at both the regional and the global level: First, the arrival of triple therapy or the "cocktail", as it was affectionately called, was the breakthrough scientific discovery that captured the attention of the world at the Eleventh International AIDS Conference in Vancouver. This breakthrough treatment meant that the progression of AIDS or death could be further slowed. Second, the first (and still the only) regional network of PLWHA – the Caribbean Regional Network of People Living with HIV and AIDS (CRN+) – was formally established.

Our mandate in those early days was simple: *advocacy*. We began to mobilize the infected community, putting a face to the disease for the first time in the region. It was no longer about the statistics but about human beings. Between 1996 and 1999, with support from many partners – the Caribbean Epidemiology Centre (CAREC), Pan American Health Organization (PAHO) and the University of the West Indies, in particular – an advocacy strategy was developed and executed that would engage persons at every level, from the political directorate to communities, the private sector, as well as the positive community. The end result was that governments began acknowledging the fact that there was an AIDS epidemic in the region and that their most precious resource (citizens) were being affected (particularly the most productive age group of persons, ages fifteen to forty-nine). While many leaders feared that the cost of treatment might overshoot their GDP, they nevertheless agreed to use their good offices to solicit external financial and technical resources. As a result, access to treatment became a reality, at first for some countries and gradually for all.

The advent of better access to treatment, however, had little or no impact on discrimination.[7] While many more persons began seeking treatment, many more stayed away. New and real challenges began to emerge. There was still a large percentage of the infected population without access to treatment. For some with access, the issue of cost was a real barrier. Other access-to-treatment issues include access to good nutrition, the quality and quantity of access and the physical location of the treatment centres. These issues, along with many others, both discourage people from seeking treatment and, in the case of those already accessing treatment, cause people to interrupt, delay or stop their adherence to treatment.

Where do we go from here? The reality is that there is no magic bullet for the issue of treatment of HIV within the framework of discrimination. It is going to take a number of different strategies to achieve the goal of universal access to treatment for all and address the issue of discrimination. In this regard, we need to continue the dialogue; however, this time around, we must include the voices of PLWHA. We must discuss and develop a strategy regarding the decentralization of care and treatment. We must ensure that PLWHA are integrated into clinical care teams at the national level. We must include "positive prevention" in our national strategic plans. Those of us who are living with the disease must be central in the response. We must continue to advocate, both individually and collectively, for the creation of an enabling environment where there is a holistic view of care and treatment.[8] If we are to see more persons seeking care and treatment, as well as embracing adherence as central to their state of wellness, how do we therefore tackle discrimination? One strategy must be *disclosure*, but this, of course, raises more issues beyond the scope of this chapter.

Notes

1. There are several studies pointing to this conclusion. See Sarah Stutterheim, J.B. Pryor, A.E. Bos, R. Hoogendijk, P. Muris and H.P. Schaalma, "HIV-Related Stigma and Psychological Distress: The Harmful Effects of Specific Stigma Manifestations in Various Social Settings", *Journal of International AIDS Society* 23, no. 17 (2009): 2353–57.
2. For human rights arguments relating to this issue, especially concerning women and children, see Jessica Byron, "Gender and Human Rights in the Commonwealth Caribbean", in *Responding to the Human Rights Deficit*, ed. Karin Arts and Paschal Mihyo (The Hague: Kluwer Law International, 2003), 166.
3. On 16 July 2011, a Trinidad and Tobago national was sentenced to twenty-five years for murdering his wife who was infected with AIDS. See Sascha Wilson, "For Killing Aids-Infected Wife, Man Jailed for 25 Years", *Trinidad Guardian*, 17 July 2011.
4. M. Dybul, A.S. Fauci, J.G. Bartlett, J.E. Kaplan and A.K Pau, "Guidelines for Using Antiretroviral Agents among HIV-Infected Adults and Adolescents", *Annals of Internal Medicine* 137, no. 5, pt. 2 (2002): 381.
5. Michael Deibert, "Hauling HIV/AIDS Out of the Closet", *Inter Press Service News Agency*, 26 September 2006.
6. Adam W. Carrico, "Elevated Suicide Rate among HIV-Positive Persons Despite Benefits of Antiretroviral Therapy: Implications for a Stress and Coping Model of Suicide", *American Journal of Psychiatry* 167 (2010): 117.
7. CARICOM Secretariat, "Background Paper for CARICOM Youth Summit: HIV/AIDS in the Caribbean", 2011, http://www.caricom.org/jsp/community_organs/aids.jsp?menu=cob.
8. For a list of other solutions, see World Bank study, "HIV/AIDS in Caribbean: Issues and Options", Washington, DC, 31 March 2001, 7.

Chapter 15

Human Rights Needs of People Living with HIV or AIDS

Suzette M. Moses-Burton

HIV/AIDS Programme Management Team, Sector Ministry of Health, Social Development and Labour, St Maarten

As I began to prepare for the symposium that inspired this chapter and reviewed its background document, one of the expected results listed caught my attention: "Recommendation of strategies for Governments to move the human rights agenda forward in relation to [PLWHA]." At first a number of issues came to mind – notably human rights concerns among people living with HIV or AIDS (PLWHA). As a PLWHA myself, having worked in this region for the past seventeen years since my diagnosis, I found myself rattling them off almost by rote:

- The right to adequate health care, particularly access to treatment
- The right to property ownership
- The right to nondiscrimination
- The right to travel and mobility
- Sexual and reproductive health rights

Of course, no discussion about the rights of PLWHA and moving the agenda forward would be complete without acknowledging that HIV-related stigma is quite possibly the main barrier to allowing PLWHA to fully enjoy their human rights. Low levels of awareness and knowledge of human rights among PLWHA are some other contributing factors. As UNFAP executive director Thoraya Ahmed Obaid said on World AIDS Day 2003, "After two decades . . . the global AIDS epidemic shows no signs of abating . . . Among the main reasons . . . is the persistence of stigma and discrimination against those infected. This outrageous violation of basic human rights drives the disease underground, crippling efforts for prevention and care."[1]

However, as I pondered the issue further, I began to wonder if the rights of PLWHA were different from the rights of any other human being. Further, if there were no inherent differences, why then was so much emphasis being placed specifically on the rights of PLWHA and not on human rights in general? At first, I ignored the question, but I soon discovered that in my quest to remain on the topic of the rights of PLWHA, I could not so easily ignore it. As I continued to do my research, I found I could not readily make a distinction. And so I decided if I were to proceed any further, I would have to consult the Universal Declaration of Human Rights, adopted in 1948, to which all the countries in this region are signatory. As I reviewed the document in its entirety, it began to occur to me that in fact there did not seem to be anything specific to the rights of PLWHA that were not in fact basic human rights. At that point I began to wonder if our governments were familiar with the contents of the declaration and who, if anyone, holds them accountable for continued infractions and, in some instances, atrocities committed by their citizens? It is bewildering that the government is mandated to protect human rights but takes no proactive measures to protect these rights from being infringed. It is only after damage has occurred or lives lost that action is taken.

Having thoroughly reviewed the document, I noted all the articles that are especially relevant for PLWHA, for while not specific to the disease, the principles were inherent in the wording:

Articles 1 and 2: Right to freedom and nondiscrimination
Article 5: Right to security of person and freedom from cruel, inhuman and degrading treatment
Article 7: Right to equality under the law
Article 13: Right to freedom of movement
Article 16: Right to marry and found a family
Article 17: Right to own property
Article 25: Right to an acceptable standard of living, including education, work and social services

As I began to focus my attentions on the rights of Caribbean PLWHA, I wondered about the implications for these rights with the impending CARICOM Single Market and Economy (CSME), and so I reviewed the revised Treaty of Chaguaramas, the provisions of which seem to echo the sentiments of the universal declaration. However, as I got to article 45, which speaks to the movement of CARICOM nationals, I made special note of the subsections which spoke specifically to movement without harassment and harmonization and transferability of social security benefits: "Article 45: Movement of

Community Nationals. Member States commit themselves to the goal of free movement of their nationals within the Community." At the end of my review, I wondered how we would deal with the further challenges to human rights made by the bold declarations for freedom of movement and provision of services articulated in the treaty.

It is apparent that human rights must be strengthened; in particular, the still existing policies and laws criminalizing consensual sex between men must be removed and laws and policies promoting antidiscrimination must be implemented and enforced.

Herein lies the crux of the matter: There is no shortage of treaties and declarations signed by all our countries to protect our inalienable, basic rights as human beings of planet earth. There is also the Political Declaration on HIV (2006), which seeks to protect and guarantee the rights of persons living with and affected by HIV. Why, then, are we still having this discourse? Why, then, have we seen so little change? Is it because our laws and policies are so deeply embedded and fashioned by our social norms, values and attitudes? Is it because these same social attitudes paralyse our political directorate for fear of "bucking the system" and losing our votes, which keep or propel them into office? If these are indeed the reasons, then how do we effectively and swiftly move away from this place of inaction and complacency?

When will we hold our governments as well as ourselves accountable for the continued violation of human rights? When will CARICOM require its member states to stop giving its citizens "free passes" in blatant disregard of commitments made in official documents?

In the absence of significant movements in the arena of human rights in this region, should we be focused solely on the rights of PLWHA, or should we be more focused on human rights in general? Does the focus on the rights of PLWHA further marginalize already marginalized populations – those infected or affected as well as those most vulnerable to HIV infection?

The honourable acting prime minister of Barbados says that with the passage of time we will see the alleviation of the offences against the rights of PLWHA. We are already twenty-five-plus years into this epidemic and the violations of the rights of PLWHA: how many more years should we be expected to wait?

Note

1. Official statement by Thoraya Ahmed Obaid, executive director of the United Nations Population Fund on World AIDS Day, New York, 2003, http://populationalert.org/news/planetwire_media_summary.htm.

Chapter 16

Human Rights, HIV and Sexual Reproductive Health

A Support Group of PLWHA Mothers Speaks to Issues of Their Reproductive Health and Health Care

Rosemary Stone

Women and Family Life Coordinator, Eve for Life, Jamaica

It seems to be universally accepted that freedom from discrimination is a fundamental right of people living with HIV or AIDS (PLWHA).[1] Nondiscrimination has to be paramount for participation and inclusion to be meaningful for persons who are infected with HIV, either in policy-level decision-making or in personal family matters that affect them.[2] Further, the state has the responsibility to create an enabling environment for PLWHA where discrimination is punishable by law.[3] The state, in enacting and enforcing laws against discrimination, should create a climate that reduces fear and ignorance. Societies should also be vigilant in protecting groups that already suffer from discrimination (e.g., women, sex workers, men who have sex with men and intravenous drug users), so that these groups do not suffer "double discrimination" because of their HIV status.[4]

There are some proponents of law who believe it is good practice to not only use a human rights approach to the issues surrounding HIV and AIDS but also include a gender equality component to these human rights. Violence against women and girls, which includes sexual assault, is a human rights concern and the right to security of person is a right that societies should strive to bestow on their citizens. But, in some societies, cultural norms and practices disenfranchise many women and girls from this basic right.[5] Gender-based analysis and prescriptions can be used to highlight the particular needs of girls and boys and men and women.[6]

Human rights that are relevant to HIV and AIDS include the following: the right to nondiscrimination, equal protection and equality before the law;

the right to life; the right to the highest attainable standard of physical and mental health; the right to liberty and security of person; the right to seek and enjoy asylum; the right to privacy; the right to work; and the right to marry and found a family.[7] Most societies see these fundamental human rights as part of the fabric of their state. Nonetheless, there is the issue of how well these rights are realized for individuals within their borders. The impact of HIV and AIDS – its scope, depth and its potential to threaten and sometimes devastate societies – has forced some to re-examine and bring to the fore these basic rights.

Initiatives to Protect the Rights of PLWHA

In 2002 in Ghana, a nongovernmental organization, AIDS Alert Ghana (AAG), along with the Ghana AIDS Commission, launched an initiative to protect the rights of PLWHA. The programme, the AIDS Alert Law Project (AALP), sought to bring policymakers and specific target groups together so that continued dialogue would provide a forum where issues pertaining to HIV and AIDS could find common ground among the participants.[8]

One intention of the AALP was to provide legal advice to PLWHA; another was to support advocacy that promoted the needs and rights of infected persons. This would also lead to a better understanding of the legal and policy issues brought on by HIV and AIDS. To this end, workshops allowed legal experts to share experiences and knowledge so that the cohesiveness of their ideas would benefit infected persons.

Deputy attorney-general and deputy minister of justice Gloria Afua Akuffo, speaking at the launch of the project in Ghana, said that the government needed to adopt a supportive legal framework and provide the avenues for relevant law that sought to protect the rights of persons living with the disease. It was also suggested that if human rights were not highlighted and protected, all the other efforts made to lessen the impact and severity on PLWHA would be eroded.

In 2004, Uganda realized that there was limited information available on the status of PLWHA in relation to human rights awareness. A cross-sectional study was conducted using several districts of Uganda.[9] Structured interviews, focus group discussions and key informant interviews were used to inform the results of the study. Eleven per cent of respondents were able to give the correct definition of the term *human rights*. The most recognized human right was the right to health care (27 per cent). The second most recognizable human right was ownership of property (22 per cent). The respondents saw nondiscrimination as the most violated human right, and 35 per cent reported that it commonly occurred at the workplace. The workplace, the community, homes and health

centres were reported as the main environments where human right abuses occurred. Sixty-eight per cent of all persons interviewed thought that the primary
advocacy issue that needed to be addressed was the right to health care.[10]

The National HIV/STI Programme (NHP) in the 2010 country progress report for Jamaica addresses freedom from discrimination, equal protection and
equality before the law of PLWHA. In order to make the general environment
and the workplace, in particular, less threatening for PLWHA, the Ministry of
Health partnered with several organizations to operationalize a redress system
for discriminatory acts against PLWHA. The National Related Discrimination
Reporting and Redress System (NHDRRS), after many collaborations and re-
finements, has been operating out of the Jamaica Network of Seropositives
(JN+). The system is designed to collect complaints, investigate complaints
and be a focal point for redress from HIV-related discrimination.[11]

Sexual and Reproductive Health Rights of PLWHA[12]

Right to Reproduction, Sexuality and Desire

Research on this topic suggests that it seems to be generally accepted that
PLWHA have the right to what is considered a normal sex life – that is, the
right to have children, the right to love and the right to be intimate.[13] Dr Kevin
Moody, international coordinator and CEO of the Global Network of People
living with HIV/AIDS (GNP+), said, "From a public health perspective,
decision-makers and service providers must recognize that people living with
HIV do enter into relationships, have sex, and bear children."[14] If PLWHA
do indeed have these sexual and reproductive health rights, then they need
to be free to make choices and decisions in relation to their sexuality and
reproduction. These choices and decisions (regarding consensual sexual
expression, reproduction, access to health care, marriage and family planning)
should be exercised in an environment that is free of coercion and stigma.[15]

Articulating Sexual and Reproductive Rights

A significant question is, how does one articulate the sexual right to reproduction
in societies where scarce resources are at a premium and health care is stretched
sometimes beyond its capacity to deliver minimum standard of care?

The factors accompanying sexual and reproductive health rights of PLWHA
are as diverse as the epidemic itself. The issues vary, depending on if you are
in a large, developed country or a small, developing country. Young PLWHA
have different needs, as they face a possible lifetime of negotiating their HIV

infection.[16] Older infected persons are trying to balance the effects of ageing merging with the effects of their HIV infection. Unmarried PLWHA face different challenges than married PLWHA.[17]

Sexual and reproductive rights violations relevant to women and girls include limited access to health care delivery services, forced or coerced sterilizations, violence, stigma and discrimination, loss of inheritance and property rights, as well as mandatory and forced testing.[18]

Young mothers who are HIV-infected face disclosure issues that might be repeated many times during their lifetime. They face the potential of recurrent sexual rejection because of their status. The dreaded feeling of infecting their unborn child with the virus is a fact that they face for the duration of their pregnancy and beyond.[19] Also, in several states, the vertical transmission of HIV from mother to child is criminalized.[20]

Prevention of Mother to Child Transmission (PMTCT)

PMTCT Plus Programme

The University of the West Indies and the Ministry of Health instituted a programme to address the fact that many children were being HIV infected by their mothers, and some were dying as a result. The transmission can take place during the actual pregnancy through maternal to foetal exchange of blood. It can also take place during labour and delivery (intrapartum). Transmission can also occur during breastfeeding. In Jamaica, a total of 884 cases of HIV or AIDS and 388 deaths in children were reported from 1986 to 2007.[21] Dr Debbie Carrington, in a presentation titled "PMTCT Plus in Jamaica", succinctly details the objectives, strengths and weaknesses of PMTCT Plus. She also outlines what the programme sees as threats and the lessons learned from 2005 to 2009. It is estimated that 1.5 per cent to 2 per cent of all antenatal clinic attendees are HIV infected. Without intervention, the rate of mother to child transmission during live birth would be about 25 per cent. The pregnant women who are placed in the PMTCT Plus programme are in exclusive positions as far as the health care sector and HIV are concerned – the programme has been afforded great attention, detailed research and is one area in which great strides have been made over the years.[22] One goal of the programme was to reduce the transmission rate from over 25 per cent to fewer than 5 per cent – that objective has been achieved. Between 2005 and 2009, the rate of mother to child transmission was reduced to less than 5 per cent.

Dr Carrington also points to future goals of the programme. According to her, it is now well recognized that HIV affects the entire family, and thus the "ultimate and ideal goal is the adaptation of a family-centred model of care emphasizing continued multidisciplinary care of women, children and partners beyond mere prevention of mother to child transmission, thus PMTCT+".[23]

The objectives of the programme include the following: testing 100 per cent of all antenatal clients for HIV; ensuring that all HIV positive pregnant women receive antiretrovirals (ARVs) to reduce the risk of HIV transmission; ensuring that all HIV-exposed infants receive a prophylactic course of ARVs; ensuring the availability of formula feed for all HIV-exposed infants, for at least the first six months; and ensuring follow-up and diagnosis of HIV status of all HIV-exposed infants.

The programme has many strengths. For example, service is implemented on an island-wide basis through the public sector (with an entrance point at an antenatal clinic). There is a multidisciplinary team approach to management, and there are multiple levels of care, with an extremely committed staff. The programme is also able to offer ARVs and replacement feeds to clients at no cost.

However, noted weaknesses of the programme need to be overcome. These include the fact that all birthing centres do not offer HIV rapid tests for unbooked mothers, the fact that there is inadequate prevention of unintended pregnancies in HIV-positive women, the fact that there is little follow-up with the mother and child, the fact that there is inadequate monitoring and evaluation, and the fact that there is inadequate social support services available. The following threats to the programme have also been identified: prevalence of stigma and discrimination within the health sector and at the community level, social vulnerability, gender inequality, cultural practices (such as early first sex or cross-generational sex between young girls and older men), low condom use and the perpetuation of myths.

In trying to ascertain how well the health care system in Jamaica has worked for a group of twelve HIV-infected young mothers, the majority of whom were newly diagnosed (for less than five years), data were taken from their files and processed. In particular, a completed questionnaire done with respondents from Eve for Life[24] personnel on the support they received from the health care sector forms the backbone of study. This information is really about a critical, crucial and venerable time in their lives as young mothers diagnosed with HIV. Ninety-two per cent of the respondents are between seventeen and twenty-two years, while 8 per cent are over twenty-five. Sixty-seven per cent of the support group was exposed to a secondary level education, while 33 per cent was only exposed to a primary level education. Eve for Life personnel classified 33 per cent of the group as literate, 47 per cent as low literacy and 20 per cent as functionally illiterate. All the respondents were school dropouts.

The findings from this sample speak to the experiences of these women only and are not representatives of other similarly situated women or of the entire health care system in Jamaica. The sample is too small to make generalizations; however, the data can point to areas of strength and weakness in the system as far as these women are concerned. We may be able to determine whether any of their human rights were violated and make some recommendations that would help to give, if not these women, but other women in the future the benefit of increased support.

Women, HIV/AIDS and Violence

Seventy-five per cent of the women in the Eve for Life group reported that they were either beaten by boyfriends or experienced sexual abuse. Eighty-three per cent of the respondents further stated that they were not offered any counselling on domestic violence by the health care programme. The Global Coalition of Women and AIDS sees violence against women as a worldwide problem that has become a public health concern, especially in relation to HIV and AIDS. The high rate of physical and sexual violence against women by their intimate partners is validated by research studies around the world.

In population-based studies on partner violence, the range is from 10 per cent in some countries to 69 per cent in others. The women report being abused by a male partner at least once in their lives. A cross-sectional study in Soweto, South Africa, of women getting antenatal care showed that women who had partners who were violent and had controlling behaviours were 1.5 times more likely to be HIV-infected than the women who did not have these partner issues.[25]

A Bangladesh study shows that men reported for physical and sexual violence were 2.5 times more likely to have STI symptoms or an STI diagnosis in the previous year. The researchers concluded that these abusive men had greater odds of engaging in premarital and extramarital affairs and thus contracting STIs – the implication being that they place their wives at greater risk of HIV infection.[26]

One obvious link between sexual violence and HIV infection is rape. Violence and fear often make women unable to negotiate condom use. A more obscure link is that women who are exposed to childhood sexual abuse are more likely to engage in high-risk behaviours like early sex, multiple partners and abuse of drugs and alcohol, which increase the likelihood of HIV infection.

The population statistics on violence against women is startling. Even though this is not a representative sample of women in Jamaica, the figures support the findings of population studies elsewhere. The following data represent the information taken from the completed Eve for Life questionnaires.

Eve for Life Questionnaire

Sexual reproductive health and rights offered counselling on

Your sexual needs and desires including discussions about how HIV would affect you as women	Yes 67%	No 33%
Symptoms to look for that could lead to psychological stress	Yes 33%	No 67%
Fertility needs and desires, including asking whether or not you were using contraceptives	Yes 75%	No 25%
Emergency contraceptive pills	Yes 17%	No 83%
Family planning methods	Yes 42%	No 58%
Prevention of sexually transmitted infections (STIs), reproductive tract infections (RTIs) on HIV transmission, on HIV re-infection, including the early management of STIs and RTIs	Yes 67%	No 33%

Given information on

The potential drug interactions with hormonal methods	Yes 17%	No 83%
Interactions between pregnancy and HIV	Yes 67%	No 33%
Risk for perinatal transmission and effectiveness of antiretroviral prophylaxis in preventing perinatal transmission	Yes 75%	No 25%
Male and female condoms and their consistent and correct use demonstrate	Yes 83%	No 17%

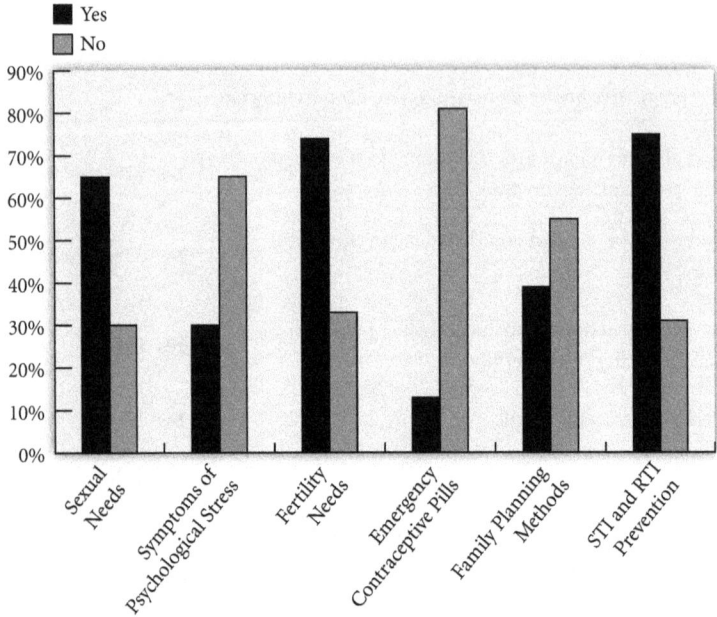

Figure 16.1. Sexual Reproductive Health and Rights

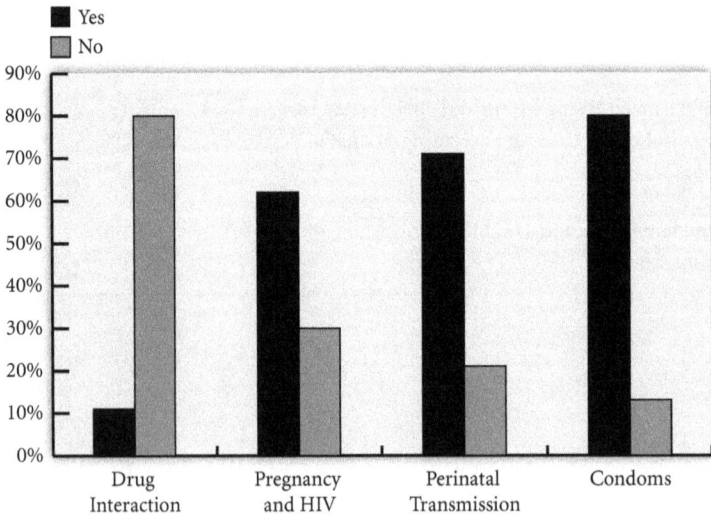

Figure 16.2. Sexual Reproductive Health and Rights Findings

Discussion of Findings

The respondents were asked if health care workers offered them counselling on several variables dealing with their sexual reproductive health. The respondents' ratings were classified as follows: (A) over 70 per cent was a high/competent rating, (B) 40 per cent to 69 per cent was medium/average and (C) below 40 per cent was low and unacceptable.

With the six variables dealing with counselling, 17 per cent were classified in the high competent rating, 50 per cent in the medium/average rating and 33 per cent fell in the low category. Regarding the four variables on information, 50 per cent fell into the high/competent rating, 25 per cent in the medium/average, and the remaining 25 per cent fell into the not acceptable level.

Diagnosis of HIV Infection

Offered counselling and information on

STI/HIV prevention and support for negotiating safe and consensual sex including dual protection	Yes 75%	No 25%
Effects of disease progression and effectiveness, availability and cost of ARV treatment	Yes 75%	No 25%
Importance of planning care of yourself, your children and your family, should you be ill	Yes 9%	No 91%
Advantages and disadvantages of disclosing HIV status	Yes 9%	No 91%
PMTCT Plus and other HIV/AIDS treatment, care and support services	Yes 67%	No 33%
Dietary and nutritional considerations	Yes 58%	No 42%
Risk reduction and supportive woman's risk-reproduction plan	Yes 9%	No 91%
Refer to services for STI screening and management	Yes 50%	No 50%

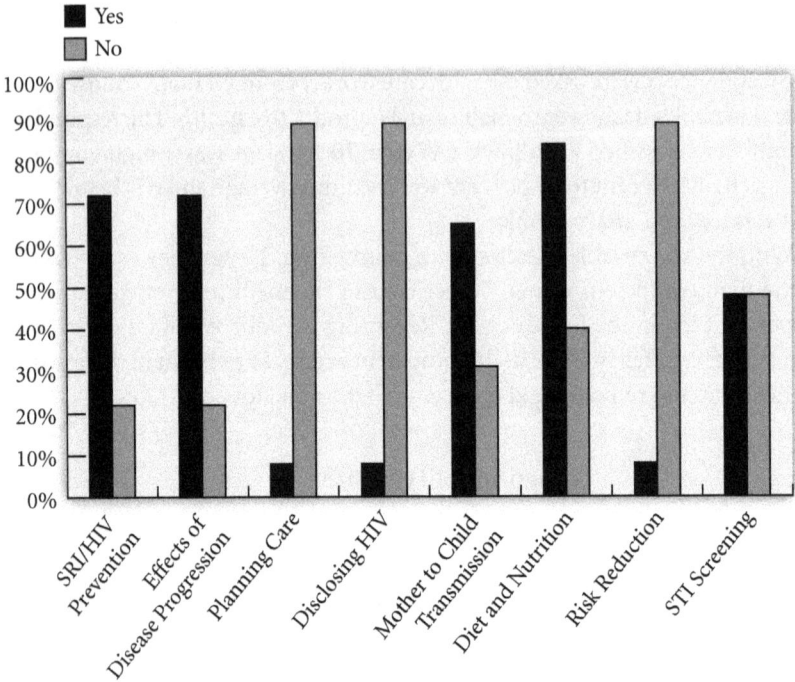

Figure 16.3. Diagnosis of HIV Infection

Discussion of Findings

Respondents were asked if they were offered counselling and information on eight variables that related to the diagnosis of their HIV infection.

Using the same classification in access to counselling and information, the eight variables used to represent HIV infection were put into categories: A (over 70 per cent), B (40–69 per cent) and C (below 40 per cent). Twenty-five per cent fell into the A category, which was high/competent, while 37.5 per cent were put into the medium/average B category and 37.5 per cent were categorized as C, low/not acceptable.

Family planning offered counselling and information on

Contraceptive choices to support voluntary, informed decision-making	Yes 42% No 58%
Ongoing infant feeding counselling and support for the woman's infant feeding choice	Yes 75% No 25%
Postpartum family planning services or nearest family planning clinic	Yes 67% No 33%

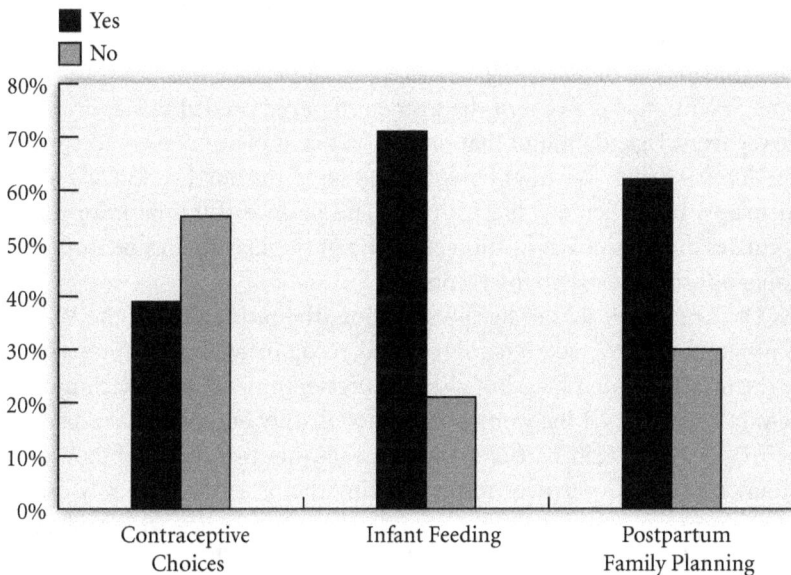

Figure 16.4. Family Planning

Discussion of Findings

The three variables provided – contraceptive choices, infant feeding (counselling and support) and postpartum family referrals – all scored in the medium to high categories. Sixty-seven per cent of responses were classified in the high/competent category and 33 per cent were in the medium/average category.

The data suggest that the health care system, in relation to the respondents, generally, was operating at a medium to average level. While this level is commendable, all the variables examined should be at the high to competent level, given the resources that have been made available, the vulnerability of the women involved and the almost universal access to HIV testing. Coupled with all this, 75 per cent of these mothers experience violence against their person, and when asked if they were offered counselling on domestic violence, the results fell into the low/not acceptable level.

Conclusion

Psychosocial support has to be made much more important and available than it seems to be presently. It has to be an integral part of the response in order to ensure optimal benefits for these young women. It has already been established that there are clear links between violence against women and HIV. A conservative estimate is that at least 50 per cent of the HIV-infected young mothers are in need of psychological therapy to address the violence against their person. Seventy-five per cent of the women surveyed needed this intervention. A survey from Uganda found that only 11 per cent of women could correctly define *human rights*. We might assume the same for our Eve for Life survey participants, given their low literacy rates. The absence of this basic knowledge perpetuates the continued violation of these rights. This can only be stopped by ongoing information-based interventions.

As Dr Carrington said in her presentation, the future goal of the PMTCT Plus programme is to make it family centred, recognizing that HIV impacts not only the infected individuals but also the affected individuals, which includes all family members. Of the women interviewed, only one-third have disclosed their HIV status to their partners, which means that two-thirds of the women are unaware of their partners' status. Making the programme family centred will help improve women's ability to handle disclosure issues, which is just one of many challenges that family-centred interventions will address.

Attitude and behavioural changes can only occur through education and exposure to psychotherapy. The young mothers surveyed will need both as they navigate a lifetime of disclosure issues for both themselves and, in some cases, their children.

Notes

1. Perhaps the most basic human right in social existence is the individual's right to nondiscrimination on such grounds as race and sex. This has now been universally endorsed and recognized in several international law instruments. See Rebecca J. Cook, "Human Rights, HIV Infection, and Women", in *HIV Law, Ethics and Human Rights: Text and Materials*, ed. D.C. Jayasuriya (New

Delhi: UNDP Regional Project on HIV and Development, 1995), 240. See also article 7 of the Universal Declaration of Human Rights and article 26 of the International Covenant on Civil and Political Rights.

2. PLWHA or those affected by it might not seek counselling, testing, treatment and support if this means facing stigma, discrimination and lack of confidentiality or other negative consequences.

3. In Jamaica, for example, a reporting and redress system exists: the National HIV Related Discrimination Reporting and Redress System (NHDRRS).

4. The incidence and spread of HIV and AIDS are disproportionately high among groups who already suffer from a lack of human rights protection and experience discrimination. This includes groups that have been marginalized socially, culturally and economically. See Program on International Health and Human Rights, François-Xavier Bagnoud Center for Health and Human Rights, Harvard School of Public Health, and the International Council of AIDS Service Organizations (ICASO), "HIV/AIDS and Human Rights in a Nutshell: A Quick and Useful Guide for Action, as Well as a Framework to Carry HIV/AIDS and Human Rights Actions Forward" (2004), 1, http://globalhealth.usc.edu/Home/Resources/Pages/~/media/3B27BC433DB44B68B161AF3B5E769032.ashx.

5. "In most societies, gender relations are characterised by an unequal balance of power between men and women, with women having fewer legal rights and less access to education, health services, training, income-generating activities and property. This situation affects both their access to information about HIV/AIDS and the steps that they can take to prevent its transmission." See Commonwealth Secretariat, "Gender Mainstreaming in HIV/AIDS: A Multisectoral Approach" (New Gender Mainstreaming Series on Gender Issues, 2002), xi.

6. "Gender analysis – a tool that uses sex and gender as a way of conceptualising information – helps to reveal and clarify women's and men's different social relationships and realities, life expectations and economic circumstances. Gender analysis involves the collection and use of sex-disaggregated data that reveals the roles and responsibilities of women and men. It is crucial to understanding HIV/AIDS transmission and initiating appropriate programmes of action, and forms the basis for the changes required to enable women and men to protect themselves and each other. Gender analysis provides a framework for analysing and developing policies, programmes and legislation, and is thus an important tool for gender mainstreaming." Ibid., xi.

7. Other rights include the right to freedom of opinion and expression and the right to freely receive and impart information; the right to freedom of association; the right to equal access to education; the right to an adequate standard

of living; the right to social security, assistance and welfare; the right to share in scientific advancement and its benefits; the right to participate in public and cultural life; and the right to be free from torture and cruel, inhuman or degrading treatment or punishment. See UNAIDS, "International Guidelines on HIV/AIDS and Human Rights" (2006), paragraph 80, http://data.unaids .org/Publications/IRC.../jc1252-internguidelines_en.pdf.

8. Lydia Ofori Abakah, "Respecting the Rights of Persons Living with HIV/AIDS" (Ghana News Agency, 29 September 2004), http://www.modernghana.com/ news/115312/1/respecting-the-rights-of-persons-living-with-HIVai.html.

9. G.W. Maina, "Human Rights Awareness and Needs amongst People Living with HIV/AIDS (PWAs) in Uganda" (paper presented at the Fifteenth International Conference on AIDS, Bangkok, Thailand, 11–16 July 2004), http:// www.iasociety.org/Default.aspx?pageId=12&abstractId=2172262.

10. Ibid.

11. The NHDRRS has a multisectoral (public and private sector) approach to both reporting and redress. An advisory group includes many partners, such as representatives of NHP, UNAIDS, human rights organizations, the Ministry of Labour and Social Security, PLWHA and NHP, among others. Representatives are ministry personnel, PLWHA, advocates, policy coordinators and lawyers.

12. Global Network of People Living with HIV/AIDS (GNP+), "Advancing the Sexual and Reproductive Health and Human Rights of People Living with HIV" (Amsterdam, 2009), http://www.gnpplus.net/images/stories/SRHR/ 090811_srhr_of_plHIV_guidance_package_en.pdf.

13. Ibid. Some jurisdictions have reacted to HIV infection by mandating that an HIV test be made a condition of the grant of a licence to marry. See UNAIDS, *Handbook for Legislators on HIV, Law and Human Rights* (Geneva, Switzerland: UNAIDS Best Practice Collection, 1999), http://www.ipu.org/PDF/ publications/aids_en.pdf.

14. See UNAIDS, "Advancing the Sexual and Reproductive Health and Human Rights of People Living with HIV" (press release, 11 August 2009), http://www .unaids.org/en/Resources/PressCentre/PressreleaseandstatementarcHIVe/ 2009/August/20090809ORPLHIV.

15. "Stigma, discrimination and punitive laws prevent people living with HIV from accessing services and making informed decisions about their sexual and reproductive futures", said Michel Sidibé, executive director of UNAIDS. See UNAIDS, "Advancing the Sexual and Reproductive Health and Human Rights of People Living with HIV" (press release, 11 August 2009), http://www .unaids.org/en/Resources/PressCentre/PressreleaseandstatementarcHIVe/ 2009/August/20090809ORPLHIV.

16. Young people below the age of majority may need parental permission to access sexual and reproductive health information and services.
17. Couples, concordant and seroconcordant with fertility intentions, for example, face differing pathways.
18. UNAIDS, "Sexual and Reproductive Health and Rights of Women and Girls Living with HIV" (paper on SRHR and HIV positive women and girls presented at the fifty-fifth session of the Commission of Women in February 2011 and the 2011 UN General Assembly high level meeting), 3, http://www.wecareplus.net/resources/UNAIDS_SRHR_positive%20_women_and_girls_CSW2011.pdf.
19. Effective ARV treatment is available to prevent the transmission of HIV to the unborn child.
20. Criminalization fails to take into consideration the socioeconomic and cultural reasons that a woman is unable to prevent vertical transmission and therefore negatively affects the human rights of women. It is often times due to their vulnerable circumstances such as poverty, gender inequality, lack of education and lack of access to and knowledge of health care. See UNAIDS, "Sexual and Reproductive Health and Rights of Women and Girls Living with HIV", 7.
21. "Paediatric and Perinatal HIV/AIDS in Jamaica", *West Indian Medical Journal* 57, no. 3 (June 2008): 187–320, http://www.adypadoe.com/Paediatric-and-Perinatal-HIV/AIDS-in-Jamaica.html#.
22. The special issue of the *West Indian Medical Journal* published in June 2008 is dedicated to paediatric and perinatal HIV and AIDS in Jamaica.
23. Debbie Carrington, "PMTCT Plus in Jamaica" (November 2007), http://www.jamaica-nap.org/docs/what%27s%20new.ppt.
24. Eve for Life is an NGO which was established in 2008 in response to a dire need for support to women and children living with or affected by HIV and AIDS.
25. Heather C. Brown, K.L. Dunkle, R.K. Jewkes et al., "Gender-Based Violence, Relationship Power and Risk of Prevalent HIV Infection among Women Attending Antenatal Clinics in Soweto, South Africa", *Lancet* 363 (2004): 1415–21. See also Heather C. Brown, Kristin L. Dunkle, Sinban D. Harlow, James A. McIntyre and Micho Yoshihama, "Prevalence and Patterns of Gender-Based Violence and Revictimization among Women Attending Antenatal Clinics in Soweto, South Africa" (5 February 2004), http://aje.oxfordjournals.org/content/160/3/230.full.
26. "Among Bangladeshi Men, Wife Abuse Is Associated with Extramarital Affair", *International Family Planning Perspectives Digest* 33, no. 3 (September 2007), http://www.guttmacher.org/pubs/journals/3314407.html.

Chapter 17

Addressing the Capacity-Building Needs of People Living with HIV or AIDS

A Critical Element in the Response

Ainsley Reid

GIPA Coordinator, National AIDS Committee, Jamaica

There is anecdotal evidence to suggest that the lack of understanding about the basic facts on HIV and AIDS among people living with HIV or AIDS (PLWHA) impacts their effective and meaningful involvement in the national response to HIV and AIDS. Education and training of PLWHA to understand their rights is critical to their quality of life, along with adequate preparation so they can be involved in the national response. Absence of this self-awareness may lead to social exclusion and the violation of fundamental rights.

Jamaica has an HIV prevalence of approximately 1.6 per cent,[1] and 32,000 people[2] are estimated to be living with HIV, with 50 per cent unaware of their status.[3] The Jamaica National HIV/STI Programme (NHP) is actively mounting a national response to achieve universal access to treatment, care and prevention services in order to address this growing concern. Among the many strategies is an approach to strengthen the participation of PLWHA in the national response. This approach includes an initiative to mobilize a cohort of twenty PLWHA per year, who then become members of self-support groups (SSGs). Two focus group discussions were conducted to examine and ascertain levels of awareness about HIV and AIDS basic facts, positive prevention, and stigma and discrimination issues.

Interventions are needed to equip the community of PLWHA to participate in existing HIV and AIDS policies and programmes that address prevention, care and support, and stigma and discrimination. Equally important is the need to improve PLWHA community leadership and the competence of PLWHA to strengthen the peer-to-peer outreach. Intervention should encourage meaningful activism among recently diagnosed PLWHA at the national level. This approach requires technical support, resources, focus and steady coordination to function within the multisectoral response to HIV and AIDS. There is evidence in other jurisdictions that the rights-based approach[4] to HIV and AIDS can be enhanced when PLWHA are sensitized and trained to understand and recognize their role as part of the wider citizenry.

The NHP created a Greater Involvement of People with HIV/AIDS (GIPA) desk for PLWHA, which is proposed to evolve into the creation of a GIPA Unit to further develop and implement a programme based on the research findings. Next steps in the process include documentation of the process to cull, cross-fertilize, and identify lessons learned in order to apply and share them regionally as a best practice.

This chapter does not seek to explore the problem but to share a practical approach which could contribute to a broader discourse seeking to address human rights issues in the context of poverty, health and the inadequate participation of PLWHA in developing solutions to the HIV crisis. It highlights the approach as an effective means to involve more PLWHA in the national response to HIV in Jamaica.

The GIPA Principles: History, Background and Development

In December 1994, leaders of forty-two nations convened at the Paris AIDS Summit. They agreed to effectively respond to the AIDS crisis by developing and supporting structures, policies and programmes. As a result, enshrined in the Declaration of the 1994 Paris AIDS Summit is a set of principles – grounded in the Denver principles of 1983[5] – recognized internationally as the GIPA principles.[6] The declaration acknowledged that in order to successfully tackle the spread of HIV and its associated stigma and discrimination, PLWHA should play a central role in the design and implementation of policies and programmes on prevention and care. It also acknowledged that for PLWHA to take on greater roles in the response, they need increased support to prevent tokenism.[7]

The role of PLWHA has to be more vital than being the token faces of the AIDS crisis. By being open and honest with others about their status and providing testimonials, PLWHA can have significant impact upon attitudes towards PLWHA; however, this should not be the extent of their involvement in the national response. PLWHA have the power, if given the appropriate support and technical guidance, to stem the tide of the HIV epidemic. Greater success can be achieved by their proactive involvement and leadership in the promotion of human rights and the response to HIV and AIDS.[8] Through GIPA, public health can also be promoted and barriers of fear and prejudice confronted.

This perspective supports the determination of the PLWHA community to contribute to achieving the Millennium Development Goals, particularly goal 6, which speaks to the halting and reversing the spread of HIV by 2015.

A GIPA desk was established in Jamaica in 2008 based on the aforementioned rationale of strengthening the involvement of PLWHA in the national response. The goal of the initiative is to complement and support existing interventions in the multisectoral response (especially the public and private sectors) in order to promote greater local recognition of the GIPA principle within the national HIV response.

The GIPA desk seeks to coordinate capacity building among PLWHA within the national programme in order to enable more effective integration and participation in all aspects of programme development and delivery. Over the years, as the response to HIV becomes more intense, PLWHA have been advocating for their roles to be more strategic and not be relegated to primarily presenting their stories and experiences of living with HIV. It was recognized that the input of PLWHA in the national response must transition from testimonials to more strategic input into every component of the national programme.

In 2009, a needs assessment was conducted by PLWHA on PLWHA and analysed by a consultant.[9] It identified gaps in the capacity of PLWHA to strategically participate in the national response. The analysis highlighted the areas of importance for the GIPA as follows: the re-education of the PLWHA in fundamental knowledge about HIV and AIDS; the creation of a formal social support system, including support groups; the acquisition and distribution of correct information to debunk many HIV- and AIDS-related myths and misinformation; the fostering of PLWHA's skills to confidently confront many of the stereotypes that have formed in the public; the fostering of PLWHA's attitudes to reinterpret living with HIV; the fostering of PLWHA's skills regarding disclosure; and advocacy of antidiscrimination legislation to protect PLWHA.

The findings illustrate that many PLWHA who desire greater involvement in the national response are untrained and may not possess the skills necessary to remain consistently and meaningfully involved. The inclusion of PLWHA therefore means providing them with the necessary tools to function as effective partners in the process. Essentially this becomes a matter of providing PLWHA with the capacity to become better advocates, as well as the technical assistance where necessary.

This capacity-building programme is led by a programme coordinator who is HIV positive. It is developed on the basis of the needs assessment, coupled with the input of PLWHA, some of which are participating in the initiative. Some staff members of the NHP in the Ministry of Health provided technical feedback.

The pilot of this programme has been developed to prepare PLWHA to participate in selected aspects of the national response. In the pilot, the workplace programme has been earmarked as the programme area for participation.

Programme Overview

Structure

The initiative begins with recruitment of PLWHA who are able to commit to their own capacity-building efforts. The work of the PLWHA involved should be considered as value added to the implementation of interventions at the level of the workplace and SSGs.

The GIPA desk at the NHP has piloted the process by selecting twenty recruits from a pool of PLWHA applicants. Future cohorts of the programme will consist similarly of twenty recruits per year over a four-year period. It will also reflect a reasonable mix of PLWHA, including men who have sex with men, women, sex workers and out-of-school youth. This provides a method of control to balance the effective mobilization and involvement of the PLWHA community.

Cost-effective psychosocial support and mentoring should be provided by relevant partners with the required competences to enable the community facilitators (who will be trained to facilitate awareness programmes in the public and private sector and train new recruits) to function at their maximum. The programme assumes that further capacity building initiatives will be required and the process might point to these needs as it continues. The actual capacity-building programme for recruits is designed to run for one calendar year for each cohort. The first six months includes the finalization of the recruitment and incorporates a series of sensitization workshops, which will culminate in the training of the participants. Participants in the programme will be deployed for six months to various worksites for their participation and involvement in the implementation of that worksite's HIV programme.

This important phase of the programme will follow a predeployment orientation exercise to help recruits prepare for their integration into the HIV and AIDS programmes at worksites. The purpose of this is to help them assume the roles for which they were trained. Deployment will enable the PLWHA community to broaden its involvement and participation in other aspects of the national response, especially in civil society, private and public sectors. However, a major expectation is that recruits will commit to representing the

PLWHA community on special advisory committees and coordinating bodies, especially the HIV/AIDS steering committees in programmes at worksites.

In recognition of the need for further capacity building to develop community facilitators into effective advocates, those interventions, which have proven to be successful, can be used as models. Therefore, those with reasonable knowledge and comfort levels with teamwork may be recommended for inclusion in advocacy initiatives. Others will be recommended for training to facilitate SSGs and as investigators in the National HIV-related Discrimination Reporting and Redress System (NHDRRS), as set up within the Jamaican Network of Seropositives (JN+) through the NHP, to collect cases of stigmatization and discrimination for the purpose of determining and providing redress.

This overall approach may be easily replicated as the PLWHA involved are trained to be community facilitators working within various sectors. Those with outstanding performance may be recruited subsequently to join a cadre of associates called the GIPA Unit. The GIPA Unit replicates the process with future cohorts. As a result, after the first phase, the process will evolve into the creation of the GIPA Unit to manage the capacity-building process. The unit should be supported by a partnership platform between the NHP; national PLWHA bodies, organizations and networks; the National AIDS Committee (NAC); and the Jamaica Business Council on HIV/AIDS National Foundation.

Detail

The GIPA capacity-building programme has four phases: recruitment, sensitization and training, deployment, and exit appraisal.

Phase 1: Recruitment

Participants become eligible for this phase of the programme when they meet the selection criteria. An orientation is then conducted to familiarize recruits to the programme and preregister them for the next phase.

Phase 2: Sensitization and Training

Six sensitization workshops are included in this phase. Accumulatively, these represent the didactic aspects of the capacity building: HIV basic facts, health education and promotion, legal literacy, HIV and AIDS and the world of work (ten key principles, GIPA and disclosure issues, human rights), stigma and discrimination, and NHDRRS. All the elements of the Positive Health, Dignity and Prevention (PHDP) curriculum are incorporated into the programme. The workshop topics are based on the needs of the HIV and AIDS programmes in the workplace, SSGs and other stakeholders in the response. While the sensitization workshops accompanied by support materials are geared to help participants achieve the cognitive and effective objectives of the workshops, the training workshop has skills-based objectives and is geared towards skill acquisition relevant to integration in the workplace programme.

The training workshop is conducted over two to three days to help trainees hone their skills in preparing and delivering various types of presentations, facilitating discussions and conducting interactive exercises. This helps enable them to deal with difficult participants and audiences, handle (constructive and destructive) feedback or criticisms, and evaluate their presentations using various tools, methodologies/approaches and technologies.

Trainees who successfully complete phase 2 (by attending and participating in all the workshops as listed) meet the selection criteria for deployment and are accepted for phase 3 (the deployment phase of the programme).

Phase 3: Deployment

Recruits who are accepted for this phase of the programme have completed phases 1 and 2 and have met certain selection criteria for deployment: They must demonstrate that they have good grasp of and capacity to present correct information about HIV basic facts, stigma and discrimination, and select topics. They must be comfortable in conducting interactive exercises and dealing with disclosure issues, and they should fully understand their role as presenters and facilitators. In addition to knowledge-related and skills-based criterion, they need to be punctual, responsible, open to functioning in a team and willing to work in various types of worksites and organizations, with key populations.

Recruits accepted for deployment are then placed in a six-month internship at a workplace HIV programme. Prior to their deployment and internship, they participate in a predeployment orientation exercise. This involves short, personal development courses conducted over two days and includes topics such as time management, deportment, self-care (maintaining adherence and hygiene), team building (including managing inter-/intra-team conflicts) and information about the partnership in which this programme is being implemented.

This phase of the programme equips the recruits to take the lead as community facilitators, representing the PLWHA community and participating in outreach, sensitization and training interventions in the implementation of HIV/AIDS workplace programmes.

Phase 4: Exit Appraisal

At the end of phase 3, the exit appraisal process will be conducted. During this phase, the community facilitators are interviewed to determine the level of success at the worksite. The assessment includes the use of the following documents:

- An overall self-assessment completed by the community facilitator
- Performance appraisal from the workplace technical officers (WTOs)
- Training assessment

This assessment helps establish the facilitator's commitment to post-programme involvement within the network of SSGs and other advocacy-type interventions. Upon completion of the programme, all community facilitators are invited to a graduation and certification exercise.

Overall Resources Required

The following is a list of necessary resources for the programme.

Events

- Consultation on universal access to prevention, care, treatment and support to set the stage for future developments of the programme and the PLWHA community
- Workshops and community facilitator's retreats
- Cadre of partners in the private, public and civil society sectors
- Annual community convention and retreat to monitor and evaluate input, outputs, outcomes and systems. This will also provide the programme with opportunities for the use of baseline information to examine more closely the social and economic needs of the programme's immediate beneficiaries, with the goal of partnering with other stakeholders to provide other products and services that are fundamental to the sustainability of the programme (e.g., an emergency medical fund).

Personnel

- GIPA coordinator to manage the process, identify lessons learned for culling and cross-fertilization and identify support (including financial) for a seamless transition from the GIPA desk to the GIPA Unit
- Experienced resource persons and presenters (initially from the NHP and its stakeholders) for the sensitization and training workshops for the first and second cohorts

- Community facilitators with outstanding performance selected from the first cohort to join the cadre of associates and replicate the entire process (recruitment/orientation, sensitization and training, deployment, and the exit appraisal/graduation with future cohorts), delivering psychosocial support through mentorship of their peers in the programme
- Overseas study visits to cross-fertilize best practices with other or similar-type interventions in other jurisdictions

Materials to Be Produced

- The standardized curriculum will outline the content with learning objectives for each session and delivery methodology for the didactic nature of the sensitization sessions. This will be accompanied by a participant's reference manual (compiled presentations, relevant handouts and other learning aids). This will be supported by instruments for analysis at the end of each workshop to determine improvements in learning.
- The skills-based aspect of the curriculum will be designed to help trainees achieve their integration in workplace interventions without significant challenges. It will help them represent the PLWHA community in Jamaica by teaching them to articulate the HIV-related issues with sound knowledge. It will also help increase their abilities to present on select topics, facilitate discussions and conduct interactive exercises.
- The community facilitators' deployment guide will outline and clarify their role in the multisectoral outreach, and "in-reach" to the PLWHA community, to address stigma and discrimination issues. It will also include the predeployment information.
- Other tools and forms for use in the programme will include tests for each sensitization session; a training assessment forms for preregistration, trainee information, and appraisal; and graduation materials.

Other (Materials, Services and Technical Assistance)

- Administrative items
- Planning meetings
- Monitoring and evaluation strategies (as part of the quality assurance of the process)
- Technical assistance on curriculum and material development

Considerations for Sustainability

The programme is designed to support the building of social capital among the should-be "primary" beneficiaries of the national response – the PLWHA – whose quality of life, existence and talents are tremendously affected by societal stigma and discrimination. The continuation of the capacity building and provision of peer-led psychosocial support are key to a proactive and engaged PLWHA community. It would be a progressive move if, at the national level, the PLWHA leaders and supporters were to advocate for a culturally appropriate local PHDP curriculum in addition to that of the health care providers. This is essential in further streamlining and unifying capacity-building initiatives targeting PLWHA.

Other facilitating opportunities that would add value to the sustainability of this initiative include (but are not limited to) the following developments: the UN Educational, Scientific and Cultural Organization (UNESCO) in partnership with the Education Development Center (EDC Caribbean) spearheaded the development and launch of "Positive Partnerships: A Toolkit for the Greater Involvement of People Living with or Affected by HIV in the Caribbean Education Sector".

There exists an active and comprehensive response to HIV and AIDS in Jamaica. The NHP, with its four components, is implemented as part of an overarching strategic plan. Developments in the NHP highlight the strategic moves of the prevention component to improve and implement the capacity building on PHDP for health care workers.

In the enabling environment and human rights component of the plan, workplace technical officers (WTOs) are assigned to entities within the private sector (umbrella organizations such as JaBCHA, JEF, JMA and PSOJ) and the public sector (government ministries and related agencies). The WTOs are responsible for the promotion and formulation of HIV workplace policies and programmes in their sectors. They work collaboratively with a management-approved Focal Point and Steering Committee in each worksite to accomplish this.

There is a GIPA desk with a coordinator under the purview of the enabling environment and human rights component. The key functions of the desk are as follows:

1. Expand the participation of PLWHA in existing interventions by delivering sessions on basic HIV and AIDS facts, GIPA and the NHDRRS.

2. Participate on special committees and panels representing the PLWHA community.

3. Coordinate the selection, sensitization and training of twenty PLWHA per year for their greater involvement in risk reduction and HIV-related discrimination reduction interventions.

4. Assist JN+ and the NHDRRS through active participation in selected interventions.

The person who is charged with the responsibility of coordinating the GIPA desk is a well-known PLWHA who has been featured in the first national antistigma campaign, "Positive, Truly Positive, and Getting on with Life" (2006). He is also the founder of JN+ and a founding member of the Caribbean Regional Network of PLWHA (CRN+). He has been involved in the response to HIV since the mid-1990s and has experience in the various phases of the management of HIV programmes – namely, assessment, planning, designing, implementation, monitoring and evaluation. He has worked with PLWHA groups, faith-based organizations and various other sectors, including the private sector, the media and the public sector.

At the regional level, advocacy training on any area of interest to the Caribbean for PLWHA activists may be an opportunity to achieve additional capacity building for the community facilitators. This includes interventions of key regional partners such as the CHART, CHLI, CBMP, CRN+ and GNP+. A proposal has already been made to UNESCO and EDC Caribbean for the establishment of a Regional Roving GIPA Institute to conduct ongoing advocacy training on a country-by-country basis, with the goal of establishing GIPA Units within the national response programmes across the Caribbean region.

Rationale for This Partnership

This approach is initiated and managed by PLWHA. The creation of a functional GIPA Unit will require additional resources as well as the establishment and maintenance of partnerships led by PLWHA with the NHP and NAC. Since this strategy requires formal organizations to operationalize an approach for GIPA, the same formality would apply to the arrangements to execute and implement the GIPA Unit – hence the consideration for NHP/NAC partnership and support for the volunteers in the programme (e.g., volunteer allowance, operational space and so on). However, work has already been done by the current GIPA coordinator, resulting in relationships with bodies such as NHP, NAC, JN+, JaBCHA, CHART, the Ministry of Labour and Social Security, and dozens of other entities. These relationships should be nurtured, supported and maintained so to keep this process alive.

The partners involved in the creation and support of the GIPA Unit include (but are not limited to) the following:

- *PLWHA bodies and networks.* The creation of the GIPA Unit requires a unified PLWHA body called the National Network of People with HIV and its network of SSGs. Through its SSG, JN+ has referred 50 per cent of recruits in the current phase of the GIPA capacity-building programme. There is a symbiotic relationship between JN+ and the GIPA capacity-building programme.
- *NHP.* This entity is the principal recipient of the Global Funds Jamaica and has the authority and capacity to assess, plan, design, implement, monitor and evaluate HIV response programmes in Jamaica. It has a staff with the competence to assist this process and help to sustain it (including a director with four components heads for prevention; care, treatment and support; enabling environment and human rights; and governance, monitoring and evaluation). NHP has a history of recognizing the need for GIPA and has supported many initiatives that enable the realization of this effort. Currently, they provide a contract, renewed yearly since 2009, which evolved into this process.
- *NAC.* This entity is the custodian of the multisectoral response to HIV in Jamaica and has the mandate to advise the minister of health about developments in the epidemic. The NAC also has a secretariat with staff (including an executive director and two officers), communications and programmes. These officers support the four committees (education, care and support, fundraising, and legal and ethical) that are made up of member organizations. There is also a local grassroots network of parish AIDS associations connected to the NAC. The NAC provides a desk within its general office space for the GIPA coordinator.
- *UNAIDS.* This entity is the joint venture of ten organizations in the UN system responding to HIV. Its goal is to help the world prevent new HIV infections, care for PLWHA and mitigate the impact of the epidemic. It is the main advocate for accelerated, comprehensive and coordinated global action on the HIV epidemic. This essentially means that UNAIDS is the chief advocate and architect for GIPA, since they were among the list of partners that formulated the GIPA principle in 1994.
- *JaBCHA.* This organization facilitates the involvement of the private sector in policy formulation and programme implementation

to respond to HIV. It provides a useful platform for the integration and utilization of the community facilitators. It has recently started a national foundation to raise a billion Jamaican dollars for the sustainability of the national response.

- The Ministry of Labour and Social Security, like dozens of others and their related entities, is currently facilitating major aspects of the response. The ministry has been involved in the response to HIV through its connection with the International Labour Organization (ILO). Current developments in the MLSS include the establishment of an HIV unit to conduct audits of the workplace to ensure integrity in the HIV policy and programmes at worksites.
- *CHART.* This agency is currently training health care workers on various aspects of the continuum of care and has an annual HIV management symposium.

Partnership with these entities will help in the deployment and training aspects of the GIPA programme. The key to the success of this process is the provision of psychosocial support, especially in the second year. The suggested NHP/NAC partnership, being the executing mechanism for the GIPA Unit, should seek out additional resources to train and supervise select associates of the GIPA Unit to provide psychosocial support, mentoring community facilitators (a peer-to-peer approach).

The resourcefulness of this approach includes re-engaging certified community facilitators as senior associates in the GIPA Unit to continue management of the programme for future cohorts. Ongoing technical assistance is going to be needed to validate the monitoring and evaluation process of the various aspects of the programme.

Notes

1. National HIV/STI Programme, Jamaica, "UNGASS Country Progress Report to the Secretary General of the United Nations" (UNAIDS, 2010), http://www.unaids.org/en/dataanalysis/monitoringcountryprogress/ 2010progressreportssubmittedbycountries/jamaica_2010_country_progress _report_en.pdf.
2. Ibid.
3. Ibid.
4. UNAIDS, "What Constitutes a Rights-Based Approach? Determining Rationale, Objectives and Areas of Focus for Our Work" (paper presented at the UNAIDS Global Reference Group on HIV/AIDS and Human Rights,

fourth meeting, 23–25 August 2004, Geneva), http://www.un.org.kg/en/ publications/document-database/article/Document%20Database/ UN%20System%20in%20Kyrgyzstan/Human%20Rights%20and%20 Human%20Rights%20Based%20Approach/113-HIV-AIDS/2175-unaids -issue-paper-what-constitutes-a-rights-based-approach-determining -rationale-objectives-and-areas-of-focus-for-our-work-eng. See also UN-AIDS, "Public Report" (presented at the Global Reference Group on HIV/AIDS and Human Rights, fourth meeting, 23–25 August 2004, Geneva), http://www.google.com/url?sa=t&rct=j&q=&esrc=s&source =web&cd=3&ved=0CDgQFjAC&url=http%3A%2F%2Fglobalhealth .usc.edu%2Fen%2FResearch%2520And%2520Services%2FPages %2F~%2Fmedia%2F59CAED3A2D144178A2F76F4849C6FBC5 .ashx&ei=hJi7TsGDMNKatwetx7SkBw&usg=AFQjCNFM7yKOsXz _ktC9DVMwc2a4rNl-xQ.

5. See "Statement from the Advisory Committee of the People with AIDS: The Denver Principles" (1983), http://www.actupny.org/documents/Denver.html.

6. See "Declaration of the Paris AIDS Summit", s. 4, para. 1, http://www.unaids .org/whatsnew/conferences/summit/index.html.

7. In the Caribbean, statements made by CARICOM, including the Roseau Declaration and the Port of Spain Declaration, have insisted on GIPA, particularly at the decision-making stage. See UNESCO, "Positive Partnerships: A Toolkit for the Greater Involvement of People Living with or Affected by HIV and AIDS in the Caribbean Educated Sector" (2010), http://unesdoc.unesco.org/ images/0018/001879/187912e.pdf.

8. UNAIDS, "A Vital Partnership: The Work of GNP+ and the International Federation of Red Cross and Red Crescent Societies on HIV/AIDS" (UN-AIDS Best Practice Collection, October 2003), 6–7, http://data.unaids.org/ publications/irc-pub06/jc961-gnp_en.pdf.

9. Matthew McKenzie, "Sensitisation and Training for People Living with HIV (PLHIV) for Their Greater Involvement in the National Response to HIV/ AIDS in Jamaica: Needs Assessment Report" (Kingston, Jamaica: Ministry of Health, National HIV/STI Programme [NHP], 2010).

www.ingramcontent.com/pod-product-compliance
Lightning Source LLC
Chambersburg PA
CBHW031130270326
41929CB00011B/1572